Child Exploitation and Communication Technologies

Alisdair A. Gillespie

Russell House Publishing

First published in 2008 by:
Russell House Publishing Ltd.
4 St. George's House
Uplyme Road
Lyme Regis
Dorset DT7 3LS

Tel: 01297-443948
Fax: 01297-442722
e-mail: help@russellhouse.co.uk
www.russellhouse.co.uk

British Library Cataloguing-in-publication Data:
A catalogue record for this book is available from the British Library.

ISBN: 978-1-905541-23-2

Typeset by TW Typesetting, Plymouth, Devon

Printed by Biddles Ltd, King's Lynn, Norfolk

Russell House Publishing

Russell House Publishing aims to publish innovative and valuable materials to help managers, practitioners, trainers, educators and students.

Our full catalogue covers: social policy, working with young people, helping children and families, care of older people, social care, combating social exclusion, revitalising communities and working with offenders.

Full details can be found at www.russellhouse.co.uk and we are pleased to send out information to you by post. Our contact details are on this page.

We are always keen to receive feedback on publications and new ideas for future projects.

Contents

About the Author

Alisdair Gillespie is Reader in Law at De Montfort University in Leicester, UK. After qualifying at the Bar (Middle Temple) he returned to academia where he read for a research degree in law at the University of Durham, where he also taught. In 2000 he moved to the University of Teesside as a lecturer (later Senior and Principal Lecturer in Law), before moving as Reader to De Montfort University in 2005.

Alisdair specialises in the law relating to the exploitation and abuse of children, particularly where it is facilitated by Information and Communication Technologies. He has worked with law enforcement and other criminal justice agencies, including providing training. He speaks at national and international conferences on this area and has published numerous articles in professional and academic journals. Apart from his interest in this area, Alisdair also has research interests in the regulation of covert investigations and legal education.

In 2001 he was appointed by the then Home Secretary to the *Home Secretary's Task Force on Child Protection on the Internet*, a body on which he continues to sit.

Preface

Who this book is for

I first started writing this book because I was asked to speak at a number of conferences and training workshops by law enforcement and child protection agencies and sometimes even at academic conferences. It became clear that whilst many professionals were aware of some of the problems of children being exploited through the Internet they were not fully aware of how this happened, why it happened and what the law could do about it. This book addresses these issues and, although it will also be of interest to the academic community, its original genesis was for key professionals in the field.

The scope of this book

I had to make a decision early on as to what the scope of this book would be. I accept that this area raises a number of issues for the civil child protection framework to consider but my expertise is in the area of criminal law and I felt this is the area that most professionals wanted to know about. Professionals I talk to have said they wanted to know what crimes had been committed, how perpetrators could be identified and prosecuted. However, I believe this book will be of interest to those who work in the civil child protection system. Many of these professionals will come into contact either with victims or offenders of the behaviour set out in this book, and many are unaware of the detail of this conduct and how the law has tackled it. Reading the book should, therefore, permit all professionals to understand the current legal framework and the limits of the law.

Children and the new communication technologies

It is a trite but true statement to say that children have engaged with communication technologies in a way that adults have perhaps not. The youth of today transit seamlessly between the online and offline worlds and this can have many social and educational benefits. Communication technologies allow people to seem closer together despite their geographical distance. One of the reasons why children have taken to modern technology so quickly is because of the social interaction it allows. Children can, through technology, share messages, pictures, sounds and even movie-clips. In 2005 three-quarters of all children had Internet access in their home and it has undoubtedly risen again by now.

New ways that children can be put at risk

Whilst technology does have obvious benefits, it also carries with it threats. Sex offenders have also been quick to use information and communication technologies.

It will be seen in **Chapters 3** and **4** that the use of modern technology has transformed the production and dissemination of child pornography, particularly abusive images of children. This undoubtedly poses a grave risk to children since abusive images of children cannot ordinarily be produced without a child being abused or exploited. Technology has also meant that it has become a global phenomenon meaning it becomes more difficult to trace the producers of this behaviour and, more importantly, makes it extremely difficult to trace and rescue the victims of this vile trade.

Offenders finding new ways of gaining access to children

Sex offenders also use communication technologies to obtain children. In this book a series of behaviours will be discussed. The behaviour that has captured the media's attention in recent years is that of 'grooming' a child. A contemporary example of such behaviour involves an offender posing as an adolescent whilst befriending another adolescent online, eventually persuading them to acquiesce to sexual activity. In **Chapter 5** this behaviour is examined in detail, including a realisation that this is simply a new way of undertaking old behaviour. **Chapter 6** discusses the phenomenon of child procurement, that is situations where offenders seek to procure a child for their own sexual gratification. There have been a number of examples of this occurring and the chapter will also discuss how offenders sometimes use communication technology to 'watch' the abuse of a child by one of their number. This theme is then taken further in **Chapter 7** which looks at the issue of child prostitution and this includes an examination of the rather worrying trend of children self-exploiting themselves.

What the law can do to counter this

This book guides the reader through each distinct behaviour and assesses how offenders can use technology to exploit a child. After the behaviour has been discussed the chapter will then identify how the law seeks to tackle this behaviour and assesses any possible deficiencies in the framework.

This book has taken a long time to write for two main reasons. The first is that a series of other commitments kept interfering with the writing of the project. The second, and perhaps more significant, was that this is a fast-changing area and throughout the writing of this book there have been major changes that have required me to re-work sections of the book. Eventually I had to decide that because this is a fast-changing environment I would have to draw a line in the sand at some point and submit the manuscript. Finally this book is now complete and fully up-to-date as regards the law in September 2007.

AAG
Leicester, UK.

Acknowledgements

I acknowledge a number of people for assistance in the production of this book. This book perhaps differs from others in that although many people were aware I was writing a book, much of the material gathered was initially used for other purposes. However, I acknowledge the following people because without their assistance I would not have had the opportunity to gather the information for whatever purpose and because they have helped me in my work in this area for some time. Some people I cannot publicly acknowledge because it is necessary for their work that they remain anonymous. I do, however, acknowledge Detective Superintendent Matthew Sarti of the Metropolitan Police and collectively acknowledge the Metropolitan Police's *Child Abuse Command*, and the particular officers who I have worked with will know who they are. I thank Bob McLachlan, formerly a Detective Chief Inspector and sometime head of the Paedophile Unit of the Metropolitan Police. I also acknowledge the assistance of the *Child Exploitation and Online Protection Centre*, a recent unit that has been set up and which is changing the way that the fight against child exploitation is undertaken. I also acknowledge the staff of the *Internet Watch Foundation* who I have come into contact with over the years. The IWF is a unique body that shows that industry and law enforcement are capable of working together in the fight against exploitation on the Internet. The IWF has made a significant difference in this field and many children have been safeguarded by their existence.

I also wish to acknowledge Esther George, senior policy advisor at CPS Headquarters, with whom I have talked about these issues over several years: I have always enjoyed talking with Esther and her wisdom has proven extremely useful. I would also like to acknowledge members of the *Home Secretary's Task Force on Child Protection on the Internet*, particularly members of sub-group (a) which considered (and continues to consider) issues relating to the criminal law. There are too many members to name but they know who they are and how they have helped to change the law relating to the exploitation of children on the Internet, making a real difference to child protection.

Outside of the law enforcement agencies I wish to acknowledge Dr Rachel O'Connell, now Head of Corporate and Social Responsibility for Bebo. Rachel was formerly the Director of the Cyberspace Research Centre at the University of Central Lancashire where she was one of the foremost experts in the area of identifying grooming behaviour online. Talking with Rachel was always both useful and hugely entertaining. I want to give special thanks to Professor Max Taylor (of the University of St Andrew's) and Dr Ethel Quayle of University College Cork. Max and Ethel created the COPINE (Combatting Pornography in Europe) project and they have become the pre-eminent authorities on offender behaviour regarding the sexual exploitation of children, particularly through the use of communication technologies. Max, and especially Ethel, talked to me on numerous occasions, suffered an amateur asking questions about forensic psychology and made available much of their work.

I wish to also acknowledge colleagues at my own institution, De Montfort University, particularly Gavin Dingwall, Reader in Law, and Professor Michael Hirst. Gavin and Michael read sections of this manuscript and discussed many of the issues contained in this book. Finally, I wish to acknowledge the *Arts and Humanities Research Council* who funded a period of research-leave during which Chapter 7 (child prostitution) was completed.

Although I was privileged in 2001 to be asked by the Home Secretary to become one of the original members of the *Home Secretary's Task Force on Child Protection on the Internet*, a body on which I continue to sit, it should be noted that the comments in this book are personal ones and should not be thought to be the considered position of the *Task Force*.

A note on referencing

It is customary in the legal profession to include page-numbers (where known) and this has been adopted throughout this book even though I am aware that other disciplines omit page-numbers from some published works.

Where page numbers are not used is in respect of modern appellate cases that are available only electronically. The biggest source of freely-available cases is BAILLII (British and Irish Legal Information Institute; www.baillii.org) and many of the cases mentioned in this book can be found here. Since electronic resources do not contain page numbers the convention is to use paragraph numbers instead. Each paragraph in the judgment is numbered consecutively and placed within square parentheses. Accordingly where, in this book, the term 'at [20]' is seen, this would mean the twentieth paragraph of the judgment. I hope this clarifies the referencing in this book and makes it easier to read.

As noted above, this is a fast-changing environment with new laws and new decisions from the courts appearing nearly every month. So far as possible this book is up to date as of September 2007. Of course it is only the law that changes and so this book will continue to be relevant when discussing the behaviour even as the law develops.

CHAPTER 1

Children and Technologies

It is trite to say that there has been a technological revolution in recent years. Society has been revolutionised by the way in which we receive information and conduct our lives. Information and Communication Technologies (ICT) have now become second nature. Technology that even ten years ago would have seemed like something from science fiction have become so standard that we barely give them a moment's thought. We have moved to an era of instantaneous communication with e-mail, SMS messages and portable telephones becoming the accepted way of undertaking social and business transactions.

Information and communication technologies

This book is quite carefully focusing on the use of ICT and the title of the book does not mention the word 'Internet' because it is important to realise, right at the very beginning, that this is only one form of communication technology that is used by children. Although the media are preoccupied by the Internet there are many more technologies that exist which can be used and abused. In this chapter a brief introduction to some of these technologies will be made. It should be noted, however, that the emphasis throughout this book concerns the legal framework governing behaviour rather than the technology. Thus this chapter provides an introductory overview for those unfamiliar with technological development and how it can be abused. Those wishing further detail on the technology should consult specialist texts in this area.

Nobody can doubt that the advance of technology in recent years has been staggering. A simple demonstration can be seen from watching an episode of the original *Star Trek* series. Asked to imagine technology suitable for the 23rd century, the designers came up with the ideas of computers that can speak and be spoken to, computers that can be carried around, and small tape cartridges to save data onto. Such technology looked at through today's eyes seems actually out of date. Voice recognition has

become quite advanced although most of us still prefer to use a keyboard to input our work. Tape technology is now completely out of date, disks replacing it, and even these are being phased out by solid-state medium such as memory cards and sticks, and we now talk about handheld computers and not portable computers. Even their communicators have been brought into reality with Bluetooth headsets and mobile telephones, and indeed most of the modern mobile telephones make the *Star Trek* communicators look old fashioned.

Computers have moved on rapidly too. The average personal computer to be found in a house has more power than the supercomputers of the 1960s and 1970s, which used to fill up large rooms and required constant cooling. In 1981 my family bought its first computer, the Sinclair ZX81. I sometimes wonder what today's youths would make of this computer. It came with the vast memory of 1 kilobyte (1 k). To put this into context, a Microsoft Word document with the single letter 'a' in its contents, will account for over 20 kilobytes. With this one byte you could, in a fashion, write basic computer games and undertake simple computer functions. The ZX81 was wholly black and white and had no real graphics functions. The Sinclair Spectrum, arguably, eclipsed the ZX81's place in computer history the following year, but it is an important example of how far technology has come. Today's computers have memory in megabytes and gigabytes, something unimaginable 20 years ago. Back then a computer was there for the family, now computers have become truly personal, with many families having a computer for each member.

The progress of technology has certainly brought with it significant social, educational and economic benefits. Arguably the Internet has transformed holidays with many people now booking direct with the airline, hotel and travel-car companies rather than bothering with package holidays. This has increased the destinations people travel to. Communication allows businesses to speak to each other seamlessly and hospitals can use technology to allow eminent physicians and surgeons to consult on complicated cases. The Internet is probably the leading educational resource; think of anything obscure, put it into a search engine and you will find lots of web pages that exist to tell you all you wanted to know about your topic.

The communication mediums that will be discussed in this book are:

- The World-Wide Web
- E-mail
- Chatrooms (including Internet Relay Chat (IRC))
- Peer-to-peer systems
- Short Messaging System (SMS) – aka 'text messages'
- Instant messenger
- 3G technology

With the exception of one or two within this list, it is likely that most readers will have used the mediums listed. The use of communication technologies in modern society has become almost essential: most of the research for this book has been gathered via the Internet and not from traditional sources. Discussions in respect of this book have taken place over the e-mail system and, like many others, I would find it more difficult to do my job without such technology.

Internet

It may be surprising to see that the word 'Internet' is missing from the list of communication technologies listed above. The reason for this is the Internet is an over-arching technology that allows the communication mediums to exist. It has been suggested that:

Although there is no official definition of the Internet, most industry commentators would agree upon a description of the Internet as a public international network of networks.
(Terrett and Monaghan, 2000: 1)

This may not seem a particularly easy definition but it is nonetheless a simple one. The Internet is merely a collection of networks, a network being a collection of computers. In other words the Internet is simply a vast collection of computers all linked together allowing the hosting and dissemination of information. The original network was established by the US Department of Defense in the 1960s and this was then linked to American academic institutions. Over the decades numerous high-capacity computer networks adopted the same protocols and were added to the Internet until the current position has been reached which is that it is 'virtually impossible to identify the physical boundaries of the Internet' (Smith, 2002: 1).

Connection to the Internet for most users is through a 'local' contact known as an Internet Service Provider (ISP). These are 'local' in the sense that they usually have a geographical location even if they are multi-national companies. Common examples of this in the UK include BT, Virgin, AOL etc. Most people will never need to know more than the fact that they can connect to this vast network of computers using their ISP and this will allow them speedy access to information anywhere on this global network.

Once a connection has been made then a person can access content housed on these networks. Content providers will range from an individual to a multi-national company (Smith, 2002: 5) and physical geography ceases to be relevant: it is as easy for a UK user to access the website of the President of the United States of America as it is to access the website of Number 10 Downing Street. Content will differ dramatically although it is realistically possible to divide it into two classifications; real-time content and downloadable content (Smith, 2002: 5).

'Real-time' is the term used to denote that an activity is viewed in actual time rather than, for example, compressed time or slowed time. Real-time in the context above means that it is content that can be viewed directly. This may be static content whereby a person locates the information and reads it on the screen. Many websites operate on the simple real-time premise: the user simply goes to the particular website and reads what is there. The content is updated as and when necessary. However real-time content need not be static and it could be a 'stream'. The easiest way of imagining a 'stream' is to think of it as a broadcast. A person joining a 'live' stream will pick up the broadcast at whatever point the broadcast is at. Contemporary examples of 'streams' can be found on the BBC website where it is possible to listen to any of its radio programmes live and certain television broadcasts for important occasions.

The term 'real-time' can also, rather confusingly, be used in connection with non-live content. If we return to the example of the streams, then it was noted that a person will hear the broadcast from the point at which they begin listening. However, what if they miss the broadcast or wish to hear it from the very beginning? Some organisations (for example, the BBC) will allow people to listen to their programmes again. Whilst this is 'real-time' in that the listener will hear the matter at the same speed as the initial broadcast, it is not 'live' in that it has already happened.

Downloadable content differs from 'real-time' content in that it can be taken from the network and saved to the computer (or other device) that has accessed the Internet to be used at a later stage. Typical examples of downloadable content will be pictures or documents that a user will wish to browse later. It is equally possible (and indeed even more confusing) for downloadable content to be something that can be heard in 'real-time'. For example, it may be that a person is able to download a video or music file that the person can watch or listen to at a later date. It is still in 'real-time' to the extent that it mirrors the actual elapsed time but it is not live since it has already happened.

The World Wide Web

It was seen above that the Internet is, in effect, simply an international network of computers. However, when one refers to the 'Internet' a person is usually referring to the World Wide Web. The World Wide Web was developed in the late 1980s and very early 1990s as a way of ensuring that the information contained on the Internet could be more easily accessed and displayed.

Prior to the development of the World Wide Web information contained on the Internet would have to be accessed by someone knowing its exact location or through a system of 'bulletin boards'. These were electronic versions of offline bulletin boards used by companies over many decades. Users would simply 'post' information on the relevant board and someone could come along and download that information and read it. The difficulty was that searching bulletin boards was not particularly easy and would sometimes require specialist software.

The World Wide Web created a new language that would be used to host information. It was known as HyperText Markup Language (HTML). In essence, this is a series of common commands that tells a page how it should look and what it should do with certain information (i.e. animate

it, show a picture that is located at a particular location in the Internet, allow a user to download information etc.). Each page would be given a specific address where it could be found. The web address is more properly known as a URL (Uniform Resource Locater) and will often begin www. – meaning World Wide Web. Alongside these important developments a protocol was developed that allowed software to be developed that would allow these pages to be readily accessed from the network servers by individual computers. This protocol was known as HyperText Transfer Protocol (HTTP) and this details how pages will be stored and retrieved.

The World Wide Web made it significantly easier to access material. Since each site would have an individual address and the HTML text would allow details of the information to be stored and sent it meant that it was soon possible to develop search tools that would allow people to locate information in a much speedier way. The culmination of this approach can be seen in sites such as Google and AltaVista where the World Wide Web can be searched extremely quickly to locate sites relevant to the information requested.

In order to access the World Wide Web it is necessary to use a 'web browser'. This is a programme that accesses HTTP and processes HTML, converting the site into the format that the author requires it to be. The most famous browser is undoubtedly Microsoft's Internet Explorer although others do exist, for example FireFox. The browser allows a user to access both 'real-time' and 'download' material. However, it also provides a series of 'fingerprints' that can be used to assist in the detection of unlawful activity. Browsers will use 'caches' to speed-up browsing. Put simply a cache is an automatic store on the local computer connected to the Internet that will automatically download information that it thinks will be helpful for future visits to the Internet. Most commonly pictures (which can take a reasonable time to download) are placed within a cache automatically since if the computer revisits the website (and nothing has changed since its last visit) then it means it can display these 'local' pictures instead of re-downloading the images. The user has no control over this and this has implications where a user has accessed indecent images of children since it will provide evidence that the photographs were viewed (since they can be found in the cache). Other forensic 'traces' left by web browsers include search terms and 'cookies' (a small data file that is automatically created by a website and stored on the 'local' computer which includes information on when the site was last visited etc.). These forensic traces can hold valuable information for law enforcement agencies when they are investigating potential misuse of technology.

Social networking sites

The World Wide Web continues to develop as technological advancements are made both on and offline. Along with this technological shift there are also social shifts in the way that the World Wide Web is used and in recent years the principal shift has been towards the use of social networking sites.

Social networking sites are the collective names for those that encourage members to produce profiles of each other and to link share this information to others in an attempt to find people of similar tastes etc., producing a network of 'friends'. A profile is created by the user and allows the person to provide details about themselves including name, location, interests (music, history etc.) and even images of themselves. Obviously this has implications for the safety of children and young people and a lot of preventative action has been taken to provide advice to children as to what information to place on the site.

The social networks then allow the profiles and pages to be 'linked' together through 'friends'. Most networks require both parties to give permission for the pages to be linked. However, by providing these links then a large network can be created with friends of friends all seeking to link to each other.

Arguably, the most famous examples of this genre are *Myspace*, *Facebook* and *Bebo*. All three of these sites are considered to be relatively mainstream but have a strong presence in the United Kingdom. *Myspace*, although not the first social networking site, was perhaps the one that caught the public's imagination and quickly became an established presence. It eventually caught the attention of major media organisations and it was bought by News Corporation, a major news provider owned by Rupert Murdoch. This proved controversial but *Myspace* retains a strong presence.

All social networking sites have been controversial. Some organisations, for example *Myspace*, have a minimum age for users before they are allowed to create a profile (*Myspace*'s is 14). However, doubts exist as to how easy it is to verify a person's age, especially a child's. Other sites do not have any minimum age profile and indeed actively target the child and young person market. One of the fastest-growing social networking sites in recent years was *Facebook* which was originally set up for schools, colleges and universities although it is now available to everyone with an e-mail address. There have been criticisms that this site, which is still largely geared towards educational groupings, have been exploited to bully or harass people, including staff (Chatterton and Neil, 2007: 12) although the organisation states that it 'takes down' such sites when discovered. Concern has also been raised as to whether children are posting inappropriate material on their profile pages (see below).

E-mail

It has been suggested that *'e-mail is the oldest and still probably the most widespread application of the Internet'* (Smith, 2002: 3). It is old because it predates the World Wide Web and has been used to facilitate the sending of messages for many years now. e-mail has become an everyday tool with people using it for social, educational and professional purposes. e-mail is used to confirm purchases, to make enquiries as to services and simply as a social tool.

Over recent years e-mail has developed to go beyond mere text. Originally e-mail was an unformatted plain-text system that was functional but was limited in scope. Modern e-mail systems allow e-mails to be sent in formats almost as extensive as word processors. It is common for 'backgrounds' to be included on e-mails, together with a wide-variety of fonts and pictures to be included.

An additional benefit of e-mail is that it is possible to 'attach' files to the e-mail. When this occurs a duplicate of the file is sent, via an Internet connection, to the other person's computer. The attachment could include pictures, documents, sounds or any other computer data. It becomes a convenient way in which data can be shared between two persons and is the electronic equivalent of sending a parcel to someone.

Further advances in e-mail technology have included the provision of encrypted e-mail. This attempts to remedy one of the more perceived difficulties with e-mail, that being that it is largely unsecure. The transmission of the messages takes place over the Internet and before being delivered to the actual user it is 'held' by the relevant e-mail provider (for most people at home this will be their Internet Service Provider) until retrieved by the user. This means there are a number of places where it is possible for someone to try and intercept the e-mail before it is delivered by the user, not least because a copy of the message is ordinarily retained on the e-mail provider's server for a considerable period of time. Encrypting the message will not necessarily prevent the message from being intercepted but it will mean that it becomes more difficult to understand the contents of the message.

Like a web-browser, e-mail contains a number of useful forensic traces. One of the more usual is to be found in the 'header' of an e-mail. This is ordinarily now hidden from general view (although it is easy to see it) and includes information on who sent the e-mail, at what time and where it originated from. Forensic examination can recover this information even after it has been deleted. In order to disguise the origins of an e-mail (either for legitimate or illegitimate purposes) it is possible to use an anonymiser service. These are special servers that exist on the Internet who will forward an e-mail to a recipient without it being possible to trace who the original sender was. Obviously, this does raise issues in terms of its potential application to malicious communications.

Chatrooms

Of all the communication mediums that exist perhaps the one that has, in recent years, received a relatively bad press is that of chatrooms. Chatrooms exist in two principal ways. The first are on websites available on the World Wide Web. The second is through a completely different programme known as Internet Relay Chat (IRC). Both operate in similar ways but IRC is perhaps less easy to control.

Within a chatroom (of whichever type) users are able to 'talk' to each other in real-time, i.e. they are talking to each other live. Most chatrooms are text-only based with the users talking by typing messages to each other. Some chatrooms encourage the use of webcams to allow users to speak to each other, but this can be problematic where there are large numbers of people within a chatroom.

Ordinarily, users will all start in a general chatroom although in IRC this is commonly

referred to as a 'channel'. When a user types a message and submits it to the chatroom everyone within the room/channel can see the message and reply to it. This does mean that in particularly popular rooms a large number of people can be 'speaking' at the same time, causing difficulty in maintaining message structure. In IRC it is easy to create a private channel that is restricted to those that are aware of its existence and are invited to join. A particular difficulty with IRC is that the 'channels' are transient: once the channel has been closed and all users leave, then it ceases to exist until it is recreated. This can cause problems for gathering evidence of conduct within chatrooms. However, law enforcement agencies do have other specialist tools available to them, including a system that allows them to covertly enter chatrooms and monitor discussions. The difficulty is that there are so many chatrooms in existence that identifying which rooms to monitor is not easy and is often based on intelligence.

Peer-to-peer systems

It was noted above that the Internet is, in essence, a global network of networks. This means that a person who accesses the Internet can gain access to information that is contained within all of these networks (subject to issues of content-control etc.). Peer-to-Peer systems (often abbreviated to P2P) work on the basis of sharing information contained on individual computers rather than servers. Instead of gaining access to a wide global network a connection is simply made between two computers, with a person allowing others to gain access to information contained within a specific part of the 'host' computer. That said, there is still a broad network since otherwise it would be difficult to know how to gain access to the information. Many Peer-to-Peer systems have a network/server that allows users to search for content. However, in order to access this content connection is made between the computers. The connection may be direct (i.e. the two computers will speak exclusively), but more often an Internet connection continues to facilitate the connection.

Arguably, the two most famous Peer-to-Peer systems were *Napster* and *KaZaA*. Napster originated as a file-sharing system but evolved into a Peer-to-Peer system. It was predominantly a music-based system that allowed participants to swap 'pirated' music files. Napster differed from many Peer-to-Peer systems in that it maintained a central server. This, as discussed above, allowed for details to be kept of where files were located and, therefore, who should be contacted directly to share the appropriate files. Napster was the subject of several legal challenges because the essence of the system was that it allowed persons to trade 'pirate' versions of music without having to pay royalties or purchase a licence to use the music (c.f. the popular iTunes system where songs are 'purchased' so royalties etc. can be paid). In the mid 2000s Napster re-emerged but this time as a legitimate business that would allow music to be shared solely on a commercial basis.

KaZaA is perhaps the next most famous Peer-to-Peer system and is arguably more of a 'classic' Peer-to-Peer system. It was, in essence, a structured File Transfer Protocol (FTP) i.e. a system that allowed two computers to upload or download files to each other. Whilst Napster had a reputation for being music-based, the same was not strictly true with KaZaA which, although it included music within its listings (and thus was the subject of legal action in the same way as Napster) also included movies, video clips and other files.

Peer-to-Peer networks grew popular because they were considered to be 'urban' and thus there was something slightly rebellious about them. The fact that they included a significant library of music, videos and pictures also led to their exponential growth. However, the controversy of Peer-to-Peer was not just that it permitted pirated material to be included within it, there was also concern that it allowed illegal material to be disseminated. Although many may be searching only for music it was known that a considerable proportion of the material contained within Peer-to-Peer networks was pornographic, including child pornography. Since the transfers do not use the World Wide Web it was also more complicated to identify where material was stored and, therefore, how to remove illegal material.

Freenet

In very recent years one of the most notable technological developments is that of 'Freenet'. Compared to the Internet, Freenet is a relatively small operation but its implications are quite profound. Freenet is considered to be a response by those who think the Internet has become

'conventional' and succumbed to regulation. In the early days of the Internet there was a considerable debate as to whether the Internet should be regulated at all or whether it should be free from censorship. Realistically the latter was never likely and individual countries have attempted to regulate the Internet, with the debate in 2006/7 concentrating on how search engines such as Google agreeing to censor material for countries such as China.

Freenet does not rely on global networks in the same way that the Internet does but is, in essence, an attempt to create one of the biggest 'true' Peer-to-Peer networks in existence. Freenet will use the spare computer capacity of its members. Those who participate will reserve a part of their computer for Freenet and this will be encrypted. When all of these spare capacities are added together it produces a vast amount of data-storage capability. Since the capacity is encrypted the person who 'holds' the computer cannot access the material or indeed know what is contained on the drive. The network created does not rely on single-user location (i.e. Person A stores his data on Person B's computer, with Person B storing his data on Person C's) but rather files are allocated across the grouping.

Those who administer Freenet are determined that it will be without rules as to content and it should, in essence, be the ultimate example of free speech. The difficulty, of course, is that it becomes extremely attractive to those who wish to host or disseminate illegal material and it is believed that Freenet is certainly being used to disseminate child pornography. The anonymity of Freenet also means that it would be extremely difficult to identify and trace who is disseminating such material. The encryption on each computer will also be problematic for identifying and removing the illegal material.

Freenet is undoubtedly something that the law enforcement community is starting to turn its attention to but infiltrating the grouping will not be easy. Also, questions may be raised as to whether it would be cost-effective to do so since the grouping remains relatively low. Given that there are only finite resources it is quite possible that some will take the view that it would be better to target these resources on the Internet (especially the World Wide Web and chatrooms) where more material and offenders are likely to be found.

Short Messaging System (SMS)

The advent of the Short Messaging System, or 'text messaging' as it is better known, has certainly been one of the most noticeable shifts in technology in recent years. It probably needs little explanation to readers and is, in effect, a simple way that allows users to send a message from one mobile telephone to another. It is not dissimilar to a crude e-mail system for telephones, something that is arguably taken further by MMS (Multimedia Messaging System) which allows pictures, music or other documents to be sent.

SMS originated in the early 1990s although realistically it did not take off until the mid-to-late 1990s, not least because that is when the mobile telephones equipped to deal with SMS became more affordable and contract 'packages' started to bundle free messages as part of the overall contract. SMS is now one of the largest methods of instantaneous communications with some estimates suggesting that nearly one billion SMS messages are sent world-wide every day, with the figure in the UK being estimated at 100 million SMS text messages a day. SMS continues to have an advantage for instant communications over e-mail because few people have truly portable e-mail services (e.g. *Blackberry*) due to the cost. It is also thought that SMS messages are more secure than e-mail, in part because it is possible to delete messages from a handset without them being easily recoverable (although it is now possible to forensically recover some messages from the memory or SIM cards within a telephone).

Instant messenger

Arguably this is a misnomer because many communication mediums provide instant messages but this is sometimes more luck than purpose. It is likely that readers who use either SMS or e-mail will have at least one message which has been delayed. Although it is common to believe that both are instant communications, because more likely than not there will be no discernable delay between transmission and delivery, they are not designed to be this way and nor are there any guarantees about how quickly messages will be delivered.

Instant messaging (known as IM) is different to this and is purposely a real-time communication, i.e. a person is communicating then and there with the communication taking as long as it requires to chat. Whilst IM messages will typically use an Internet connection they use a special programme known as an IM connection and it allows two or more users to be connected through the networks allowing instantaneous communication to be made. IM predates the Internet although its popularity has almost certainly increased with Internet connections. IM is similar to a chatroom but it does not require a room *per se* and by using an IM programme (Microsoft's Instant Messenger being one of the more popular since it is free) it is possible to continue working on other programmes etc. whilst 'talking'.

In the early days of IM (1980s and 1990s) the communication was real-time to the extent that you could see the individual keys being transmitted as a person was 'talking'. Whilst this looked good, and at least meant you could see when someone was 'talking', it was frustrating in that you had to wait for a message to be completed before knowing exactly what it meant and if a user wanted to edit the message (i.e. delete a wrong character) this could cause confusion. Modern IM packages tend to allow a user to produce and edit a message until submitted, usually by pressing the 'enter' key. This message is then instantaneously sent to the other connected members who read it as a complete message.

Many argue that IM is the equivalent of a telephone call whereby people are having a 'conversation' whereas e-mail is often considered to be the electronic version of a letter. Whilst this is not strictly correct it is a useful analogy. It will remain to be seen how popular IM remains now that Internet telephony (e.g. 'Skype') is possible. Will people now decide to 'ring' each other using an Internet connection allowing more personable contact whilst retaining the advantages of Internet communication? Those advantages principally being cost since most providers now operate a 'flat-fee' Internet package, and speed.

A feature of IM is that it can detect when contacts are available. This could occur through social-networking sites (see above) where people who are listed as 'friends' also log onto the site and there is the option for them to communicate via EM. Alternatively, and perhaps more frequently, it could occur through the IM programmes itself. Most IM programmes will allow you to establish a set of 'contacts' and the system will automatically poll the Internet to find when the person comes online. Once that person does log onto the Internet a message is sent to indicate that both are online and they can then communicate if they so wish.

A difficulty with IM is that it can be used to hide from more public communication systems. As will be seen later in this book there have been occasions where a person has begun to contact a child in a chatroom but have quickly tried to persuade the child to either enter IM or a private chatroom. The advantage of this is that it is a private communication: no-one can see what is being said. However, this advantage also poses a risk to children since it becomes more difficult for someone to identify whether the contact is being subjected to unwarranted sexual communications. The privacy also brings with it difficulties in obtaining forensic evidence to demonstrate what the communications were. Whilst e-mail is a separate file and accordingly can be recovered even after deletion, the same is not true of IM where unless the user specifically requests otherwise, no transcription would be saved.

3G technology

The latest development of mobile telephones is known as '3G', standing for third-generation. This is rather confusing since many are not familiar with what the first two generations were. In essence, it is often said that the first generation were the analogue mobile telephones that first appeared. Second generation were then digital mobile telephones. Some people refer to second-and-a-half generation telephones which is when GSM was invented and which allowed for much quicker access to the Internet and related resources. It was often considered comparable to Broadband but others have suggested that 3G is more equivalent since it is 'always on'. Later additions to 2.5G were camera telephones and many 'organiser' features, transforming a mobile telephone from a simple communication device into an organiser and music player.

3G has still not developed fully in the United Kingdom, in part because the main networks have not yet moved to this technology. That said, one dedicated network exists ('3') and others will gradually move towards it, especially when the technology becomes easier. The higher speeds and bandwidth means that one selling point for 3G was video-phones. The technology allows for video-calling to be realistic on a 3G network with the quality being acceptable. However, some debate exists as to whether users are particularly

bothered at being able to see the person they are talking to, especially given that many people talk on the telephone whilst doing something else.

However, 3G does offer potential in the future. Since, like Broadband, 3G technology is 'always on', it should mean that there is a more integrated approach to the use of mobile Internet. It is easy to see how Internet radio will become increasingly popular on the move, as will television broadcasts, something that is being pioneered already. Concerns have begun to be raised that the adult entertainment industry are targeting 3G technology, thinking it could be a way to increase their market share by providing pornography on demand wherever a person is. To a customer who wishes to access pornography this carries the additional advantage that it is largely private, with people not being able to tell what content is being accessed. It does raise concerns as to whether the technology will also be used to transmit illegal content.

3G will, in effect, allow a mobile telephone to do many of the things that the Internet allows computers to do at present. This may also mean that many of the concerns raised by the use of the Internet (e.g. chatrooms etc.) could be replicated on 3G telephones but with a smaller forensic footprint so that it would be more difficult to tackle such abuse.

Children and communication technologies

This book is not focusing on the law relating to technology or indeed the law relating to sex offences on the Internet. Its focus is principally on how the technology can be used to facilitate the exploitation of children. Before examining how this may occur it would be prudent to discuss how children use communication technologies.

It would be trite to comment that children and young people are arguably at the centre of technological advancement: it is common to hear people commenting how their son or daughter is a 'wizard' at computers and can do things that they cannot. It is quite clear that young people are becoming involved in technology from an early age and the price of communication technologies often means it becomes accessible to them both at home and school.

In 2002, some 46 per cent of households had access to the Internet (O'Connell, 2002: 3) and since that time it has been increasing, with recent figures suggesting that by 2010, 80 per cent of households will have broadband Internet access, providing 'always-on' coverage to the online world. When Internet access at home and school are examined it was seen, in 2002, that 73 per cent of children had Internet access at home (O'Connell, 2002: 11), and by 2005 this had risen to 75 per cent (Livingstone and Bober, 2005: 8), with almost 92 per cent of children having access to the Internet at school (ibid.). The placement of the Internet access is interesting with only 19 per cent of children having direct access to the Internet in their bedrooms (ibid.) but this will undoubtedly grow in future years. The ISP's have been increasingly promoting 'wi-fi' technology in recent years. Wi-fi allows more than one computer in a designated area (e.g. the home) to have access to the same Internet connection rather than the traditional single computer connected via a modem. Where a child has their own computer it is more likely that they will increasingly have independent access to the Internet thanks to the ISP desire for everyone to gain access to wi-fi broadband.

Parents do appear to recognise some of the dangers of the Internet and it has been reported that approximately one-third of computers have some sort of filtering system contained within them (O'Connell, 2002: 11), although this will only prevent them accessing age-inappropriate material and not, for example, prevent them from using other forms of the Internet connection such as chatrooms. Despite these filters, over 50 per cent of children have seen pornography on the Internet (Livingstone and Bober, 2005: 20), with the majority of these children coming across the pornography unintentionally (ibid.). Of course, this does demonstrate that a minority of children will actively seek pornography on the Internet.

The World Wide Web is certainly not the only communication technology that is used. Despite media presumptions, it would seem that children engaging in chatrooms remains an activity of, an albeit significant, minority. In 2002 approximately 19 per cent of children used chatrooms (O'Connell, 2002: 22) and this had only risen to 21 per cent by 2005 (Livingstone and Boder, 2005: 22). This is perhaps surprisingly stable, and although a two per cent jump in three-years may be considered significant, it does still demonstrate that approximately only one-fifth of children will use chatrooms. Of those children who do use chatrooms, the majority use it in order to hold conversations with existing social contacts

(Livingstone and Boder, 2005: 16), although in a minority of situations people will meet someone they have only met online (Livingstone and Boder, 2005: 22; O'Connell, 2002: 32).

The popular perception on the use of Instant Messenger programmes is also perhaps slightly challenged with research suggesting that they are used by approximately one in eight children (O'Connell, 2002: 22), but it was notable that this was across all age-groups. When an analysis is made of the different age-bands then it is clear that the figure for teenage children increases significantly, with up to one-fifth of that group using them (ibid.). Again, it would appear that for the majority of users, instant-messenger programmes are principally used to converse with people already known to the child (Livingstone and Bober, 2005: 16), although again this appears to differ slightly depending on the age-profile, with older children being more willing to speak to strangers. That said, there remains a suspicion of them. One interviewee for the *UK Children Go Online* survey summarised this as:

> *If you're talking to someone on the Internet, who's a friend, you actually talk to them saying stuff, but feelings and everything are real . . . but if you're talking to someone you haven't met, how do you know if what they're telling you is the truth.*
> (Mark, 17, in Livingstone and Bober, 2005: 16)

One issue of concern to many, however, is whether the concept of 'friends' or 'knowing someone' online is flexible. For example, can a person become a friend even if they have never met but have a social discourse over the Internet? Research certainly suggests that this phenomenon does exist (see 'Rosie', 13, in Livingstone and Bober, 2005: 22), and children, particularly older children, are more prepared to give personal information about themselves out (O'Connell, 2002: 20). Indeed, arguably, the 'friendship' can go further:

> *I have had a very close relationship with a young lady over the internet for about a year.*
> (Oliver, 17, in Livingstone and Bober, 2005: 16)

This does raise questions as to whether children understand issues of identity over the Internet: i.e. did 'Oliver' know for certain that his friend was a young lady? This is one of the issues that, as will be seen in this book, does cause concern because it is possible for a person to be 'tricked' into believing a person is a different age or even sex (a good demonstration of a real-life example of this is presented in 'Jenny's story' produced by Childnet International).

Perhaps the greatest technological shift for young people has been in respect of their use of mobile telephones. Research suggests that 80 per cent of children own their own mobile telephone (Livingstone and Bober, 2005: 8), and this is not just older children, one-third of children aged 7–11 own a mobile telephone (O'Connell, 2003: 32). Much of this growth was within a short period of time. It rose from 17 per cent to 36 per cent of ten-year-olds owning a mobile telephone in one year (Cormie, 2003: 96), and it is likely that this trend will only continue. The majority of children in this age-range own 'Pay-as-you-Go' telephones which perhaps best demonstrates how this technology has adapted.

'Pay-as-you-Go' was originally designed for those people with poor credit rating who telecommunications companies would prefer not to extend credit to as contract customers (since, in essence, contract customers pay in arrears). Yet the British public took to using 'Pay-as-you-Go' in a way that was not expected, and during the early days of the telecommunications growth many preferred such handsets since it provided them with a cheap, cost-effective system without the need for being tied into contracts etc. Parents also saw it as a way in which mobile telephones could be provided to children without too much financial risk being present. It was not just the possibility that they could accrue vast telephone-bills, but if a phone on contract is lost or stolen the person is still liable to pay the contract.

SMS messages continue to be one of the most popular uses for mobile telephones, and again there appears to be research which suggests that it is likely to remain that people use SMS within a small circle of pre-existing friends (Livingstone and Bober, 2005: 16). However, the ways in which SMS technology is being used is changing. SMS, and its multi-media cousin MMS, can be used to access 'screen-savers' or 'wallpapers' for mobile telephones (changing their appearance when switched on) and ringtones. It is also being increasingly used by the entertainment industry to participate in voting etc. (Cormie, 2003: 97),

although the implications of such technological shift became apparent in 2007 when there were a number of 'scandals' where it was shown the integrity of some of this technological shift was questionable. This perhaps does demonstrate one difficulty with technological movement. The pressure is on improving the technology and getting the next uses 'out there', but it does not always appear that the social and corporate responsibility implications of such movements are given the same attention.

Of course, mobile telephones themselves are changing and 38 per cent of mobile phones operated by children includes access to the Internet (Livingstone and Bober, 2005: 8), and this rate will almost certainly increase as technology shifts towards the third-generation telephones (3G). In other countries where this growth has been more significant, the future can perhaps be identified. In Japan, a similar number of children have mobile telephones (83 per cent) (O'Connell, 2003: 36), but with a much more significant usage of 3G telephones. Nearly 20 per cent of female Japanese children have used dating services operated over the 3G network (ibid.), and 50 per cent of children had admitted to meeting someone they first met over a mobile telephone (ibid.). Whilst there may be cultural differences that could explain some of these factors, the mobile communications industry is moving towards producing telephone-specific social networking activities including instant-messenger, chat and other services.

However, it should also be acknowledged that the communications industry is also trying to be proactive in its dealings with child protection. The industry approached the Home Office to become part of the *Home Secretary's Internet Task Force on Child Protection* which is a government-led body that brings together law enforcement, child protection agencies and the communication industry (both computer and now mobile telephone providers) to discuss ways of ensuring the virtual world is safe for children. It has to be recognised that this was a significant step by the mobile telephone operators and it has involved protocols and policies being established to, for example, restrict access to age-inappropriate material (Cormie, 2003: 99). Thus the telecommunications industry, or at least the responsible side of that sector, are learning from the experiences of the Internet companies.

Behaviours online

As has been noted, this book is principally concerned with behaviours online. The majority of the book is from an offender perspective, i.e. what the person who is abusing or exploiting a child does online. Each behavioural type is given a distinct chapter although it will be seen that much of the behaviour is similar. However, at the outset it is important to realise that we are focusing on the behaviour of the individual and not that there is anything intrinsically problematic with communication technologies. It has been suggested:

> New technology makes many children far more accessible to those who wish to abuse [children]. It is more anonymous and it may act as a vehicle for groups of abusers to communicate with one another and provide mutual legitimisation ... New technology [also] introduces new features to the way in which abusers organise their abuse ...
>
> (Palmer, 2004: 11)

This is an important quote because it reinforces that it is not the technology *per se* that poses a danger but the way that the technology can be used by children and offenders in such a way that it can harm children. Child abuse has a long history and technology is simply the latest development in this sad behaviour. People will always find ways of abusing or exploiting children and it is important to note at the outset that the focus is very much on the person and not the technology. It will be seen that some offenders seek to displace their offending behaviour onto technology (see, for example, Taylor and Quayle, 2003: 92) suggesting that technology was either the cause of their behaviour or allowed them to do things they would not ordinarily do. This is a false premise and should be tackled. Technology is inert: it facilitates only that which people create and thus any blame or abuse of technology is the fault of the offender and should be recognised as such.

Behaviour of children

The use of ICT by children has already been discussed (above) but the behaviour of children on ICT should also be touched upon. This behaviour will be discussed in certain individual chapters but perhaps some general points need to be made here.

The conduct of children cannot excuse abusive or exploitative behaviour against them if only because adults are expected to know what is right and wrong, and therefore understand that they should not be complicit in such behaviour with children. Whilst recognising that strong point, it should be acknowledged that some children do exhibit problematic behaviours on the Internet and this does serve as a challenge to those seeking to protect them. This will perhaps be most noticeable in Chapter 2 which discusses cyber-bullying and harassment, where it would appear that a relatively high proportion of the offenders are themselves children. This should perhaps not be too surprising since, unfortunately, childhood bullying has a long history in society. However, problematic behaviour is not only restricted to bullying, but can also include sexually inappropriate behaviour.

One issue to consider at the beginning is who decides what is inappropriate? The law takes a very rigid stance and decides that, for example, the age of consent is 16 and that any sexual contact between children under the age of consent is illegal. The *Sexual Offences Act 2003* (SOA) is sometimes wrongly accused of criminalising teenage 'experimentation' but this is not strictly correct. Whilst it is true that the SOA 2003 introduced a specific offence relating to sexual activity between minors (s.13, SOA 2003), it did not follow that such activity was legal before the introduction of this offence. In fact, sexual activity was illegal under the previous legislation (most notably the *Sexual Offences Act 1956*) since that legislation did not recognise any difference between a child and adult defendant. Accordingly, a child over the age of criminal responsibility, that being 10 (s.34, *Crime and Disorder Act 1998*), would be liable for the offence as an adult (e.g. unlawful sexual intercourse with a girl under 16 (s.6, SOA 1956) or indecent assault of a male (s.14, SOA 1956)) and would be liable to the same punishment (subject to the proviso that a child under 18 does not go to gaol but rather youth detention).

The SOA 2003 therefore continues to stake the (legal) claim that children under the age of 16 are breaching the criminal law although, of course, that is not to say that they will necessarily be prosecuted for such matters since that will be a matter ultimately for the Crown Prosecution Service (CPS). Other aspects of the law continue this approach. A good example is the accessing of indecent images of children (see Chapter 4). The law does not recognise any 'defence' for a child accessing the images or indeed whether the images are of children of the same age as the child, and at least some studies suggest that youths are likely to seek 'age-appropriate' images (see Quayle, 2005: 207), although again this is likely to be relevant to any decision to prosecute.

There may be good reasons for adopting such policies, but it does cause us difficulties in deciding what is appropriate or inappropriate behaviour since sexual experimentation has occurred for many years. Technology provides a new opportunity for this experimentation to exist but also for this behaviour to come to the attention of the law enforcement or child protection communities. Prior to the advent of digital cameras it was known that some teenagers would use 'instant photograph' cameras (colloquially known as 'Polaroid cameras' because the company Polaroid pioneered their development and were the largest manufacturer) to take pictures of each other. The chances of this being detected was reasonably small because effectively only one copy of the image would exist and that would be in the physical possession of a person. Digital technology changes this and as many adults, especially celebrities, have discovered, it is no longer possible to guarantee that only one person has access to an image. If a person takes a sexual photograph using either a mobile telephone or digital camera and sends it to their 'sweetheart' then this can be distributed by the 'sweetheart' to others who may then distribute them once more. Once a sexual image is on the Internet research suggests that it is highly unlikely it will ever be recovered since it will be copied and distributed in an exponential fashion.

Children do not always understand the risks of some of their behaviour and this is considered to be one of the reasons why the law adopts the approach of setting absolute limits rather than more dynamic ones. In certain countries, behaviour will not be illegal if the two parties are consenting and they are within a fixed number of years, usually two or three of each other).

Can their behaviour always be excused as ignorance or sexual experimentation? At one level it can be argued that it is. For example, it is known that some children are looking for pornography on the Internet (Livingstone and Bober, 2005: 20), although this appears to be a minority of people and the indication appears to be that it is adult pornography, and is in essence the electronic equivalent of storing 'adult' magazines. Where indecent images of children

are concerned some studies argue that the images that are sought are more likely to be 'age-appropriate' (Quayle, 2005: 207), although this is certainly not universal. There is also the danger that some children will, in their search to find 'age-appropriate' material demonstrate a willingness to cross boundaries. One limited example is a case that I was involved in as a legal consultant. The child concerned, aged 15, was convicted of the downloading and distribution of indecent images of children. Whilst he claimed his intent was to obtain 'age-appropriate' material, that is, girls aged 13–15, he eventually admitted that in order to obtain these pictures he would 'swap' pictures of much younger children involved in pornography. Whilst the ultimate intention may have been teenage curiosity – and it is certainly accepted that the purpose of a teenage boy is to find teenage girls – he cannot be considered anything other than complicit in the trading of material involving younger children. The boy concerned knew it was 'wrong' so where does this behaviour fit into our model of understanding?

The behaviour is not necessarily fully isolated (something confirmed in other studies, see Quayle, 2005: 207), and perhaps demonstrates a worrying trend. In addition to this, within the 'negative complicity' range there have been reports in the media of schoolchildren filming non-consensual sexual attacks and then broadcasting these images to others. Clearly, those who undertake such acts are criminal but what of the behaviour of those who receive the resultant images (which are often obviously non-consensual) and, after watching them, forward them to additional friends. Is this behaviour not bordering on complicit and so should the law intervene?

Within the more 'innocent' range of behaviour there appears to be a worrying trend towards self-exploitation. There have been isolated examples of children taking indecent images of themselves, often as part of a 'dare' (see Quayle, 2005: 208), and this does demonstrate a complete lack of realisation as to what the consequences of such activity can be. However, this appears to be the 'mild' level of such behaviour. In Chapter 7 the phenomenon of 'camgirls' will be discussed. This is where children will undertake to either sit before a webcam in a sexually provocative way or even perform a sex act in front of a webcam for money or presents. Unlike prostitution, where it will be seen that young people often have no real choice but to enter the sex industry, it would appear that the 'camgirls' are exercising choice, with a BBC Radio investigation showing that they were often induced by the financial rewards that this offered:

> *The Xbox 360 had just come out and games were about 50 quid. I was thinking, 'If I could do this on a regular basis, I could have a lot of games'.*
> (Nick, Fivelive Special Report, June 2007)

The *Child Exploitation and Online Protection Agency* (CEOP) who have a national responsibility concerning child sexual exploitation facilitated by the Internet, have warned that the children are potentially breaching the law, but of more concern is the naivety shown by the children. There is a perception that the activity is 'safe' online because of a belief that nobody can be traced over the Internet and yet that is simply not true. In any event, the images broadcast over the webcam can be stored and distributed, meaning that they could have cause to regret their activities. For the rest of their lives those pictures will exist and they will never know whether someone they come into contact with has seen the pictures or, as some celebrities have discovered, whether they will re-appear decades later if the subject comes to national prominence.

It is important, at the end of this chapter, to remember that the naïve behaviour of certain children should not justify any of the activities of the perpetrator. The courts have sometimes suggested that the law exists to save children from themselves as much as from others (see, for example, *R v Corran et al. [2005] EWCA Crim 192*). This is an astute point and it is justified on the basis that adults are individuals with a sense of responsibility. An adult may well be tempted by the behaviour exhibited by certain teenagers but an adult should be in the position to know that it is legally wrong and not to engage in conduct that is not appropriate. The following chapters will explore not only this behaviour but also the conduct of those adults who realise the vulnerability of teenagers and prey on the behaviour exhibited by teenagers, seeking to turn their experimentation into inappropriate sexual contact.

CHAPTER 2

Bullying and Harassment

It may be thought that the risks to children on the Internet are all sexually related, and indeed the vast majority of this book will be taken up with sexual risks, but they are not exclusively sexual. It has been argued that there are a number of risks to children, including cyber stalking or online bullying and harassment (O'Connell et al., 2004: 2). This chapter will focus on how the law can react to the problem of bullying and harassment.

Cyber stalking

The term 'cyber stalking' is becoming generally accepted within society and conveys the idea that a person can be stalked through the Internet or related communication technologies. It has been suggested that although anyone can be a victim of cyber stalking it is more prevalent against women and children (Bocij and McFarlane, 2002). Research would appear to confirm this, with one children's charity reporting that 14 per cent of 11–19 year-olds had been threatened or harassed through SMS messages on mobile telephones (NCH, 2005: 2) and another report finding that 20 per cent of 9–16 year-old children had been bullied within an online chatroom (O'Connell, 2004: 4). Childline, one of the major child protection charities, reported that incidents of bullying *by* children had increased by 41 per cent in a single year[1] and realistically this, coupled with the expansion in the use of this technology together with the pace at which the technology develops means that its prevalence will only become more common.

What is cyber stalking? Some argue that it is not a separate branch of behaviour:

> Cyber stalking [sic] ... is simply an extension of the physical form of stalking, [and] is where the electronic mediums such as the Internet are used to pursue, harass or contact another in an unsolicited fashion.
> (Petherick in Bocij and McFarlane, 2002)

whereas others suggest it can be classified as distinct:

> Whilst some may view cyber stalking as an extension of conventional stalking, we believe cyber stalking should be regarded as an entirely new form of deviant behaviour.
> (Bocij et al., 2003: 3)

Two principal arguments have been advanced for the suggestion that it is a separate form of behaviour. The first is that if it is simply an extension of offline behaviour then arguably this creates the impression that it is simply a tool used by those who are already harassing people. There is, however, no evidence to suggest that cyber stalkers are restricted to those who would have otherwise harass people offline. The second argument is that the impact on the victim is minimal. Some suggest that because there is remoteness between perpetrator and victim then although the behaviour is a nuisance it is not inherently harmful to a victim (Bocij et al., 2003: 3). It will be seen below that this is not the case and that some victims, particularly vulnerable groups such as children, do suffer direct harm from this behaviour.

The official definition of cyber stalking is that used by the Crown Prosecution Service (the principal prosecuting body):

> Cyber stalking generally takes the form of threatening behaviour or unwarranted advances directed at another using the Internet and other forms of online communications. Cyber stalkers can target their victims through chat rooms, message boards, discussion forums and e-mail. Cyber stalking can be carried out in a variety of ways such as: threatening or obscene e-mail; spamming (in which a stalker sends a victim a multitude of junk e-mail); live chat harassment or flaming (online verbal abuse); leaving improper messages on message boards or in guest books; sending electronic viruses; sending unsolicited e-mail and electronic identity theft amongst others.
> (cited in O'Connell, 2004: 4–5)

This is a wide definition and one that encompasses a whole range of behaviours. Many would probably disagree with the definition since it encompasses such a broad scope of behaviour but, as will be seen, this is the difficulty with this conduct. What the definition also raises however is whether the label 'cyber stalking' is necessarily appropriate. It is suggested it is not because 'stalking' carries its own 'emotional baggage' and the behaviour discussed here, whilst distinct, is much greater than that which would ordinarily be considered stalking. It is for this reason that this chapter has been referred to as 'bullying and harassment' and not stalking.

Identifying the behaviour

The preceding section has identified that cyber bullying and harassment is a separate category of behaviour but what is its prevalence and what form can this behaviour take? One commentator has suggested that 'cyber bullying' ranges from 'flaming' (the posting of provocative or abusive posts) to 'outing' (where personal information about a subject is posted on the Internet) (Bamford, 2004: 2–3). This reinforces the fact that there is a wide body of behaviour that amounts to harassment and bullying online. In this section a series of case-studies will be presented demonstrating some of the behaviour.

Flaming and harassment

The first issue to examine is online harassment and this will be presented through a case-study known as 'cutie-girl'. This study was identified by O'Connell et al. and features the online harassment of children *by* children (O'Connell et al., 2004: 12–6). Their report discusses abuse found in a chat room, one of the more popular mediums for children, particularly because it gives them the opportunity to discuss life with other children from across the world. The technology can be useful and interesting, but can allow abuse too. The transcript provided of the chat is as follows:

cutie-girl	hi any1 wanna chat?
Reaper boy	hey cutie_girl . . we meet again!! I looked at ur pic in ur pro . . .
SwApR	hi Reaper boy . . been awy 4 a while
Reaper boy	u must have hit evry branch on the way down cutie gurl :-)
Reaper boy	u need ur face rearranged
Reaper boy	SwApR look at her pic in pro
SwApR	hey and fat too :-)
cutie-girl	who are u and why are u picking on me? Leave me alone please
Reaper boy	no chance u whining excuse 4 a grl . . what do u think SwApR angel!!!

Angel	not every1 can b an oil painting :-) but I see what u mean :-)
Reaper boy	I know ur home alone right now I can see u in ur school uniform
cutie-girl	ur frightening me . . . please stop
Reaper boy	I can be there in five minutes and then I will make u scream u fat **** . . .
SwApR	gurl . . . if u look like ur mom I'm surprised u even exist.
Angel	r u scared u stupid whiner
Reaper boy	did u get my txt msg whimp b***h
Reaper boy	my mission is to rid the world of crap like u. I will seek u out and destroy u
cutie-girl	please stop this
Reaper boy	I'm watching u all of the time see I can see which websites u access.
	(O'Connell et al., 2004: 12)

A common response to such abuse is for people to state that all 'cutie-girl' must do is to leave the chat room and then the abuse will stop. However, this is a fallacy because it is possible to be tracked on the Internet and this is what happened in this case (O'Connell, 2004: 14). 'Reaper boy' tracked her movements and abused her when he had the opportunity. The tracking normally occurs because of the use of Instant-Messenger (IM) systems which work on the basis of alerting users when someone comes online; indeed the system can be set up to allow a user to be paged when someone they have identified comes online. Whilst it is possible to switch IM systems off, why should a victim have to do this as this prevents them from accessing the services that they wish to enjoy? In essence, such an approach is the virtual equivalent of telling someone who is being stalked offline not to go out of their house.

That said, some simple educational steps can help reduce online harassment and there is undoubtedly a need for an online education programme to work alongside any legal solutions, the law should always be the last line of defence and not the first. The 'pro' referred to in the transcript is the person's 'profile' which allows people to enter personal details of themselves and, like cutie-girl, provide a photograph. Research has suggested that children remain somewhat sanguine about the release of personal information including sex, age and telephone numbers (Livingstone and Boder, 2004: 39) yet it undoubtedly places them at risk.

Children need to be alerted to the fact that telephone numbers should not be given out online because it allows users to abuse that technology (see below) and locations should normally be generic rather than specific (e.g. 'North-East England' rather than 'Middlesbrough'). Educational programmes should also exist to show children what the effects of bullying are, so that the bullies are shown what the effect of their actions are, but we should not lose sight of the fact that victims are entitled to use the Internet in a way that does not cause them to be harassed and that the emphasis, therefore, should not be on restricting access by victims.

The case study also identifies the effects of harassment. It was noted above that some have argued that online harassment is largely harmless but in this particular case 'cutie-girl' developed an eating disorder and psychological distress (O'Connell et al., 2004: 14). It is clear, therefore, that it can lead to actual abuse and harm, and is not a remote, innocent pastime.

Mobile telephones

This case study is a composite study in that it focuses on a number of individuals that have appeared in media reports or who I have come into contact with during my work for child protection organisations. In 2002, NCH reported that 16 per cent of children between the ages of 11 and 19 had received bullying or threatening text messages, and *Bullying Online*, a web-based UK charity, has reported that at least one child has committed suicide after being bullied over a mobile telephone.

Whilst many bullying messages may come from people connected to them, e.g. a school etc., this need not be the case and if someone's mobile telephone number is found on the Internet then some people, like, for example, Reaper boy from the previous case study, will send abusive text messages to them and it therefore becomes more difficult to identify the perpetrator. Another difficulty with the use of text-messaging is that it is possible to disguise or anonymise the number it was sent from. The very nature of the mobile telephone means that the apprehension of a child can be heightened, since when someone says, 'I can see you' the child cannot know whether this is true or not.

Mulkerrins, in an insightful feature in the *Times*, shows how technology allows blame for

bullying to be displaced onto others. She reports how a 12-year-old girl was accused of sending abusive text messages to one of her friends, and how this led to herself, in turn, suffering abuse and bullying. The mother could prove, via telephone billing evidence, that the daughter had not sent the messages and she eventually found out that computer Internet sites can be used to send SMS messages. The sites require the user to enter their telephone number, but this is purely for display purposes and, accordingly, any number could be entered and this would show up on the phone. This is almost certainly what happened in this case, but the damage was done and the girl accused remains feeling harassed.

A particular difficulty with mobile phone harassment is that it provides no escape. Carrie Herbert, a teacher who specialises in dealing with bullied children, makes the point:

> *Children who are being bullied in the classroom and in the playground can at least get some kind of sanctuary at home. With this kind of bullying, the text messaging can come up while you are watching television, while you are having a family meal. It is extremely invasive.*
> (BBC News online, 15.iv.02)

Switching off may seem an answer but, notwithstanding the point about the impact this can have on the victim's enjoyment of their life noted in the first case study, this does not necessarily help with mobile telephones. Text messages are stored on the server and delivered when the telephone is switched on so by turning off the phone, the victim is only delaying the delivery of the message, not stopping the harassment. Also, some mobile telephones also have, in effect, 'read receipts' whereby the sender's phone is told when a message is delivered. Accordingly, a user will know when the victim's telephone has been switched on (because they will be notified the text message is delivered) and they can then send more messages, knowing that the victim will read them immediately.

Mobile telephone operators have traditionally been reluctant to deal with nuisance telephone calls or messages, arguing that the solution is to change the victim's number. Whilst this is a solution it will not be a particularly effective solution if the bully is someone known to the child as it is inevitable that the number will reach them again. Also, changing a number is not particularly convenient, again causing disruption to a person's private life. In recent times, telephone companies have been getting better and they will work alongside the police to gather evidence for prosecutions etc. or, if the perpetrator is also on the same network to bar them. Recent advances that have been mooted have included users being able to bar calls and text messages from an individual number, something not easily achievable at the moment.[2]

Posting

Like the second case study this is a composite study. The Internet, and related mediums, can be used to harass people through posting messages or images. Bocij et al. note that a neighbour subjected a US-based family to harassment. Part of the harassment involved them receiving late-night telephone calls from men asking to speak to their 9-year-old daughter. It became apparent that the neighbour had posted a message on the Internet that purported to solicit the child for sexual purposes and provided their telephone number as a contact point (Bocij et al., 2002).

Within the United Kingdom there are reports of children taking pictures of children and posting them onto the Internet, frequently with sexual references. The children probably do not understand the potential consequences of this action, including making the child a target of a sex offender. It is undoubtedly a threatening, or harassing, action and can cause extreme distress to the child. More seriously, however, are reports that children are prepared to take indecent images of each other and post these to the site. The pictures may well be taken by camera phones when people are getting changed for recreational activities, or by making a composite image through using graphic manipulation software to fuse the head of a real person onto the naked body of another, thus conveying the impression that the victim is posing nude.[3]

The embarrassment that this can cause is extreme and it can feature as part of a sustained campaign of bullying or harassment. When the images are linked to mobile telephone numbers or e-mail addresses, the victim also has to deal with unwanted telephone calls or e-mail messages from people seeking to sexually exploit the person, making many victim's lives seem unbearable.

A more sustained level of harassment is the creation of Internet sites that are designed to bully or harass children. In 2003, a 15-year-old girl was subjected to such online bullying when classmates created a site known as 'Jodi's Fat But' [*sic*][4] which contained abusive comments about her, and her appearance, and culminated in it posting the date that she would die. The victim of this activity was left extremely distressed by the site and the knowledge that people from a global audience could see such sites makes it more difficult to come to terms with. Unfortunately, it appears that these sites are increasing. It is very difficult for ISPs or web-hosts to detect such sites but most providers will close the site down when it is notified to them. That said, there are an increasing number of sites that are set up in jurisdictions where they are less strict on the content of their sites, and so increasingly it is quite possible that victims will not be able to rely on hosts taking these sites down.

The legal framework

Bullying and harassment, especially when it is perpetrated by children, is always difficult to regulate. However, in all of the circumstances above, it is quite possible that it would be an adult that is trying to make contact with the child. Also, the case studies that were discussed above did not make reference to those adults that pester children etc. with the ultimate intention to sexually exploit them. In part, this is because this action will be discussed elsewhere (Chapter 5) but also because, as was noted above, it is not possible to detail every type of abuse. When considering the legal framework, it is important to consider the various aspects of this abuse and to return to the definition of cyberstalking as used by the CPS which does define the key behavioural aspects.

In terms of the legal framework there are two aspects to consider. The first is the use of the criminal law and this will require examining three headings of liability:

- Offences against the person.
- Communication offences.
- Harassment.

The civil law may also be able to assist individual perpetrators although, as will be noted, there is an argument that this may not be appropriate since it may only address the issue in respect of a single person and not tackle the wider problem (see below).

Criminal law

It was noted in the introduction that this book is primarily focused on the use of the criminal law and the reasons for this were set out. In terms of the criminal law there are a number of different types of offences that could be applicable here although where it is another child undertaking the bullying or harassment it is perhaps more open to question whether this is suitable.

Offences against the person

Assault, contrary to popular perception, is not restricted to the idea of physical contact. Indeed, in its technical sense, an assault does not refer to any bodily contact, but rather the apprehension of immediate unlawful bodily contact (*R v Ireland; R v Burstow [1998] AC 147*). Accordingly, if the harassment or bullying causes a person to fear the immediate apprehension of unlawful bodily contact, the perpetrator would be liable for the crime of assault. However, assault is triable only summarily and punishable by a maximum of six months' imprisonment (to be eventually increased to twelve months' imprisonment).

Whilst assault is an offence in its own right, it is only one of a series of non-fatal offences, all of which are linked by the concept of an assault. The more serious offences relate to bodily harm. Three offences are of note: assault occasioning actual bodily harm (s.47, *Offences Against the Person Act 1861 (OAPA)*), inflicting grievous bodily harm (s.20, OAPA 1861) and causing grievous bodily harm with intent (s.18, OAPA 1861). The courts have held that psychiatric illness amounts to 'bodily harm' (*R v Chan Fook [1994] 1 WLR 689* and *R v Ireland; R v Burstow* (op. cit.)) and thus where psychiatric harm is caused by the bullying or harassment more serious offences may apply. However, it is important to note the limitations of these offences. It must be psychiatric harm and thus medical evidence will be required to prove this and transient symptoms such as distress and anxiety will not suffice (Ormerod, 2005: 552).

In order to explore the potential applicability of bodily harm to the issue of harassment, it is necessary to consider the offences in two classes; actual bodily harm and grievous bodily harm.

Actual bodily harm

Section 47 of the 1861 Act creates the offence of an *assault occasioning Actual Bodily Harm*. Whilst

Ireland; Burstow has ensured that psychiatric harm can amount to bodily harm, this does not necessarily mean that all psychiatric injury will contravene s.47 as an assault or battery is required to be the tool by which such harm was occasioned. It will be remembered from above that it was held that an assault is causing someone to apprehend immediate application of unlawful bodily contact. It has been suggested that in many 'stalking' cases the application of s.47 will not be possible because, whilst there may be psychiatric harm, there will be no apprehension of immediate unlawful violence or, potentially, of any unlawful violence at all (Gardner, 1998: 35).

Others have developed this issue of immediacy further, by making the useful point that the requirement is not that a person is immediately fearful of violence, but rather, that the person is in fear of immediate personal violence (Smith, 1997: 811), something which is not necessarily the same. However, immediacy cannot mean instantaneous, a point decided by the House of Lords in *Ireland*. It was accepted in this case that the victim receiving the telephone calls experienced the fear of immediate violence, even though she was on the telephone so instantaneous violence was unlikely. The extension of 'immediate' to include the very short-term was welcomed and is in any event inevitable in the era of mobile telephones where one need not be in the sanctity of a house to receive a call, and where the caller may be anywhere without the receiver knowing where precisely the caller is (although of course this is subject to the proviso that if the caller knows that the person is several miles away then they cannot apprehend immediate and unlawful violence and so no assault would exist).

Realistically, the concept of assault will only help us so far. It is unlikely that a threat, or harassment, by e-mail would suffice as it is difficult to see how the recipient would fear immediate unlawful violence, given that the person must be somewhere capable of transmitting an e-mail message. Instant messaging via the Internet is also unlikely to be fruitful given the manner in which it is completed. Where text-based harassment may come within this line of reasoning, however, would be SMS text messages since a message, 'I can see you. I'm going to get you' could, conceivably, be sent from someone very near to you.

Thus the concept of actual bodily harm would appear to draw a distinction between mobile technology and fixed technology, with the former more easily coming within its breadth. Even where mobile technology is used, however, there must be the immediacy requirement. In *Kelly v DPP [2002] EWHC Admin 1428* the Divisional Court was called upon to consider the status of 'voicemail' messages. This case will be discussed in detail below, but the case concerned threatening messages being left on a 'voicemail' service. This, it is submitted, is a paradigm example of Smith's point about the notion of immediacy. Whilst the victim in *Kelly* was undoubtedly immediately in fear, there was no question of her fearing immediate violence given the gap between placing the call and listening to it. Accordingly, assault could not have been contemplated.

Grievous bodily harm

Whilst an assault and, accordingly, actual bodily harm could be somewhat restricted in the area of harassment, it does not follow that the extension of liability in *R v Ireland; R v Burstow* is similarly limited in scope. It will be remembered that there are two offences relating to grievous bodily harm; inflicting grievous bodily harm (s.20) and causing grievous bodily harm with intent (s.18).

Ireland; Burstow confirmed that bodily harm can include psychiatric harm, and in *DPP v Smith [1961] A.C. 290* the House of Lords held that 'grievous bodily harm' meant 'really serious'. Accordingly, if a person causes or inflicts really serious psychiatric harm onto a person then they could be liable for a conviction under sections 18 or 20. Section 18 is the least troublesome as this refers to inflicting grievous bodily harm with the intention of causing grievous bodily harm. Unlike s.47 there is no requirement that there be an assault, merely that a person has inflicted the harm with the requisite intent. The test for intention is usually common to all offences although it has been noted that this may not always be true (Ormerod, 2005: 101). The accepted test is usually encapsulated in murder cases, with the leading test being set out in *R v Wollin [1999] AC 82*. The test is twofold:

1. that the person intended to cause grievous bodily harm (intention being given its ordinary dictionary meaning) or;
2. that the person did an act that was virtually certain to cause grievous bodily harm, and the defendant appreciated that this was the case.

In the majority of situations it is likely that liability will proceed under limb (1), but it is conceivable that in cases of harassment the second limb could also be used. How often s.18 would be used is highly questionable since it is unlikely that many people would harass a person with the intention of causing a *serious* psychiatric injury (e.g. doing an act intending to cause a nervous breakdown), but it does remain a possibility.

The more likely charge (although it should be noted that it would be extremely rare for grievous bodily harm to ever be found because of the high threshold of injury required) would be section 20, i.e. inflicting grievous bodily harm. This, unlike s.18, does not require intention but can be satisfied by recklessness, that is to say foresight of grievous bodily harm, yet some have suggested this will not be easily proven:

> *How do you prove that a person foresaw that his act would or might cause a neurotic illness, something identifiable only by expert evidence, as distinct from mere fear or anxiety?*
>
> (Smith, 1997: 811)

Whilst this point is sound, and foresight of fear or anxiety would not suffice for liability under this section, it may not be as difficult as Smith believed; since the foresight of some bodily harm, rather than grievous bodily harm, will be sufficient (see *R v Savage and Parmenter [1992] AC 699*). Accordingly, if the perpetrator foresaw that the victim may be traumatised beyond fear and *might* suffer a recognisable psychiatric injury then liability would arise.

It is crucial when talking about grievous bodily harm not to lose sight of the 'gross' threshold. Section 20 is not about someone causing psychiatric harm to a victim, it is about someone inflicting *serious* psychiatric harm to a victim and in many situations it will be difficult to demonstrate this. Although it has been noted that victims may develop, for example, eating disorders, it is not clear that this by itself would amount to a 'serious' psychiatric injury (although it is a matter of fact for the jury and thus, depending on age etc., it is possible). Another difficulty with harassment and psychiatric harm is that alternative liability for offences against the person is not available. The House of Lords has held that actual bodily harm is normally an alternative to s.20 (*R v Ireland; R v Burstow* (op. cit.) at [159–61]), i.e. where the bodily harm is not serious it would amount to actual bodily harm. This avenue is not possible with psychiatric harm since it was noted above that in harassment cases it is unlikely that there would be an assault. Without an initial assault then s.47 liability cannot accrue.

It has been seen in this section that offences against the person may be of some use in this sphere but realistically they will be of relatively limited assistance because of the difficulties discussed above.

Communication offences

It will be seen in this book that the general rule in the criminal law is that there are no specific 'Internet' offences. The general principle is that if something is illegal offline then it is also illegal online. A slight exception to this rule, however, is in respect of communication offences. These do not break the rule in that they are not Internet-specific but they are specific offences that are designed to cover the use of communication technologies.

There are two offences of particular relevance here. The first is s.127 of the *Communications Act 2003* (which replaced s.43, *Telecommunications Act 1984*) and the second is s.1 of the *Malicious Communications Act 1988*. Both offences are similar and, arguably, overlap with each other.

Section 1 is the older offence and it creates an offence, inter alia, as follows:

(1) Any person who sends to another person:
   (a) letter, electronic communication or article of any description which conveys:
     (i) a message which is indecent or grossly offensive;
     (ii) a threat; or
     (iii) information which is false and known or believed to be false by the sender; or
   (b) any article or electronic communication which is, in whole or part, of an indecent or grossly offensive nature.

is guilty of an offence if his purpose, or one of his purposes, in sending it is that it should, so far as falling within paragraph (a) or (b) above, cause distress or anxiety to the recipient or to any other person to whom he intends that it or its contents or nature should be communicated.

Whereas s.127 of the 2003 Act states:

(1) A person is guilty of an offence if he:
   (a) sends by means of a public electronic communications network a message or other matter that is grossly offensive or of an indecent, obscene or menacing character; or
   (b) causes any such message or matter to be so sent.
(2) A person is guilty of an offence if, for the purpose of causing annoyance, inconvenience or needless anxiety to another, he:
   (a) sends by means of an electronic communications network, a message that he knows to be false,
   (b) causes such a message to be sent; or
   (c) persistently makes use of a public electronic communications network.

Both offences are triable only summarily (i.e. in the Magistrates' Court) and are punishable by the statutory maximum which, at the time of writing, is six months' imprisonment (s.1(4), MCA 1988 and s.127(3), CA 2003). Although the powers of magistrates to impose custodial sentences will soon alter to allow imprisonment for up to twelve months (s.154, CJA 2003) there are currently no plans to raise the maximum sentence for either of these crimes (see, by implication, Sch.27, CJA 2003).

As noted previously, s.127 replaced s.43 of the Telecommunications Act 1984, and learned writers had previously argued that s.1 of the 1988 Act would be preferred over s.43 because it offered a wider versatility.[5] However, it must be doubted whether the same can be true of the relationship between sections 1 and 127 because, at least in terms of electronic mediums, s.127 appears more versatile. Section 1 can be used for letters and/or notes, something that s.127 cannot, but where an electronic medium is introduced (and s.32, CA 2003 makes it clear that this includes '*electrical, magnetical or electro-magnetical energy, or signals of any description*' (s.32(1)) which would include most communication mediums, including telephone and satellite) it is likely that s.127 is now the more versatile.

Interestingly, on the face of it, s.127(1) does not include any *mens rea*[6] requirement, whereas s.1 potentially does as there is the requirement that the purpose is to cause distress or anxiety. Accordingly, it could be argued that the mental requirement is that of intention or knowledge (i.e. sending a message intending to cause distress or anxiety or sending a message knowing that it would cause distress or anxiety) although the counter-argument is that Parliament intended the offence to be one of strict-liability since they expressly include *mens rea* in other sections (most notably s.127(2)). However, the courts are normally loathe to permit a crime of strict liability (Ormerod, 2005: 141 *et seq*.) and it is certainly more likely that the courts will, for example, require evidence that a defendant knew or intended the message to be sent.

It will be remembered that s.127 covers three classes of communications, those being:

- Indecent or obscene.
- Grossly offensive.
- Menacing.

In *DPP v Collins [2005] EWHC 1308* the Divisional Court was asked to consider the meaning of these terms. Sedley LJ, giving the judgment of the Court, stated that indecent and obscene messages were to be judged objectively and according to *'contemporary standard of decency'* (at [10]). This follows the long-established rule applied by the courts (see, for example, *R v Stanford [1972] 2 QB 391*) (and this will be examined in more detail in Chapter 3). A menacing message was, according to his Lordship, one that is threatening and *'seeks to create a fear in or through the recipient that something unpleasant is going to happen'* (at [10]). It has been noted that this expression means that it is not restricted to the recipient of the person but could include threats made to someone or something known to the recipient (Ormerod 2005: 795). Sedley LJ thought that for menacing messages, *'the intended or likely effect on the recipient must ordinarily be a central factor in deciding [guilt]'* ([2005] EWHC 1308 at [10]) which certainly implies foresight, meaning that *mens rea* is present, supporting the suggestion noted above. Perhaps more importantly, it also potentially means that a person could be convicted of the offence even if the recipient was not *in fact* menaced (Gillespie, 2006a: 127).

The majority of the decision was, however, focused on the meaning of the term 'gross offensiveness'. It should be noted at the outset that the decision in *Collins* was appealed to the House of Lords ([2006] UKHL 40) and it is thus incumbent to examine what the House decided in respect of this decision (since the decision of the House of Lords was restricted solely to the issue of gross offensiveness). The House, agreeing with

Sedley LJ in the Divisional Court, suggested that in order to decide whether something was grossly offensive require the courts to consider the *'standards of an open and just multiracial society'* ([2006] UKHL 40 at [9]).

Where, however, the House of Lords and Sedley LJ differed was over the context of the message. Sedley LJ held that gross offensiveness had an 'added value' to offensiveness ([2005] EWHC 1308 at [5]) but even this would not be sufficient to convict since the justices would be entitled to look at the context in which the message was sent (at [11]). Sedley LJ believed that *'it is the message, not its content, which is the basic ingredient of the statutory offence'* (at [9]) meaning that sometimes something that is objectively grossly offensive would not be depending on the circumstances. His Lordship provided the example of two barristers talking about the case at hand, including the very words complained about, and suggested that it would be inappropriate to suggest that there would be criminality here (at [9]).

The House of Lords disagreed and stated that the legislation prohibited the sending of a message that *'contravened the basic standards of our society'* ([2006] UKHL 40 at [7]) and held that it was irrelevant who sent the message or indeed whether it was delivered at all (at [8]); it was sufficient that it was sent. This could potentially capture a broad range of behaviour, including barristers discussing a case, but the House of Lords anticipated this problem by requiring *mens rea*. The House stated that a grossly offensive message would only be culpable where the person intended to send a grossly offensive message or was reckless as to whether it was grossly offensive (at [10]–[11]); however they then quantified this by suggesting that messages that *'went beyond the pale'* would not require *mens rea* (see Gillespie, 2006a: 127).

The decision of the House of Lords in *Collins* has ensured that s.127 is a broad offence and indeed it could be suggested that it has become too wide an offence in terms of its general scope (Gillespie, 2006b). Nevertheless, in terms of cyber-bullying and harassment it is suggested that s.127 could be an extremely useful offence, especially where the message is grossly offensive or menacing. However, it has been suggested that the principal difficulty with the communication offences is that they do not necessarily capture the behaviour that is occurring (Finch, 2001: 257). This is an important point and whilst it can be seen that harassment in real-time communication will almost certainly be within the scope of s.127, it is unlikely that the bullying and harassment will be a single message but rather a pattern of abuse. Finch has argued that the difficulty that this could bring is that this might under-play the abuse suffered and call into account the adequacy of the punishments available.

Further questions exist as to whether the communication offences could cover all harassment and behaviour. A good example would be the creation of a website where questions must be raised as to whether this would constitute 'a communication' within the meaning of s.127. It is suggested that the term 'a communication' implies a message that is sent from one person to another. It is known that in some instances of online bullying and harassment the victim will be the subject of a website and the URL (website address) may be distributed, including to the victim. Whilst the e-mail containing the link is a communication can it be said that it is offensive, menacing, indecent or offensive? The site may be but the message is innocuous as it includes only the URL. It could be argued that, although the URL is the content, the actual message is wider and encompasses the website to which the URL relates. However, this construction could lead to many difficulties, especially where the sender of the e-mail did not create the site, and may also be arguably stretching the interpretation of s.127 too far.

Harassment

Arguably the most obvious solution to the problem would be to use the *Protection From Harassment Act 1997* which was enacted as a specific response to the problem of stalking and harassment (Finch, 2001: 217). The Act is interesting in that it is a piece of hybrid legislation covering both civil and criminal law wrapped around a common definition of 'harassment'. This definition is contained within s.1 which states:

(1) A person must not pursue a course of conduct:
   (a) which amounts to harassment of another, and
   (b) which he knows or ought to know amounts to harassment of the other.
(1A) A person must not pursue a course of conduct:

(a) which involves harassment of two or more persons, and
(b) which he knows or ought to know involves harassment of those persons, and
(c) by which he intends to persuade any person (whether or not one of those mentioned above):
   (i) not to do something that he is entitled to or required to do; or
   (ii) to do something that he is not under any obligation to do.
(2) For the purposes of this section, the person whose course of conduct is in question ought to know that it amounts to harassment of another if a reasonable person in possession of the same information would think the course of conduct amounted to harassment of the other.

There are, therefore, several aspects to this definition but it should be noted that this does not establish the crime, this is created in Sections 2 and 3 which will be discussed below. Subsection 1(1A) was added by s.125, *Serious Organised Crime and Police Act 2005* and was primarily designed to tackle animal rights extremists (Owen et al., 2005: 93–4), although it could apply in a wider way. However, it is more likely that for the purposes of online bullying and harassment of children and young persons the original s.1(1) would be more relevant.

It is quite clear from s.1(1)(b) and s.1(2) that *mens rea* must be present for criminal harassment that being, at the very minimum, objective recklessness, since a person will be deemed to know that a course of conduct amounts to harassment if a reasonable person with the same knowledge would. It is necessary that a person must in fact be harassed (see s.1(1)(a)) and this is defined in s.7(2) as causing someone to be alarmed or distressed. This requirement means that where a course of conduct would lead a reasonable man to consider it would amount to harassment but the victim was not in fact alarmed or distressed then no liability can arise (*DPP v Ramsdale [2001] EWHC Admin 106*).

The final point to note about s.1 is that it requires a 'course of conduct' to lead to the harassment. Section 7(3) makes clear that this means conduct that occurs on at least two occasions, but the courts have consistently stated that pure mathematics is not sufficient and they will look to see whether there is a pattern of abuse (Finch, 2002: 707). In other words, the fact that there have been two incidents of harassment will not necessarily mean any criminal offence has been committed. In *DPP v Lau [2000] 1 FLR 799* the High Court stated that the fewer incidents there were, the less likely it is that the courts will consider that the defendant has pursued a *course* of conduct. It has been suggested that a nexus must exist between the incidents in order to demonstrate a course of conduct (Ormerod, 2006: 581), and the analogy of a person attending a hospital on two occasions can be used. This, by itself, would not amount to a course of treatment since it may have been to treat separate ailments (Ormerod, 2006: 582), but where there is a link it becomes easier to demonstrate a course.

Similarly, the courts have also held that a series of separate events that take place close together may in fact be considered a single act and not a course of conduct. An example of this is *DPP v Ramsdale [2001] EWHC Admin 106* where the defendant followed the complainant home, rang the doorbell and tried telephoning her. He then left, before returning and breaking into her house. He then left the house but returned fifteen minutes later. At his trial in the magistrates' court he was acquitted because the magistrates argued this was a single act and not a course of conduct. The High Court did not disagree with this assessment (at [20]–[21]) and so his acquittal stood. However, it is important to be clear about what the High Court actually said. It did not state that this could not amount to a course of conduct but instead that it was not unreasonable or wrong for the magistrates to conclude that it was only a single act. In other words, a different bench of magistrates' could consider similar actions to be a conduct if the facts suggested a course of conduct.

The lack of certainty that exists over when closely related activities occur could be problematic in the field of cyber-bullying and harassment. If a person is in an internet chat room or using instant messaging software then it would appear logical to say that each comment within this room will be taken as a part of the whole; i.e. the entire conversation would be a single act and not a course of conduct by itself. What happens where the person is being tracked through different chatrooms though? It was noted above that this sometimes happens. Is this a course of conduct or similarly still one transaction? For example, D harasses V in chat-room X. V leaves that chat room and joins chat room Y. D discovers V's location and starts to harass V in chat-room Y. It could be argued that this is now two separate acts of harassment (and potentially a course of conduct). The alternative argument, however, is that this is still one transaction, especially where the harassment is close in time.

Where matters become even more complicated is in respect of SMS messages or e-mails. In *Kelly v DPP [2002] EWHC 1428* a defendant sent three abusive and threatening messages to the victim within five minutes of each other. The telephone calls were not picked up by the victim immediately but were recorded onto her voicemail service. When the victim listened to them, she reported the matter to the police and the defendant was charged with harassment. The Divisional Court rejected an argument that these telephone calls should just amount to a single act of harassment notwithstanding the fact that the victim listened to all three messages at once, because they were separate calls, and therefore separate actions. This decision has been criticised because of the proximity of the acts (Ormerod, 2003: 47) and it is certainly difficult to reconcile this decision with, for example, *Ramsdale* (above). The answer lies in the fact that in both cases the courts were simply being asked whether it was reasonable for the magistrates to conclude the way that they did but the contradictions certainly do nothing to help the certainty of the law. Ormerod suggests that the difficulty with *Kelly* is that it could mean that two immediate telephone calls are considered to be harassment (Ormerod, 2003: 47) and yet this would seem to rely purely on mathematics rather than consider whether it amounts to a 'course' of conduct.

The decision in *Kelly* has implications for the online world since Burton J. expressly suggested that separate e-mails could be considered separate acts and thus a course of conduct ([2002] EWHC 1428 at [23]). Yet it is easy to see how e-mails could be sent very quickly. Would it make any difference if the victim responds? For example, what is the position if D sends an e-mail to V which is capable of amounting to harassment to which V replies 'stop it'. D immediately sends another e-mail saying he will not stop and including more harassing behaviour. *Kelly* suggests that this could be two actions and thus capable of coming within s.1 but surely it is more comparable to *Ramsdale* with it being considered one conversation and, therefore, a single act rather than a course of conduct.

Potentially the same difficulty could be experienced with the creation of a website. Some websites have a single page, whilst others have numerous pages that are hyper-linked together. In *Chiron Corporation Ltd v Greg Avery [2004] EWHC 493* the High Court decided that harassment could take place through the Internet. In that case it was clear that numerous sites had been used, but what is the position where a single website is created for the purpose of harassing or threatening another. Is this a single act or a course of conduct? It could be argued that, where it is authored over a number of days, this amounts to separate acts, but is this not an example of a continuing act? Also, if D creates the site but also creates a 'comments' section where the comments of posters are automatically published then is this just a single act because the subsequent posts will be by other individuals and not by D? Section 7(3A) arguably solves this difficulty since it provides that conduct that is aided, abetted, counselled or procured by another will be considered a course of conduct for both the principal and the accomplice. Allowing individuals to post abusive messages about a person would arguably come within aiding and abetting, especially where the site was created with the very purpose of harassing another (see, for example, Posting, above).

Criminal offences

It is not necessary for the course of conduct to be illegal *per se* and indeed it has been noted that the 1997 Act was drafted in such a way as to ensure that otherwise innocent activities could be captured within its remit (Finch, 2002: 707). This is an important point because some aspects of harassment behaviour in the offline world could appear to be innocuous save for the fact that it contributes to the harassment of the victim (e.g. sending flowers to the victim). On the online world it is perhaps less easy to see how legitimate actions would form part of the behaviour but certainly non-illegal acts may. Good examples of this would include posting pictures onto a website. Assuming the pictures are not indecent then this would not, by itself, lead to a criminal offence but could form part of the course of conduct leading to a harassment charge.

There are two principal criminal offences contained within the *Protection From Harassment Act 1997*, which are to be found in Sections 2 and 4 of the Act. Section 2 is the 'simpler' offence and Section 4 is the more serious. The Section 2 offence simply criminalises someone who pursues a course of harassment defined in s.1 (s.2(1)). It is a summary offence and is punishable by a maximum sentence of six months' imprisonment. The more serious offence is Section 4 and the marginal note for this offence states that it is an offence of 'putting people in fear of violence'. The offence is defined as:

> *A person whose course of conduct causes another to fear, on at least two occasions, that violence will be used against him is guilty of an offence if he knows or ought to know that his conduct will cause the other so to fear on each of these occasions.*
>
> (s.4(1))

'Ought to know' is defined in the same way as in s.1, i.e. it is an objective test for reasonable persons (s.4(2)) and the offence is triable either-way carrying a maximum sentence of five years' imprisonment. It is important to note that s.4 is a tighter offence than s.2 since not only must there be a course of conduct but also on *each occasion* the victim must fear violence. Also the fear of violence must be in respect of the victim and not someone known to him regardless of the relationship that exists between them (Finch, 2001: 263). The requirement to fear violence on each occasion could arguably take the issue of proximity further than that which caused confusion in s.2. Ormerod uses the facts of *Kelly v DPP* (op. cit.) as an example and poses the question:

> *By listening to the recorded messages in quick succession, has the victim only been caused to fear violence on 'one occasion'? Would it be legitimate for the police to tell her to go away and listen to the saved message again so that [a] s.4 prosecution can be brought?*
>
> (Ormerod, 2003: 47)

This is an important point and demonstrates that the natural language of the Act does contemplate that a person listening to the same message could, presumably, be in fear on two separate occasions. It would clearly be absurd for this to occur but this would mean that the notion of 'course of conduct' would mean both the perpetrator and victim must be examined so that there is a correlation between incidents. This could have repercussions where non-instantaneous modes of communication are used.

It is submitted that D commits no offence under s.4 where . . . he posts threatening letters on Monday, Wednesday and Friday all of which arrive on Saturday and are read by the victim consecutively.

(Ormerod, 2003: 47)

This, it is submitted, must be correct but this undoubtedly has an implication for the concept of cyberstalking. If the victim is away from their computer for a few days and an offender has sent a number of e-mails to the victim, which they read consecutively, causing fear, is a conviction valid? Applying the reasoning of Ormerod, the answer would appear to be that a conviction under s.2 is possible since there are two transactions (applying the logic of *Kelly*) but a conviction under s.4 would not be sustainable because the victim would only apprehend violence on one occasion.

Lord Steyn, almost certainly in *obiter* comments, identified another significant weakness in s.4. The 1997 Act requires a person to fear that violence *will* occur and not just *may* occur (*R v Ireland; R v Burstow* [1998] AC 147 at [153]). It has been suggested that a person does not need to fear immediate violence (Simester and Sullivan, 2002: 398) and so to this extent it compares favourably with non-fatal offences (see above). However, it has been suggested that the requirement of fearing violence will occur could cause difficulties for charging s.4 (Finch, 2002: 710–11) since it requires a certainty that may be difficult to achieve. Some go further and suggest that it could be a fatal flaw when coupled with the requirement that a person must fear violence twice. The argument is based on the premise that if a person is in fear of violence the first time but nothing happens how can they believe that violence *will* occur on the subsequent occasions (Addison and Lawson-Cruttenden, 1998: 41). Whilst this is an interesting argument it must be one that is based on too literal a reading of s.4 and without a full understanding of the psychology of victims. A person is, it is submitted, perfectly capable of being in fear that violence will occur even though on the previous occasion the violence did not materialise.

In the context of cyber-bullying and harassment it would appear that the threshold for s.4 will, in many cases, be too high. In part this is because of geographical proximity. Where the perpetrator and the victim are not known to each other and are talking in an internet chat room is it likely that a victim could fear that violence will occur if the person does not know their address? However where the victim and perpetrator are known to each other this issue is perhaps less significant and it is possible that s.4 could be used. That said, even where s.4 may be possible it is notable that the prosecution agencies appear to prefer a charge under s.2 (Finch, 2002: 711), perhaps because of its simplicity.

Restraining orders

Given that Section 2 is punishable by a maximum of six months' imprisonment it could be questioned why this should be preferred to the communication offences noted above. The answer is partially to do with the full sentencing powers of a court when dealing with a case of harassment and the fact that under s.5 of the Act it is possible for a court to also issue a restraining order.

A restraining order is the equivalent of an injunction and '*prohibits [the offender] from doing anything described in the order*' (s.5(1)) for the duration of the order, which is for a determinate period specified in the order or for an indeterminate period, i.e. until a further order is made (s.5(3)). Breach of a restraining order is punishable by up to five years' imprisonment (s.5(6)) and breach could be through a single prohibited act rather than through a course of conduct. The restraining order is therefore potentially a very powerful tool since it would allow a court to impose a higher sentence for a repeated s.2 conduct (in that they could prescribe that a person must not harass V). The use of restraining orders will be considered later in this book since they are comparable to SOPOs (Chapter 9 below).

Civil law

Although the criminal law would appear to cover this behaviour, there may be concern as to its use. It is possible that the victim could seek to invoke the civil law, at least initially, in order to tackle the behaviour of a harassing or bullying perpetrator.

Law of tort

The law of tort is perhaps the most notable area of civil law that may be of assistance here. This involves examining two principal torts, that of public nuisance and harassment.

Public nuisance

The tort of public nuisance, *inter alia*, covers those situations where an unwarranted act interferes with morals or with the comfort of the public (Deakin et al., 2003: 489). Since harassment undoubtedly interferes with the comfort of the public this may appear relevant but realistically it is not, because the actual application of public nuisance is uncertain and bears little resemblance to a traditional tort (Deakin et al., 2003: 489). The primary difficulty in its use is that it focuses on the public at large rather than any specific victim. Where a victim can show 'special damage', i.e. conduct above and beyond that experienced by other members of the public, it is possible that a remedy could be obtained (Finch, 2001: 137–8), but proving this could be complicated.

Harassment

Where an individual victim wishes to take action then it is quite possible that they could refer back to the *Protection From Harassment Act 1997* which, as was noted earlier, creates both civil actions and criminal offences. An advantage of using the 1997 Act is that it can be used even if no prosecution is brought.

As noted above, the Act is based on the definition of harassment contained within s.1. A statutory tort of nuisance is created by the Act (s.3) and the principal remedy that is likely to be sought by an applicant is an injunction restraining the offender from pursuing harassing behaviour. An advantage of the 1997 legislation is that ordinarily proving a breach of an injunction is for the victim to prove, but a breach of an injunction under the 1997 Act amounts to a criminal offence and is thus the responsibility of the police and Crown Prosecution Service (Finch, 2001: 244). This quasi-criminal approach led to a debate about whether the standard of proof for making an injunction should be the civil or criminal standard (Finch, 2001: 244–5). However, the matter appears to have been resolved by *Hipgrave v Jones [2005] 2 FLR 174* where the High Court held that the civil standard of proof should be applied on the basis that the process was sufficiently different from, *inter alia*, an anti-social behaviour order ([2005] 2 FLR 174 at [195]).

The primary justification for using the lower standard of proof is that whilst the restraining order and anti-social behaviour orders are both civil orders, the order under the 1997 Act is a private law application made by an individual whereas an anti-social behaviour order is a public law application by the state ([2005] 2 FLR 174 at [187]). This is an important distinction and is akin to other private law torts where parties bear only a civil burden when making the application. Where it is the state seeking to control the activities of an individual member of society then it is perhaps easier to justify a higher standard (in part to comply with the equality of arms principle enshrined within Article 6 of the *European Convention on Human Rights*).

However, using this legislation could still pose a difficulty when used for online bullying and harassment. Whilst it is likely to be of assistance in those cases where the perpetrator of the abuse is known to the victim, it may be of less assistance in those cases where the perpetrator of the abuse is not known. Whilst Internet Service Providers (ISPs) are willing to co-operate with the police, they do not, generally, co-operate with individuals as regards naming offenders. They prefer to impose their own sanctions. However, such action is frequently ineffective, not least because it is easy to change an ISP or indeed use a non-ISP service. In these circumstances, a victim is unlikely to have anyone to serve an injunction on, effectively ruling out private civil actions.

Anti-social behaviour

It has been suggested that harassment and bullying on the Internet is anti-social behaviour, with society being replicated within cyberspace (Bocij and McFarlane, 2004: 204–5). If this is correct then it could be argued that state agencies have one additional tool available to them, that being the anti-social behaviour order (ASBO).

The term ASBO has become entrenched in every-day language and their use in the offline world has increased significantly in recent years (Fitzpatrick, 2005: 591). The background to the introduction of ASBOs was perceived unsocial behaviour by youths in public places such as streets and housing estates, and whether this behaviour impacted on the right of the general public to a peaceful life (Collins and Cattermole, 2004: 2–6). However, this background need not prevent their use within cyberspace.

It has been suggested that there is a 'right' to use the Internet without harassment (O'Connell et al., 2004: 10). Whilst this right has not yet been upheld by the courts there is considerable logic behind such an argument. The UK has traditionally adopted the position of treating the online and offline world as the same, and recent government and judicial initiatives have demonstrated that they are not shy of attempting to regulate the Internet. The test for an ASBO is simply whether the respondent has acted in an anti-social manner. This, according to s.1(1)(a) includes, '. . . .[acting] in a manner that caused or was likely to cause harassment, alarm or distress to one or more persons . . .' An interesting feature of this definition is that, unlike for the *Protection From Harassment Act 1997*, there is no need for the person to actually be harassed, alarmed or distressed, merely that it was *likely* to do so.

An interesting question that arises over the use of an ASBO in cyberspace is what happens if the victims are outside of the jurisdiction? Section 1 simply states that the victims are to be outside of the perpetrator's household, but statutes are normally considered to be territorial and it is submitted that this is the most likely construction to be placed on the statute not least because recent legislative terms expressly include phrases such as 'in any part of the world' (e.g. the *Sexual Offences Act 2003*). Where the victims are within the jurisdiction, however, nothing within the Act appears to specifically require any geographical proximity and accordingly it could be argued that the anti-social behaviour takes place in the location where the perpetrator logs onto the Internet, since this is where the harassment, alarm or distress is caused.

An ASBO application is a public law remedy in that it is an application by the state rather than a private individual. The usual applications are the police (although local authorities and certain other public bodies are also able to make an application, see s.85, *Anti-social Behaviour Act 2003*) and they would also be the more likely applicant for cyber-bullying. The standard of proof for an application is the criminal standard of proof (*R (McCann) v Manchester Crown Court [2003] 1 AC 787*) which raises the question why the police should proceed for an ASBO when the same evidence may lead to a conviction for an offence under s.2 of the *Protection From Harassment Act 1997* or a communications offence. The answer is that it is not infrequently a policy decision and some forces take the approach that it is better to apply for an ASBO since a breach of one is punishable by up to five years' imprisonment (s.1(10) *Crime and Disorder Act 1998*), considerably higher than the more likely alternative criminal charges. Where the

perpetrator is an adolescent, another advantage of preferring an ASBO over a prosecution is that as a civil rather than criminal remedy the subject will not have a criminal conviction. That said, the use of ASBOs on juveniles remains controversial. One problem noted is that some juveniles look on ASBOs as almost a 'badge of honour' (Lovell, 2005: 16). Whether this would apply to those in cyberspace is perhaps more open to question.

If an ASBO is imposed, the Magistrates' Court can prohibit the respondent from doing anything stated on the order. This would appear to mirror s.5, *Protection From Harassment Act 1997* and provides the court with wide discretion. In *R v McGrath [2005] EWCA Crim 353* the Court of Appeal held that the requirements need not be restricted to the direct prohibition of conduct that would cause harassment, alarm or distress. Accordingly, an order could be used to curb the wider online activities of the respondent. Proportionality must remain central to any prohibitions, but where the cyber-bullying has been intense, and to a number of victims, then it is quite possible that significant restrictions could be put in place. It may be difficult to police these restrictions but this should not by itself prevent the imposition of an order (by analogy see *R v Beaney [2004] 2 Cr App R (S) 82*) since detection is possible in a number of different ways (e.g. the ISP contacting the police) and the deterrent value of an order is also a factor to take into account.

Notes

1 (2004) *The Times*, 25 August, News.
2 (2004) The *Daily Telegraph*, 17 July, News.
3 The resultant image is known as a 'pseudo-photograph' and the next chapter discusses their legality in the context of child pornography.
4 See (2003) *Nottingham Evening Post*, 24 May, News.
5 See the editorial *Cybercrime Overview* at www.jisclegal.ac.uk/cybercrime/cybercrime.htm.
6 Loosely translated this means the mental requirement for a crime. Most crimes require a mental, as well as physical, element to them. For a discussion of *mens rea* see Ormerod, 2005: ch.4.

CHAPTER 3

Child Pornography 1

Of all the 'threats' or 'abuses' that can be facilitated by ICT perhaps the one that has, in recent years, commandeered most public attention is that of child pornography. Certainly the introduction of ICT appears to have revolutionised the way that this material appears and recent research has demonstrated that the rate of new images is increasing as is their severity (Quayle et al., 2006: 2). Chapters 3 and 4 of this book discuss what child pornography is and how the law operates in respect of it. The issue is divided between two chapters for ease of reading (as it would otherwise be a very long chapter) but also because, as will be seen, the law draws a clear divide between the types of child pornography.

The nature of child pornography

Before focusing on the legal solutions to child pornography it is first necessary to define the subject and discuss the scope of the law's interest in it.

Terminology

It should be noted at the outset of this chapter that although this chapter has been called 'child pornography' this is an extremely controversial label and one that, for good reason, has tended not to be used by professionals. The principal argument against its use is that it minimises what is being portrayed. When one thinks of 'pornography' one imagines titillation or erotica, that is material presented for the sexual stimulation of the person viewing it. There has been a significant debate over the years about the appropriateness of pornography, with many leading feminist writers arguing that pornography is about the sexual subordination of women (Easton, 1994: xii), but others arguing that it is the portrayal of consensual sexual behaviour between adults. The pornography industry has certainly grown in recent years and many countries have had to adopt a more liberal approach to the regulation of pornography as its place in society has changed (Travis, 2000: 290).

However, at the centre of the disagreement over the label 'child pornography' is the belief that this is intrinsically different to adult pornography. Central to this argument is the premise that children should not be considered erotic and portraying children as sexual objects is wrong. A common, yet powerful, point in respect of this is to state that every image in child pornography is a picture of a crime scene (Carr, 2001: 13), a point reinforced by others:

> The term 'child pornography' is an oxymoron. 'Child Pornography' is a record of the systematic rape, abuse and torture of children on film and photograph and other electronic means.
>
> (Edwards, 2000: 1)

What both Carr and Edwards are saying is that child pornography is not about titillation or adults obtaining sexual gratification from images but of children being abused, and evidence of this abuse being distributed. This is undoubtedly correct in terms of those images that include physical contact with a child (including persuading a child to pose in a sexual manner or touch themselves), but others argue the objection goes further than this and applies to all forms of child pornography, including those where there is no contact, because there is an inherent power imbalance involved in these issues (Taylor and Quayle, 2003: 4). Whilst this will normally be correct, it is important to note that there are exceptions. A worrying trend is that there are reports of children being used to take photographs of other children, most notably in school gymnasiums, leisure centres etc. Sometimes the motivation for such behaviour is financial, at other times it is to bully or harass the child. In each situation it is unlikely that the children fully understand the consequences of what they are doing.

Because the label 'child pornography' carries with it various problems, the law enforcement agencies have traditionally used terms such as 'abusive images' or 'images of sexual abuse' as a more preferred title (Taylor and Quayle, 2003: 7). Whilst this is undoubtedly a preferred label, it is interesting to note that there is the immediate emphasis on image-based material rather than other material. At the 5th COPINE Conference a debate arose as to this notion of labelling. Many speakers made the point that whilst the term may have a number of negative connotations it is readily recognisable in a global-context. This is an important point and, realistically, more effort should be spent on combating the material rather than trying to decide what to call it. In any event, perhaps 'child pornography' has, like the term 'paedophile', accrued a colloquial definition which co-exists with its technical meanings. On that basis the term 'child pornography' will be used throughout its chapter and this is one reason why the chapter is so-titled. That is not to detract from the points made above, particularly that by Edwards, as they are undoubtedly correct, but as it is an accepted label it is used for ease of understanding.

Accessing the material

When one mentions the 'dangers' of the Internet, child pornography would be one of the first issues that people would raise. Some suggest that the Internet has now become the primary medium for the distribution of child pornography (Palmer, 2004: 11), something that would seem difficult to argue against. The advantage of technology is a degree of anonymity that it brings to offenders. Historically, accessing child pornography was very difficult, relying on a visit to a specialist shop or finding a mail-order company (Quayle and Taylor, 2003: 9). Both of these carried significant risks in that some sex shop owners would report such behaviour to the police and mail order parcels may be intercepted.

A significant difference between old mediums and new technologies is the quantity of the material. It was comparatively rare for an offender to have a significant collection, not least because of the difficulties involved in obtaining the material. Research has shown that the behaviour of offenders has altered since the development and wide-scale use of the Internet. Offenders who previously had collections of tens, and occasionally hundreds, of images suddenly grew to encompass collections of tens or even hundreds of thousands of images (Taylor and Quayle, 2003: 159–68). Initially, the images to be found on the Internet were simply scans from magazines etc. (Taylor and Quayle, 2003: 161), but as the demand for new material increased, so

material was created specifically for dissemination on the Internet.

In recent years there appears to be an increasing amount of commercial-based child pornography, although the majority of material continues to be created for non-commercial reasons (Taylor and Quayle, 2003: 8). The advance in technology now allows child pornography to have become something of a 'cottage industry'. Whilst even a decade ago it would have been relatively difficult to create child pornography without specialist equipment, now, with the advent of digital technology, the production of pornography is simple. A digital camera or digital video camera plugged directly into a computer, with a Broadband connection, and the results can be placed onto the Internet directly.

The result of this situation is that the amount of material available on the Internet is increasing all the time, and, rather worryingly, the average age of the children being portrayed in the pornography is getting younger (Taylor and Quayle, 2003: 95). This is perhaps something of a surprise to some people as there is still an element of ignorance with the general population about what child pornography is, perhaps because of the labelling factors discussed above. Many people from outside of the child protection professions tend to think that child pornography involves teenagers close to the age of consent. Whilst some of this material is undoubtedly available, a significant proportion of the material involves pubescent or pre-pubescent children, and there appears to be an increase in the involvement of very young children, who can be categorised as babies or toddlers.

The 'cottage industry' theory is implicitly confirmed by research that suggests child pornography is increasingly of a domestic/familial nature (Palmer, 2004: 11). One of the reasons for this may be the growth of online communities. Whilst we are familiar with the term 'paedophile ring' which is a term often bandied around the media, the Internet does allow for users to come together and produce virtual communities, allowing them to share images amongst themselves (Taylor and Quayle, 2003: 120–47). One of the most famous of these communities was the 'w0nderland club', which until the law enforcement community infiltrated it, was a secretive trading association. Admission to the club was not through money but through trading unique images; each member had to provide 10,000 images. Although this community was perhaps the first high-profile example of such a community, it was not, and is not, unique. The difficulty with such groups is that it promotes the behaviour that concerns Palmer and Taylor and Quayle. If someone wants access to the group but has a shortfall of images needed, what do they do? The temptation, where they have a child, is to photograph their child or their child's friends. This is what happened with the w0nderland club, and arrests and referrals subsequent to this club confirm this happened.

Type of material

When one talks about 'child pornography', it is usually in relation to photograph-based images, but it is important to note that child pornography is not limited to this. Interpol provide the following definition:

> Child pornography is created as a consequence of the sexual exploitation or abuse of a child. It can be defined as any means of depicting or promoting the sexual exploitation of a child, including written or audio material, which focuses on the child's sexual behaviour or genitals.
>
> (Carr, 2001: 9)

This definition expressly considers other forms of material, including written and audio material, something that is important. Within this chapter it will be necessary to distinguish between a variety of different types of material.

Photographs

Perhaps the most obvious form of child pornography are photographs. These can be of a variety of types from still photographs to full moving film. However, the position is not always clear since quite often still photographs are actually 'still captures' from a moving film and distributed accordingly. This material does lead some types of offenders, particularly those who are cataloguers, to attempt to find an entire series (Taylor and Quayle, 2003: 161), including offering other material in their collection as 'swaps' to achieve this aim.

It will be seen below that there are specific laws relating to photograph-based child pornography. The advent of communication technologies has not, however, simply led to a change in the dynamics of production and dissemination, but has also introduced a new species to the collection, the pseudo-photograph.

Pseudo-photograph

It has been suggested that a pseudo-photograph comprises a photograph or collage of photographs altered by a graphic manipulation package (Akdeniz, 2001: 253), or possibly images that do not involve actual children (Akdeniz, 1997: 228). Examples of the latter are relatively easy to conceive. Images can be produced by manipulating an image of an adult to look like a child (for example, slimming the hips, 'airbrushing out' pubic hair etc.) or through 'cutting' the head of a child and 'pasting' it onto an adult body (see, for example, *R v H [2005] EWCA Crim 3037*). It has been questioned whether it is appropriate to criminalise such images in that they do not actually result in a child being abused but it is not necessarily this simple. As has been noted already, where a real child's face is being imposed onto the body then although it may not be true to say the child is being abused, it is certainly possible to say that the child is being exploited. Even where it is a modified adult the 'fuel' argument has been used to support criminalisation in that such material encourages a demand for indecent images of children (Edwards, 2000: 284).

A separate argument to this is that pseudo-photographs could be used to persuade children that it is 'normal' to become sexually active (Taylor and Quayle, 2003: 158). A sophisticated pseudo-photograph may be to superimpose a smiling child's face onto the body of a child being abused so as to convey the impression that the child is enjoying the abuse. However, whether this is sufficient to justify the possession of such images is perhaps more questionable. This is considered elsewhere in this book (Chapter 5), as it could be argued that the more appropriate solution to this problem is to criminalise the use of such images, but others do suggest that it can justify criminalising possession.

Non-photograph images

Photographs are not, of course, the only type of image that could potentially amount to child pornography. The specific law relating to indecent photographs (*Protection of Children Act 1978*) are restricted to photographs and pseudo-photographs which were discussed above. The definition of a pseudo-photograph is something that *'appears to be a photograph'* (s.7(7),

PoCA 1978) and thus although there is no authority on this point yet, it is submitted that images which do not appear to be a photograph (i.e. do not look materially like a photograph) will not count. Accordingly, drawings and cartoons etc. would be outside the remit of PoCA 1978.

One slight exception to this rule is contained within s.7(4)(b), PoCA 1978, which states that a photograph includes *'data stored on a computer disc or by other electronic means which is capable of conversion into a photograph'*. This was thought to cover situations whereby a photograph is scanned into a computer but it will also have a more modern use.

Computer graphics programmes currently exist that will allow a photograph to be converted into a drawing, be it a line drawing or other form of 'art'; indeed some mobile telephones have such 'filters' as standard. The product of this conversion would, if it is possible to reverse engineer the conversion, continue to be a photograph since it comes within s.7(4)(b). It is important to note that this would not be a pseudo-photograph but rather a photograph and thus it will be irrelevant whether it *looks* like a photograph. However, sometimes this image will not be capable of reverse-engineering (e.g. because a person 'cuts' the resulting image and pastes it into a simpler graphic manipulation programme, or because the picture is printed out or printed and then re-scanned), and in these circumstances it cannot be said to be a photograph since it is not *'capable of conversion into a photograph'*. Neither can it be said to be a pseudo-photograph since it does not look like a photograph.

Tracings

Law enforcement agencies have, in the past, discovered what can best be described as 'tracings' when searching for indecent photographs of a child. At the most basic level, a tracing is where tracing paper is placed over a photograph and a copy of the image is made. This tracing, like any tracing, can then be copied to another piece of paper so that it produces a duplicate image. Why would offenders do this? For some, it is the recognition that the product – be it the tracing or the duplicate – is neither a photograph nor a pseudo-photograph and is thus outside the remit of PoCA 1978, although there are plans to amend PoCA 1978 to extend its remit (see *Criminal Justice and Immigration Bill 2007*).

By mixing tracings with other images it is possible to create the equivalent of a pseudo-photograph on paper. For example, a tracing is taken of a young girl and this is then added to a tracing of an adult pornographic picture to make it look like the child is participating in sexual activity. These tracings raise similar issues to those identified above in respect of photographs in that they are either the product of a photograph or the pursuance of the exploitation. Whilst the child may not necessarily be as identifiable to others from a tracing, it does not necessarily mean that the child cannot be identified or, indeed, that if the child saw the image that they would not encounter the psychological difficulties noted above.

Computer generated images

Recently, law enforcement agencies are starting to identify an increasing number of computer-generated images (CGI) of child abuse. These images are created by a computer using graphic packages and do not represent a real child. They are, therefore, the product purely of fantasy. The CGI images are rarely of a naked child but are instead usually of children depicted in sexual activity, often with adults, and mostly involving situations that, if it occurred in real life, would involve extreme pain and probably personal injury.

The quality of CGI images varies quite markedly and certain CGI images would appear to be almost photograph-quality. Outside of the area of child pornography it is certainly possible to see examples of graphics packages where considerable time has to be taken to decide whether the image is computer-generated or real. The test for a pseudo-photograph is whether it appears to be a photograph and accordingly some of the high quality images may be within PoCA 1978. However where the images do not appear to be photographs, i.e. they are obviously computer-generated images, then it is unlikely they would come within PoCA 1978.

Drawings, paintings etc.

Obviously the sexual representation of children can be portrayed by any media form and it is not unusual for law enforcement officers to identify drawings or paintings involving children in sexually inappropriate poses etc. This is outside the remit of PoCA 1978 and would be dealt with according to the obscenity legislation.

Sound

It will be remembered that the definition of child pornography suggested by Interpol expressly included sound files. Law enforcement agencies have, during numerous operations, identified sound files on suspect's computers. The files will often depict children being abused but it is not always sexually, something that was brought into the public domain thanks to the BBC Panorama programme on the 'w0nderland club'.[1] The programme included an interview with Nick Webber, a law enforcement computer consultant who described one file:

> On [a suspect's] computer, there was a voice of a little girl. She sounds to me to be English, probably 8 or 9, being repeatedly beaten by her mother and saying, 'No more, no more'. But the beating just continues, again and again and again, and she's crying and screaming . . .

Other recordings have been recovered and some of these involved an audio tape of a child involved in sexually explicit behaviour. It is known that some offenders will find audio tape recordings sexually arousing (Quayle et al., 2006: 60), and this includes recordings of physical abuse. A difficulty with this material is that it is not always immediately clear whether the sounds will be of actual abuse since they could be recordings from legitimate settings (television, film, etc.) or indeed whether it is an adult posing as a child. However, where forensically it is possible to identify that the voice is a child, then this again raises issues about child abuse and exploitation.

Whilst it is perhaps more difficult to use the 'fuel' argument with sound recordings since there has not been any significant research undertaken as to the prevalence of this material, the argument about secondary victimisation (below) will remain true. This will be true even when the recording is not sexually explicit since it is undoubtedly exploitation to use the child's distress as erotica.

Text

Perhaps the most obvious non-photograph-based form of abuse will be text-based. The difficulty raised by text has already been mentioned in passing, but there is unquestionably a significant amount of material available on the Internet that concerns text-based child-pornography. Perhaps

the largest resource is that created by organisations similar to NAMBLA (North American Man/Boy Lovers Association). The essence of man/boy love text was perhaps first brought to the UK public's attention in the Channel 4 documentary 'A Devil Amongst Us'.[2] The programme followed 'Rob' who went to a site on the Internet to download a story prefixed by the following warning:

> his story contains acts of consensual intercourse between an ADULT male and a MINOR male. If that's not your cup of tea don't read it as you have been warned.

'Rob' referred to the fact that the Internet contained significant quantities of what he referred to as 'cross-generational' sex stories (the term 'cross-generational' being one of the more usual self-justifying terms used by child sex offenders to justify what they perceive as their sexuality). Whilst this may be undoubtedly troublesome, the difficulty with the law is that many respected works contain similar themes, Nabokov's *Lolita* being a prime example, and the Marquis de Sade's *Juliette* perhaps being one of the most infamous. It has been suggested that the latter work represents the transformation within liberal society in the United Kingdom in that the book, which was for so long banned, featured prominently in the office of a recent Director of Public Prosecutions (Travis, 2000: 11).

It could perhaps be argued that the law could draw a distinction between the type of material referred to by 'Rob' and literary works but how would such a distinction be drawn? It will be noted below that this distinction is arguably drawn in the obscenity legislation but without much obvious success.

It is not only fictitious accounts that are troubling in this area. Law enforcement agencies have identified people talking about their abusive sexual behaviour to others in chatrooms and by e-mail etc. However, even legitimate documentation has been misued by sex offenders. The *Sexual Offences (Protected Material) Act 1997* sought to restrict the rules of disclosure to ensure that the witness statements of the victim or attending medical examiners would not be disclosed to the defendant in person because there was evidence that certain sex offenders were trading these reports whilst in prison as pornography. This Act has never been brought into force and reliance is instead currently placed on prison rules which would be breached by the use of such material, arguably a significantly less effective strategy.

Criminalising child pornography

Why is it that the law believes that child pornography is worth banning? It is easy to see why the law wishes to outlaw the creation of images which portray a child being actually abused, but what of simple possession? How can this be justified; is it because there is a link between possession and offending?

For many years research has tried to discover whether there is a link between the use and possession of child pornography and contact sex offences. This is not an easy area to research, not least because, as has been pointed out, *'those who are arrested represent only a fraction of all sexual offenders, and that sexual crimes have the lowest reporting of all crimes'* (Quayle et al., 2006: 1). Similarly, even when reference is made to those arrested or charged with criminal offences, the research relies on discussing prevalence with offenders and they may not wish to disclose the full truth. The research is divided on any link. Some studies have shown that it is not possible to identify a link (for a useful summary see Quayle et al., 2006: 62–3), yet other studies show a high correlation (Hernandez, 2000).

What appears less open to debate are the links between child pornography and abuse and exploitation. Where a real child is portrayed being abused then there can be no question that a child has been abused to produce the image. A reason for criminalising even the possession of such images is the repeat damage that this can cause. Research demonstrates that once an image has been posted on the Internet it can never be retrieved since it will be downloaded, copied and distributed throughout the world-wide web (Taylor and Quayle, 2003: 24). The consequence of this is that the child has to come to terms with the fact that as they grow older the material relating to them being sexually abused will continue to exist and still be accessible (Taylor and Quayle, 2003: 211). This can best be illustrated by the presentation from an extract of Pete, who as a 13-year-old had pornographic pictures taken of him:

> I didn't realise what the photographs would be used for, I didn't know he'd put them on the net. Now I can't walk down the street without wondering who's seen them . . .
> (Palmer, 2004: 30)

This uncertainty undoubtedly causes further harm to the victim, something that the courts have eventually began to understand. In *Beaney [2004] EWCA Crim 449* the Court of Appeal stated:

> . . . the psychological harm which the children in those images would suffer by virtue of the children's awareness that there were people out there getting a perverted thrill from watching them forced to pose and behave in this way.
> (at [9])

This demonstrates that child pornography is a crime which has long-term consequences and *Beaney* shows an understanding that the harm the victim is subjected to is more than just the physical activities of sexual abuse. These effects include the knowledge that exploitative images are being used for gratification. It will be seen that not every image necessarily involves the abuse of a child as some images may be taken from a distance or may involve a composite image whereby the face of a child is morphed onto an adult's body or two images are brought together to appear as though sexual contact is occurring. A classic example of the latter is where a child's photograph is altered to provide a sexual context. For example, a picture of a child eating an ice-cream may be altered so that the ice-cream cone is 'airbrushed' away and the resulting image is pasted onto a pornographic photograph so that it now looks as though the child is engaging in oral sex with the adult. It cannot be said that this image is abusive *per se* in that the child was never in contact with an adult, but it is undoubtedly exploitative and it is unlikely the psychological issues discussed above will be any less since it is unlikely a person viewing such images would stop to ponder whether they are real or a manipulated image.

Separate to this argument is the simpler 'fuel' argument. The courts have remarked on a number of occasions that one reason why even possession is a criminal offence is that the possession and downloading of images creates a demand for new images (see, for example, Taylor and Quayle, 2003: 161). It would appear that there is some evidence to support this. It has already been remarked upon that the number of images appearing on the Internet has increased significantly in recent years and this cannot simply be that producers have suddenly decided to 'advertise' their behaviour but because the demand for material leads to new material being created (Quayle and Taylor, 2003: 7). Another issue with the 'fuel' theory is that research also suggests that 'users' of child pornography (as distinct from collectors) may *'get bored by the images that they have downloaded'* leading them to not only find fresh images but also to *'seek more arousing images which may include sexually more explicit or violent pictures, or images that depict younger children'* (Quayle et al., 2006: 61). Thus not only is there the problem of new images being created but the images are becoming increasingly explicit and the ages of the children are becoming younger (Taylor and Quayle, 2003: 95).

The legal framework

It has been noted already that the law draws a distinction between photographic (including pseudo-photographs) forms of child pornography and other forms. Chapter 4 of this book will examine the legality of photograph-based forms of abuse and the remainder of this chapter will focus on the legality of the other forms of pornography.

Realistically, there are two primary areas of law that are applicable to these forms of pornography; communication offences and the obscenity legislation.

Communication offences

Communication offences were introduced in the previous chapter within the context of cyber-bullying and harassment but they are not restricted to just this area and will cover a much broader spectrum of activity. Within the context of child pornography it is likely that only s.127, *Communications Act 2003* will be relevant since s.1, *Malicious Communications Act 1998*, which could cover some relevant activity in that it refers to indecent or grossly offensive messaging, would only be triggered where it is intended to cause distress or anxiety to the recipient (s.1(1), MCA 1998). Given that the communications relevant here are more likely to be between sex offender and sex offender it is unlikely that requirement for distress or anxiety would be met.

However, s.127 has a much wider remit in that it criminalises those messages that are sent via a public communications network that are of a grossly offensive, indecent or obscene nature. The meanings of some of these terms were examined earlier in this book but to summarise here, the

key terms of relevance to us will be 'indecent' and 'obscene'. In the Divisional Court Sedley LJ said that:

> . . . obscenity and indecency, too, are generally in the eye of the beholder; but the law has historically treated them as a matter of objective fact to be determined by contemporary standards of decency.
> (*DPP v Collins* [2005] *EWHC Admin* 1308 at [10])

The ruling of the Divisional Court was ultimately reversed by the House of Lords ([2006] UKHL 40) but on different grounds and it is submitted the comment above remains good law. In essence, this means that the magistrates (since the communication offences are triable only in the Magistrates' Court) would be asked to examine each communication and identify whether they are indecent or obscene. These terms are used elsewhere in the law and they bear the same definition here. The precise meanings of these terms are set out later in this chapter, below, and Chapter 4 (indecency).

Obscenity

The other key legislation that is relevant to this behaviour is the *Obscene Publications Act 1959 (as amended)*. Realistically, this is the more appropriate charge because the disadvantages of communication offences have been noted above and in the previous chapter. That is not to say that the obscenity legislation is the ideal legislative tool since it has had a somewhat controversial history (Travis, 2000 provides an illuminating history of obscenity through the ages) and its use has declined over the years (Edwards, 1998). However, in recent years it has achieved a renaissance when it was rediscovered as a possible solution to some of the issues surrounding websites (see, for example, *R v Waddon* [2000] *All ER(D)* 502 and *R v Perrin* [2002] *EWCA Crim* 747).

The principal relevant offence is contained within s.2(1) of that Act which states:

> . . . any person who, whether for gain or not, publishes an obscene article or who has an obscene article for publication for gain (whether gain to himself or gain to another) shall [commit an offence].

The offence is triable either-way and is punishable by a maximum sentence of up to five years' imprisonment which, as will be seen, is significantly less than the photograph-based offences (Chapter 4), but is significantly more than the communication offences outlined above. In fact, the offence is more than one offence since it can be committed in different ways, but to understand the applicability of this 'offence' it is necessary to consider the definition of 'obscene', 'article' and 'publication'.

Article

The basic offence is to, publish *inter alia*, an obscene article but what is an article? It is arguably the easiest to define, not least because of the wide definition provided by s.1(2), OPA 1959:

> In this Act 'article' means any description of article containing or embodying matter to be read or looked at or both, and any film or other record of a picture or pictures.

The *Obscene Publications Act 1964* amended this Act to include, for example, negatives and reproductions or the manufacture of material. In *R v Fellows and Arnold [1997] 1 Cr App R 244* the Court of Appeal had no difficulty in deciding that computer data stored electronically was an article for the purposes of s.1(2). This followed an earlier ruling (*Attorney-General's Reference (No 5 of 1980) (1981) 72 Cr pp R 71*) where the Court had ruled that video cassettes were included within the Act and that the purpose of s.1(2) was to bring all forms of media within the Act. It is quite clear, therefore, that electronic data, stored on any communication medium, is within the Act.

Obscenity

The key term to be defined is that of 'obscene' which is obviously central to the whole offence. It has been suggested, somewhat amusingly and somewhat astutely, that a typical jury direction in the 1970s would be:

> Obscenity, members of the Jury, is like an elephant. You cannot define it, but you know it when you see it.
> (Robertson, 1979: 45)

This does not, of course, help a jury to decide what obscenity is but it does perhaps demonstrate some of the difficulty that has arisen in this area. The legislation itself provides a definition of sorts:

> ... an article shall be deemed to be obscene if its effect or (where the article comprises two or more distinct items) the effect of any one of its items is, if taken as a whole, such

> as to tend to deprave or corrupt persons who are likely, having regard to all relevant circumstances, to read, see or hear the matter contained or embodied in it.
> (s.1(1), OPA 1959)

In *R v Anderson [1971] 3 All ER 1152* the Court of Appeal felt obliged to remind judges of the fact that the Act provided a definition and that the dictionary definition of obscenity was both unhelpful and inappropriate. It becomes easy to see why Robertson's elephant analogy is somewhat incisive. It is further complicated by the fact that since 1965 'obscenity' is no longer defined simply in respect of sexual content but can include other forms of behaviour such as drugs (*John Calder (Publications) Ltd v Powell [1965] 1 QB 509* and see Ormerod, 2005: 945). However, for this book the examination will be restricted to sexual material.

Key to the definition of obscenity is 'deprave and corrupt' but this does lead to a rather peculiar argument in this area, known as the aversion argument. This can be summarised as:

> If the article were so revolting that it would put someone off the kind of depraved activity depicted ... then it would have no tendency to deprave.
> (Ormerod, 2005: 946)

However, as Ormerod notes, this argument can only be used in limited circumstances, and certainly where material is being 'advertised' as being desirable to persons seeking that sort of material (ibid. and *R v Elliot [1972] 1 QB 304*). Within the premise of the material under discussion it is likely that this will feature here. Child pornography on the Internet is frequently placed there to allow 'like minded individuals' to access, download or replicate (Taylor and Quayle, 2003: 120 *et seq.*). On that basis it is unlikely that the aversion argument would succeed.

Deprave and corrupt

Arguably the key to the issue of obscenity is the concept of 'deprave and corrupt' but what does this mean? In *R v Martin Secker and Warburg [1954] 2 All ER 683* it was held that it meant more than mere shock or disgust. Perhaps the key definition was provided by *R v Penguin Books Ltd [1961] Crim LR 176* where it was said:

> To deprave means to make morally bad, to pervert, to debase or corrupt morally. To corrupt means to render

morally unsound or rotten, to destroy the moral purity or chastity, to pervert or ruin a good quality, to debase, to 'defile'.

(177)

Accordingly, the definition has more to do with ethics and morality than legal certainty (Edwards, 1998: 851), something perhaps confirmed in *DPP v White [1972] AC 849* where the House of Lords stated that it did not require any overt sexual activity to take place, the deprivation and corruption could take place through fantasy.

The difficulty that arises with a definition based on morality or ethics is that it is extremely subjective. What one jury considers obscene, another may believe is decent. This leads to one of the criticisms that can be levelled at the obscenity legislation. Since a finding of obscenity will not set a precedent it means that material will never be criminalised *per se* but always subject to individual decisions (Itzin, 2001: 404). Conversely, however, a finding that an article is not obscene will almost certainly be taken as a precedent, albeit *de facto* and by the prosecuting authorities, as it will be difficult to meet the prosecution tests where a tribunal of fact has already decided it to be decent. Some have suggested that the repercussions of the *Inside Linda Lovelace* case (where there was an unsuccessful prosecution in respect of a sexually explicit book) in effect, marked the end of any attempt to prosecute books under this legislation (Edwards, 2000: 182). This is supported by others who suggest that text-based literature would be very difficult to now prosecute (Travis, 2000: 255–7, 262–4). These suppositions may no longer be strictly true since they are slightly dated and pre-date the expansion of the Internet. This issue will be explored further below.

Persons to be depraved and corrupted

The more relevant part of the test is who must be depraved and corrupted. There remains a degree of confusion over this (Ormerod, 2005: 948) with the courts in *R v Calder and Boyars Ltd [1969] 1 QB 151* suggesting that the correct test was whether a *'significant number or proportion of those persons likely to read it'* would be corrupted. This was a case that concerned a book and in *DPP v White [1972] AC 849* the House of Lords suggested that this test may not be transplanted into other forms of publications.

The scope of this chapter is, realistically, the Internet and these matters were discussed by the

Court of Appeal in *R v Perrin [2002] EWCA Crim 747*. This is an important case and one that we will return to later, but as regards who are to be depraved and corrupted the court stated in respect of this kind of material:

> *... we see no reason why the task of the jury should be complicated by a direction that the effect of the article must be such as to tend to deprave and corrupt a significant proportion, or more than a negligible number of likely viewers ... it is much better, in our judgment, for the jury to be directed simply in accordance with the words of the statute.*
>
> (at [30] per Kennedy LJ)

The statute itself does not suggest a minimum number of persons but simply asks the jury to consider whether likely viewers will be depraved and corrupted. In the context of websites it is suggested that this is the more appropriate test because it will be extremely difficult to ascertain who have accessed a site. An interesting feature of the *Perrin* case is that it has led to speculation about the importance of age verification or automatic payment systems since in *Perrin* the defendant was convicted only of material that was contained on a free 'preview' page rather than material that required a credit card to obtain access to the site. The Court of Appeal itself considered that the distinction between 'preview' and 'by payment' materials may explain the verdict (at [11]), the clear implication being that it is less likely vulnerable persons would 'view' such material and therefore could be corrupted.

However, in the subject matter of this chapter, child pornography, it is highly unlikely that this logic would work since most people would find child pornography depraving and corrupting. But what of a situation where a 'ring' chooses to exchange paedophilic material only amongst itself and has security within the site to ensure that others cannot access it? In *DPP v White [1972] AC 849* the House of Lords stated that being corrupted was not a 'finite' state: i.e. it was possible to be further depraved and corrupted (something reiterated by the Court of Appeal in *R v O'Sullivan [1995] 1 Cr App R 455*). Accordingly, it would not be possible for members of this 'ring' to avoid prosecution by arguing that they were already depraved and that this material would not make them more so.

Publishes

Apart from 'obscene' the issue of most controversy in the area of obscenity on the

Internet are the related words 'publishes' and 'publication'. Section 1(3) of the OPA 1959 states that publication occurs where a person:

(a) distributes, circulates, sells, lets on hire, gives or lends it, or who offers it for sale or for letting on hire, or
(b) in the case of an article embodying or embodying matter to be looked at or a record, shows, plays or projects it, or, where the matter is data stored electronically, transmits that data.

A crude definition could be said to be the process by which one person makes the article available to another. It is important to note that whilst s.1 does not criminalise pure possession (cf. the position with indecent images of children (Chapter 4 below)), neither does it require the article to be published, it is sufficient for a person to be in possession of material intending to publish it. In *Fellows and Arnold (op. cit.)* the Court of Appeal was called upon to consider the position as respect a person who made his electronic collection of obscene articles available to others by providing a password to gain access. The Court argued that this could be publishing within the meaning of the Act, noting that this was the equivalent of providing a key to a library.

The Internet itself has been considered by the courts. In *R v Waddon (op. cit.)* the Court of Appeal agreed that the transmission of data between a computer and an Internet server would amount to publication within the meaning of the OPA 1959. This was later confirmed by the case of *R v Perrin (op. cit.)*. This would seem to be a logical step and is certainly in line with *Fellows and Arnold* and therefore it can be concluded within the context of modern communication technologies that the transmission of articles or making such articles available (through P2P or inclusion on an FTP site) could be considered publication. However, it does raise an interesting issue in terms of jurisdiction.

Jurisdiction

It has been argued that:

> The unique geography of the Internet creates serious jurisdiction difficulties for both the civil and criminal courts. Territorial frontiers do not exist in cyberspace, and territoriality based laws may seem out of place in such an environment.
>
> (Hirst, 2003: 186)

Law normally operates on a territorial basis, i.e. the law will only seek to regulate that which occurs within its own territories. There are exceptions to this, which are known as extraterritoriality, and sex offences is perhaps one of the more prominent examples of this where recent legislation has sought to tackle 'sex tourism' (Hirst, 2003, provides a detailed and comprehensive analysis of jurisdiction in his text). However, the OPA 1959 does not purport to be extraterritorial, meaning that the ordinary jurisdictional norms should apply (i.e. unless a matter takes place within the jurisdiction of England and Wales the court cannot act).

However, as Hirst notes, modern communication technologies transcend geographical boundaries, indeed that is the very purpose of the Internet. How does the law react to such a phenomenon? The usual rule in English law is that whatever is illegal 'offline' is illegal 'online', i.e. that the law will not provide for specific laws that relate solely to cyberspace (something noted when discussing 'grooming' in Chapter 6). This means, therefore, that any jurisdictional basis has to be based on the premise that a crime occurs within England and Wales.

The first case to deal with this jurisdiction within this context was *R v Waddon* (op. cit.) where the Court of Appeal held that using the Internet to publish obscene articles could occur within the jurisdiction. The facts of *Waddon* were that the defendant was the director of a company that hosted a website based in the United States of America. It was alleged that either the defendant himself or an agent acting on his behalf transmitted data (which amounted to indecent photographs) to and from America and it was this which brought it within the jurisdiction of the courts. The court stated:

> ... there can be publication on a website abroad, when images are there uploaded; and there can be further publication when those images are downloaded elsewhere.
>
> (at [12])

However, this did not adequately address the point about where this publication took place: i.e. where it was hosted or where it was downloaded. This omission became relevant again in the case of *Perrin* (op. cit.). The facts of Perrin were that the defendant was a French national, albeit resident within England and Wales. The website in question was based in North America (where such material was legal) and although a search of his home found and identified some relevant material, it was not proven where the material originated from, although it was conceded by the defendant *'that he was legally responsible for the publication of the articles . . .'* ([2002] EWCA Crim 747 at [5]). This was not suggesting he conceded jurisdiction, however, but merely that as the director of the company he was ultimately responsible.

The concession does appear to have ensured that the Court of Appeal did not consider the issue of jurisdiction, merely accepting that publication occurred. However, it has been suggested that in the absence of any proof that the images were transmitted from the United Kingdom to America, then the only publication could be the receiving of images:

> s.1(3)(b) [of the OPA 1959] . . . *provides that data may be published by transmitting it, but that does not mean (nor even does it suggest) that the act of publication occurs where the transmission is received. If it did, it would impose rules of English criminal law on foreigners . . . in respect of conduct that may be committed entirely abroad, and which may not necessarily be considered unlawful there.*
> (Hirst, 2003: 190)

The argument put forward by Hirst is quite persuasive: the verb 'to publish' suggests that the action takes place where the data is *transmitted* rather than received. However, the courts perhaps argue that this is the only way in which such material can be policed for citizens of the United Kingdom. It would appear possible to limit website content to people from within a certain jurisdiction and perhaps the suggestion of the courts is that unless persons do this then they should expect to be judged by the standards of those countries that can access the material. This could be construed as extremely harsh but is perhaps compatible to how countries have historically policed obscenity.

Before leaving this issue a note of caution should be raised. Hirst criticises *Perrin* as potentially taking jurisdiction too far but it should be remembered that the Court of Appeal did not actually rule upon jurisdiction since the defendant in that case made a formal admission that he was *legally responsible* for the material that was published. The essence of the decision was, therefore, more to do with obscenity rather than any challenge to the courts jurisdiction. Accordingly, the only statement of jurisdiction remains the *obiter dicta* statement made by Rose LJ in *Waddon*.

Defences

The OPA 1959 includes a defence of acting 'in the public good' which is frequently referred to as the defence of artistic merit. Section 4 sets out the parameters of this defence:

> . . . *the publication of the article in question is justified as being for the public good on the ground that it is in the interests of science, literature, art or learning, or of other objects of general concern . . .*

In *DPP v Jordan* [1977] AC 699 it was held that the terms 'or of other objects of general concern' had to be construed alongside the previous terms and thus the argument that hard-core pornography may have some sort of sex-therapeutic benefit would not be applicable as this is a different category to those listed. Notwithstanding this, the existing list is broad and some have argued that after the collapse of the prosecution in respect of the book *Inside Linda Lovelace*, the provisions, at least in respect of books, became unworkable with the argument being that if it were not possible to secure a conviction for that work, it would be difficult to see how any work could proceed (Travis, 2000: 262). This is a view supported by other eminent commentators who suggest that the turning point was arguably in 1991 when the Director of Public Prosecutions refused to prosecute a publisher who created an imprint of the infamous novel *Juliette* by the Marquis de Sade, even though this portrays the sexual abuse and killing of children and women (Fenwick, 2002: 284).

If we return to our context for this chapter, modern communication technologies, it is highly unlikely that sounds of real children being abused could come within this defence (unless it was alleged that they were taken from a legitimate artistic film but even then the context would become important). It is easier to see how drawings could perhaps more easily be included within the defence although it would require some external verification as to their artistic quality. In the 1980s there was a reaction to an exhibition of works by Tierney Gearon in the Saatchi Art Gallery, London where the police sought to investigate pictures that included naked children posed (Ost, 2002: 445). The gallery was investigated under both the obscenity and indecency legislation, although only the former has any defence.

It has been suggested that the police investigation to this exhibition was *'out of proportion to any possible harm that the exhibition posed'* (Ost, 2002: 445). However, this shows the importance of context. If the exhibition was to take place solely to sex offenders would this still be true? If obscenity is judged solely in respect of the images it should not make any difference, but arguably part of the reason here is the fact that the wider audience may appreciate the artistic measure of this. What if this were applied to the Internet however? Could these same images be posted on the Internet even though this would provide easier access to sex offenders?

It should also be noted that although the Gearon exhibition included images of naked children, they were not sexually explicit. The type of pictures and CGI images that are being found by law enforcement contain depictions of brutal sexual interaction between adults and children and it may be more difficult to find an expert who would be willing to suggest the artistic integrity of such images. Also, the jury (as the ultimate tribunal of fact) would have to decide that the images did serve the public good and not just that someone believes that.

The most complicated area for the defence remains text. Whilst it would be hoped that the stories produced by NAMBLA et al. would not be considered to have the same artistic merit as *Juliette* or *Lolita* can it be said that this is necessarily the case? The latter are, of course, published by respectable publishing houses but in this electronic era, it is not unusual to see some texts that are only published electronically so should the law adapt to this? Some argue that during the obscenity trials there was no difficulty in producing witnesses to testify as to the literary merits of a text and so could the same be true here? It may be difficult to argue this in respect of the stories found by 'Rob' highlighted above as this would arguably be analogous to the situation found in *Jordan* (*op. cit.*) but it remains exceptionally rare to proceed solely on the basis of text.

Notes

1 Originally broadcast on 11 February 2001. A transcript of the programme is available on the BBC website (last accessed 26 February 2007).
2 This was first broadcast on 8 January 1998 and formed part of the 'Witness' series of documentaries.

CHAPTER 4

Child Pornography 2: Indecent Images

It is estimated that the majority of child pornography available is likely to amount to photographs (or pseudo-photographs) and the law has created a distinct area of law to cope with this, that of indecent images of children.

The law has changed several times over the past years and at the time of writing it is expected that future legislation is likely to be forthcoming. Whilst the law has, to an extent, kept pace with technology, constantly changing the law is not necessarily helpful as there is a danger that it could lead to confusion (Gillespie, 2004).

The legal framework

There are two principal offences relating to indecent images, together with three recent subsidiary offences. All have common definitional features. Unlike with obscenity legislation, the possession of images is illegal and not just the creation and dissemination of the material. The two principal offences are contained in s.160, *Criminal Justice Act 1988* (possession) which states:

(1)   . . . it is an offence for a person to have an indecent photograph or pseudo-photograph of a child in his possession.

Since 2001 this offence is punishable by up to five years' imprisonment and is a relevant offence for the purposes of the notification requirements (see Chapter 8). The second offence is the more serious and is contained within s.1, *Protection of Children Act 1978*.

(1)   . . . it is an offence for a person–
    (a)   to take, or permit to be taken or to make, any indecent photograph or pseudo-photograph of a child; or
    (b)   to distribute or show such indecent photographs or pseudo-photographs; or
    (c)   to have in his possession such indecent photographs or pseudo-photographs, with a view to their being distributed or shown by himself or others; or

    (d)   to publish or cause to be published any advertisement likely to be understood to be conveying that the advertiser distributes or shows such indecent photographs or pseudo-photographs, or intends to do so.

Since 2001 this offence is punishable by a maximum of ten years' imprisonment and, like s.160, is an offence that attracts the notification procedures. It can be immediately seen that s.1 is the much wider offence and indeed s.1(1) creates seven separate offences (paragraph (a) creates three (takes, permits to be taken and makes), paragraph b creates two (distribution and showing), and paragraphs c and d create one each), or more properly, seven separate *actus reus* through which the crime can be committed.

The *Sexual Offences Act 2003* altered some of the definitional aspects of the two principal offences, but it also added three new offences (ss. 48–50). These will be discussed later in this chapter and in the book, but for summary are (*inter alia*):

- Causing or inciting a child to become involved in pornography (s.48).
- Controlling a child involved in pornography (s.49).
- Arranging or Facilitating a child involved in pornography (s.50).

These are relatively distinct offences and accordingly will be dealt with separately at the end of the chapter.

Indecent photographs

It has been noted already that the principal offences are Sections 1 and 160 and it would seem at first sight that the division between these two is relatively easy to explain; s.160 relates to possession and s.1 to the creation and dissemination of photographs. However, when communication technologies, especially the Internet, is involved, the distinction becomes slightly blurred.

Downloading

The action of downloading a photograph from the Internet has caused problems for the law in differentiating between the offences. It can be argued that downloading an image is not any different to storing a photograph that has been obtained from a source. The hard disc becomes, in essence, the storage box and so instead of a box or album full of photographs the hard disc stores them. It would be thought, therefore, that an offender who downloaded an image would be liable to conviction under s.160, CJA 1988. However, a landmark decision in *R v Bowden [2000] 1 QB 88* decided that an offender could also be liable under s.1, PoCA 1978.

The logic of this decision is understandable if it is viewed in a strictly literal way. The image that has been downloaded to the computer did not exist at that location before. Accordingly, a new image has been 'made' by the process of downloading (the image being the file now stored on the computer). The Court of Appeal in *Bowden* used this logic to suggest that under these circumstances the correct charge would be s.1 (p. 95). In doing so, they rejected the submission of defence counsel that 'make' meant 'create', i.e. an image that had never been known before came into existence (pp. 94–96). Instead, they held that the duplication of an existing image would suffice since there is now undoubtedly an additional photograph. Literally speaking this is correct and can indeed follow the logic of the offline world:

A contacts B, a known child pornographer, and asks him to sell an indecent image of a child. B, wishing to continue to profit from his photographs, copies the photograph and sends it to A.

In this example, A would be guilty of possessing child pornography because he now owns an indecent photograph of a child. B would be guilty of two offences under s.1. The first would be that he has distributed the indecent photograph of the child (sending the copy to A) and the second would be the making of the duplicate copy. This is uncontroversial since there are now two copies of the photograph instead of one, i.e. a new one has come into existence.

This logic was applied to the issue of downloading and whilst there is no distribution *per se* there is still the making of an image, a new duplicate of that image has come into existence. However, this time, it would be B that has made the photograph rather than A who has posted it. In both examples an indecent image has been made and thus liability appears to arise under s.1.

Whilst this logic is literally correct it has been questioned whether this was an appropriate action since it would be possible for this liability to be triggered where a person has the exclusive access to a photograph and yet who catalogues it electronically (Ormerod, 2000b: 383). A good example of this would be where someone transfers a photograph from a floppy disc to his hard-drive or to a CD-ROM, or where someone electronically scans a photograph that he previously had only in a physical format. In all these situations it does not necessarily follow that this is the preparation for dissemination and could, indeed, be an attempt to facilitate cataloguing (it has been noted that some child pornographers appear almost obsessive in their cataloguing and indexing of images, see Taylor and Quayle 2003: 156–70). Ormerod has suggested that this is analogous to someone who is cataloguing physical media and thus could be as easily dealt with as possession rather than making.

The points raised by Ormerod are compelling and it could be questioned whether if *Bowden* was heard now instead of in 2000 the same decision would have been made. At the time the case was heard the maximum sentence for possession was six months imprisonment, and the penalty for making was three years. Given that there had been significant concern as to the prevalence of child pornography on the Internet it could be possible to argue that *Bowden* was a creature of necessity in that the courts believed that a summary-only offence was not sufficient to combat Internet behaviour, whereas, of course, five years' imprisonment (the current penalty for possession) may have been.

In any event, the decision in *Bowden* has been confirmed and indeed expanded. In *R v Smith; R v Jayson [2003] 1 Cr App R 13, 212* the Court of Appeal decided that, subject to the appropriate *mens rea* requirement, deliberately calling up an image to the screen or opening an e-mail attachment that contains an indecent image of a child, would be sufficient to attract liability under s.1. The reasoning behind this is because of the way the Internet works. A computer, when it accesses a website, will actually create a duplicate of the images accessed in its cache store. The computer does this automatically, but this means, of course, that an image that did not exist is now created and, accordingly, could be considered 'making' for the purposes of s.1(1)(a) (pages 220–1 of the judgment provides a succinct analysis of the technical process through which the image is created).

A similar process exists for the opening of an attachment via e-mail, where the contents will be written to the computer's hard disc, irrespective of whether the user wishes this or not. The case was again criticised for blurring the distinction between Sections 1 and 160 (Ormerod, 2002b: 662), and certainly the extension made in *Smith; Jayson*, whilst being literally correct, does raise concerns as to whether the correct balance between possession and making has been struck. However, the Court of Appeal has attempted to resolve this, in part, by stating that the downloading of images will be treated for sentencing purposes as though it was downloading (*R v Oliver et al [2003] 1 Cr App R 28*, 463 at [12] and [15]), but as will be seen later in this book this is not quite the same and there are significant differences to the way that offenders may be sentenced (see Chapter 8 below).

Irrespective of the merits of the decision it is clear that the current legal position is that downloading an image, or recalling an image onto a screen, can amount to 'making' and thus within s.1, PoCA 1978. However, it is important to be clear what the legal position is. Where an image is downloaded it will also be in the defendant's possession. Whilst it would not be appropriate to charge both offences (although theoretically this is possible since possession is a continuing offence), prosecutors do have the option of whether to charge s.160 or s.1. It will be seen that this duplication has led to a number of instances where the law has developed in ways it need not have done, potentially creating further uncertainty.

Definitions

Sections 1 and 160 share common definitions (see s.160(4)) and it will be necessary to consider these before the offences. The principal aspects to define are:

- Indecent
- Photograph
- Child

Indecent

The legislation itself does not define the term 'indecent' but in *R v Stanford [1972] 2 QB 391* it

was said that indecency and obscenity are at opposite ends of the same spectrum, with obscenity being the graver of the two (p. 398). In *R v Graham-Kerr (1988) 88 Cr App R 302* the Court of Appeal ruled that the meaning of indecency was an objective question that was solely within the remit of the jury, i.e. not something that an expert witness should be allowed to testify on.

The effect of a purely objective test is that it focuses on the image and not the intentions of the offender. That is to say, it does not matter *why* a person does a prohibited act (e.g. taking a photograph or showing a photograph), it is sufficient that the person knowingly does the act. It may be thought that this is an appropriate situation but it can cause difficulties, as can be seen from two examples:

Example A (family photograph)
   In certain circumstances it is quite possible that a family photograph of a child in a bath may be construed as indecent. This is almost certainly purely innocent and an everyday activity but depending on what is shown in the photographs, prima facie liability may arise and all the family has to safeguard against prosecution is the dicta statement of the Court of Appeal that it would probably not be in the public interest to prosecute such offenders.
                                                           (Ormerod, 2001: 658)

Example B (children on the beach)
   If a person takes photographs, or a video recording, of young children playing nude on a beach it is quite unlikely that this will be considered indecent (assuming that there is no focusing on the child's genitalia etc.). What happens, however, if the person then takes this film and shows it to several sex offenders with the intention of them all receiving sexual gratification from it? If the image is not indecent then this showing is perfectly legitimate notwith-standing the purpose for which the showing takes place.

The alternative to the objective test would be to create a subjective test where the circumstances of the *actus reus* help define whether an image is indecent or not. Arguably the easiest way of achieving this would be to use the test developed by the courts for the offence of indecent assault (ss. 14 and 15, *Sexual Offences Act 1956*). These provisions were subsequently repealed and replaced by s.3, SOA 2003 (Sexual Assault)). This test was formulated in *R v Court [1989] AC 28* where the House of Lords decided that indecency (for assault) could be broken down into two categories. The first are those acts that, because of their circumstances, are always indecent, and the second is where an act may or may not be indecent (e.g. spanking) in which case it is indecent if the purpose of the perpetrator is indecent.

This approach was recently given statutory recognition (s.78, SOA 2003) and is the standard test for most sexual 'contact' offences. What would the position be if it were adopted for indecent images? In the first example above it would be hoped that no parent would take photographs that are obviously indecent, so they are more likely to be placed in the second category where the legitimate purpose would be taken into account. With the second example, this would automatically fall into the second category and would allow such activity to be captured by the criminal law as socially and morally wrong, whilst at the same time not criminalising the legitimate showing of pictures (e.g. between family).

However, whilst this would seem a useful and sensible approach to take, in *R v Smethurst [2003] 1 Cr App R 6* the Court of Appeal dismissed an argument that this approach should be adopted, and rejected the suggestion that not to do so would be contrary to the European Convention on Human Rights. It is submitted that the Court was correct to reject the ECHR argument, but it is unfortunate that it did not consider it more appropriate to use the *Court* test. Realistically the Court did not provide any convincing argument for rejecting this approach and it is likely that it owes more to the doctrine of precedent than to any substantive legal principle. It would seem now that any change would have to be introduced by legislation rather than through the courts and it is to be hoped that time will be given to considering such a proposal as it could ensure the law is brought into line with other offences and could also bring consistency to this area.

Until Parliament legislates we are left trying to decide how to apply the objective test. It is clear that the objectiveness must be in respect of the actual article and not related material. In *R v Murray [2004] EWCA Crim 2211* the Court of Appeal reinforced this when it was called upon to rule on a video in two halves. The first half contained a medical examination of a child's genitalia by a doctor with a commentary explaining the doctor's action. The second half was a manipulation of the first part and was where images of the child's genitalia had been spliced together to form a sequence and the commentary had been deleted. The defendant sought to argue the point that as the first half of

the question was not indecent (because it was a *bona fide* medical examination), the second half could not be considered indecent as it consisted of images that were found from within the first half.

To further this argument the defendant argued that using the 'pause' button on the remote control could produce the equivalent image. The Court of Appeal rejected this argument stating that the two halves were quite distinct and that the tribunal of fact, in this case the jury, could legitimately consider the two halves separately and decide whether the second (manipulated) half was indecent. This is an interesting decision, but one that does reinforce the fact that it is not the motives surrounding the taking of an image that is relevant, but rather the image itself.

The issue of indecency has reared its head once again because of a sentencing decision. As a strict matter of law, for the purposes of Sections 1 or 160 it does not matter how indecent an image is, so long as it meets the indecency threshold, a conviction under s.1 can arise. However, as a matter of public policy, it is desirable to differentiate between the level of indecency for the purposes of sentencing, something that the Court of Appeal considered in *R v Oliver et al. [2003] 1 Cr App R 28, 463*. The full implications of this decision will be seen later in this book, but it is worth noting that the Court of Appeal decided to adapt the COPINE scale for its purposes. The COPINE scale was created by Taylor et al. at the University of Cork, perhaps the leading centre within Europe on child pornography on the Internet, as a way of describing the different types of pornography available (Taylor et al., 2001). The original scale had ten points within it (see Table 4.1):

This is a useful and valid description of the material but it must be clear at the outset what its purpose was. The COPINE unit made clear that it has created 'ten levels of severity of photographs' but they were not suggesting that this necessarily bore any relationship to the illegality of the material or that collecting such images were necessarily indicative of anything, stressing that the context of the production and possession of the images is crucial (Taylor et al., 2001: 102). Indeed, the authors of the scale were quite clear that it cannot be said that a person collecting Level 1 images is necessarily any less problematic than someone who collects higher scaled images (Taylor et al., 2001: 103). The scale is, therefore, a description of material and not an indicator of dangerousness.

Table 4.1   The COPINE scale

	Name	Description
1	Indicative	Non-erotic and non-sexualised pictures showing children in their underwear, swimming costumes etc.
2	Nudist	Pictures of naked or semi-naked children in appropriate nudist settings, and from legitimate sources.
3	Erotica	Surreptitiously taken photographs of children in play areas or other safe environments showing either underwear or varying degrees of nakedness.
4	Posing	Deliberately posed pictures of children fully, partially clothed or naked (where the amount, context and organisation suggests sexual interest).
5	Erotic Posing	Deliberately posed pictures of fully, partially clothed or naked children in sexualised or provocative poses.
6	Explicit Erotic Posing	Emphasising genital areas where the child is either naked, partially or fully clothed.
7	Explicit Sexual Activity	Involves touching, mutual and self-masturbation, oral sex and intercourse by a child, not involving an adult.
8	Assault	Pictures of children being subjected to a sexual assault, involving digital touching, involving an adult.
9	Gross Assault	Grossly obscene pictures of sexual assault, involving penetrative sex, masturbation or oral sex involving an adult.
10	Sadistic/Bestiality	(a) Pictures showing a child being tied, bound, beaten, whipped, or otherwise subjected to something that implies pain. (b) Pictures where an animal is involved in some form of sexual behaviour with a child.

Taylor et al., 2001: 102

The Court of Appeal, relying on the advice of the *Sentencing Advisory Panel* (see Gillespie, 2003), decided not to rely on this scale in its entirety, and interestingly it decided that Levels 1 to 3 of the COPINE scale would not be considered because the Court argued that it would not meet the threshold for indecency (*Oliver et al.*, op. cit.: 467). However, in *R v Carr [2003] EWCA Crim 2416* the defendant was charged, *inter alia*, in connection with a collection of 12,000 pictures of women and children's bottoms, including a number of 'upskirt' pictures that were, presumably, obtained surreptitiously. This behaviour, known as scopophilia, is usually caught by the common law offence of outraging public decency, but since some of the pictures related to a child it was decided to use PoCA 1978. The Court quashed the sentence in respect of these counts and did not impose a new sentence (at [27]), but this is something significantly different to quashing the conviction, something they failed to do. Quashing a sentence does not alter the convicted status of a person,

and thus the Court of Appeal was, albeit implicitly, upholding the conviction of the appellant for this collection. Whilst the transcript of the judgment does not go into detail about the particulars of this collection, it is highly likely that 'upskirt' pictures could not be considered anything other than COPINE Levels 1 to 3 and thus the Court appears to have contradicted its earlier belief that these levels were exempt from the criminal law. This can only add another layer of uncertainty into this area.

Photograph

The second definition aspect is that it must be a photograph. This aspect has been touched upon already when it was noted that the legislation is restricted to photographs and pseudo-photographs, but what do these mean? Section 7(2), PoCA 1978 Act states:

References to an indecent photograph includes an indecent film, a copy of an indecent photograph or film, and an indecent photograph comprised in a film.

In *R v Fellows; Arnold [1997] 1 Cr App R 244* the Court of Appeal held that scanning a photograph into a computer created a 'copy of a photograph', but notwithstanding this, there was concern in the 1990s as to whether the legislation could cope with modern communication technologies. Accordingly, Parliament amended the legislation to specifically cater for electronic mediums. Section 7(4)(b), PoCA 1978 Act now stated that a photograph includes '*data stored on a computer disc or by other electronic means which is capable of conversion into a photograph*'.

Pseudo-photograph

The second, and perhaps more significant amendment, was the introduction of the pseudo-photograph. The concept of 'pseudo-photograph' was introduced in the previous chapter and it was noted that a possible justification for criminalising even the mere possession of such images is that it may fuel the demand for more indecent pictures, leading to children being abused or exploited. What does the law consider a pseudo-photograph to be?

Section 7(7), PoCA 1978 states:

> '*Pseudo-photograph' means an image, whether made by computer-graphics or otherwise howsoever, which appears to be a photograph.*

At the outset it can be noted that the definition appears restricted to images that look like photographs and accordingly, drawings and cartoon imagery will be outside of this scope. This was implicit within the decision of *R v Goodland [2000] 1 WLR 1427* where the Divisional Court held that a pseudo-photograph must look like a photograph. In saying this, they rejected the suggestion that a 'pitiful' image consisting of two photographs 'hinged' together by sellotape (so that when 'hinged' a child's head 'replaced' an adult's head on a pornographic image), was a pseudo-photograph.

Within the field of communication technologies it has not been immediately clear how far this definition applies with, perhaps surprisingly, few reported decisions on this definition. In *R v Fellows; Arnold [1997] 1 Cr App R 244* the Court of Appeal stated that they believed the section was concerned with adapting photographs rather than merely electronically transmitting copies of photographs (at p. 255 of the judgment). Some commentators have argued that a

pseudo-photograph comprises a photograph or collage of photographs altered by a graphics manipulation package (Akdeniz, 2001: 247) and this appears the most likely. Accordingly, as suggested in the previous chapter, it is submitted that most CGI images (although perhaps not all since some may be of sufficient quality to 'appear to be a photograph'), and certainly all cartoons and drawings, will fail to be considered a pseudo-photograph.

Child

It may be thought that the definition of 'a child' may be the easiest to note but even this can raise some issues of concern. The 1978 and 1988 legislation does not penalise indecent images, but rather indecent images of a child. Where the identity of the child is known then it is possible to lodge the birth certificate of the child as evidence, thus providing a presumption of the victim being a minor. However, it is comparatively rare for law enforcement agencies to know the identity of a child and, therefore, the precise age of the victim (Palmer, 2004: 30–1). The legislation was drafted with this in mind and s.2(3), PoCA 1978 Act states that an image is to be taken of a child if, on consideration of the evidence, it appears to be of a child, something that is replicated in s.7(8) for pseudo-photographs. In other words, the age of the child becomes an issue of fact for the jury to decide.

In *R v Land [1988] 1 Cr App R 301* it was held that age was something that a jury could decide by themselves without the need for expert evidence, and in *R v Owen (1986) 86 Cr App R 291* the courts confirmed that age was relevant in deciding whether an image was indecent. This combination led to the situation where it was comparatively rare for prosecutions to occur for post-pubescent images because the prosecution would need to prove beyond all reasonable doubt that the image portrayed a child (Tate, 1990: 22–3). This argument was something that legal commentators had noted:

> The ruling seems to envisage that, if there were, two photographs, exactly similar in all material respects, one of an 18 year-old girl and one of a well-developed 14 year-old, the jury might, on being informed of the 14 year-old's age, properly consider the latter photograph to be indecent even though they would not so regard the former.
>
> (Smith, 1998: 121)

If this observation is then linked to the ruling in *Land* it can be seen why the difficulty arose. If either image was to be put before the jury in the absence of any knowledge as to their age, could the prosecution prove beyond all reasonable doubt that the person portrayed was a child? It is submitted that it would be very difficult to do so because, as Smith demonstrates, it could as easily be someone over the age of consent. Accordingly the law enforcement community concentrated their attention on pubescent or pre-pubescent children.

Until 2004, the age of 'a child' was somebody under the age of 16, but s.45 of the Sexual Offences Act 2003 raised the age of a child to 18. The formal reason for this change was that it was necessary to comply with an EU framework decision (Council Framework Decision 2004/68/JHA), although whether this is a particularly convincing explanation is more open to question (Gillespie, 2004a: 361–2). Raising the age in this way could, arguably, help alleviate the issue about post-pubescent children above, since although Smith used the example of an 18 year-old it is perhaps easier to tell the difference between a 14 year-old and an 18 year-old than it would be between a 14 and 16 year-old.

However, given the standard of proof required, whether this will make any practical difference is unknown and, in any event, it is not clear that shifting limited police resources away from pubescent and pre-pubescent children to a wider range is either desirable or necessary. This change in the law has also created the situation where the age of a child is now beyond that of the age of consent (which is 16). This creates the situation that, apart from certain defined situations outlined below, a 16 year-old can freely choose to participate in sexual activity but cannot choose to be the subject of a pornographic picture.

There are reasons why the law should perhaps set the age at 18, most notably the fact that indecent images are, in effect, permanent. Whilst the subject of the photograph may believe that the taker will act responsibly with it, this is not always a safe assumption to hold, and there have been numerous examples where images have been misused either during or, more likely, after a relationship. It is certainly known that once an image finds its way onto the Internet then it is, in effect, a permanent feature, as it will be copied and 'mirrored' so as to ensure that it will be virtually impossible to identify every copy (Taylor and Quayle, 2003: 24). However, is this a convincing reason by itself for this change? It appears somewhat incongruous that a 16 year-old could give valid consent to other matters that

could have a degree of permanency, including, for example, unprotected sexual intercourse with someone who is HIV positive (implicit within the decision of *R v Dica [2004] EWCA Crim 1103*), and yet cannot give consent to her boyfriend to take a topless picture of her. The full implications for this change could be quite significant, although whether law enforcement agencies will go out of their way to use this extension is subject to some doubt (Gillespie, 2004a: 363).

Mens rea

Whilst neither s.1 nor s.160 mention a *mens rea* requirement, it is clear from judicial pronouncements that they are not crimes of strict liability, i.e. there is a need for a mental element to be proven to show liability. The danger of a strict liability offence can be seen when one looks to the Internet and e-mail, where, for example, 'spam' has been shown to include mild forms of child pornography, and where people looking for adult pornography have identified child pornography by mistake. If the indecent images legislation was strict liability then *prima facie* the recipient of these images would be liable because as demonstrated above, accessing such images causes a duplicate to be automatically created by the machine. Presumably innocent behaviour would come within prosecutorial discretion, but it has already been noted above that faith in such discretion is not always reassuring.

In *R v Atkins [2000] 2 Cr App R 248* the Divisional Court was called upon to rule as to the *mens rea* requirement of these offences, and they held that the true construction was that Section 1 required someone to intentionally make an image (p. 260) or to knowingly possess an indecent image of a child (p. 262). In *R v Smith; R v Jayson [2003] 1 Cr App R 13, 212* this approach was confirmed by the Court of Appeal, but they took it further arguing that the *mens rea* requirement was not only someone intentionally making an image, but accessing an image knowing that it was likely to contain an indecent image of a child (p. 216). The idea of intention or knowledge is not particularly controversial and, indeed, would help to alleviate any concerns as regards the example given above. However, it has been suggested that extending the concept of knowledge to include material 'likely to contain' indecent images of a child is somewhat problematic because this is, in effect, making the *mens rea* one of foresight and recklessness

(Ormerod, 2002a: 661). The difficulty that is identified with this approach is that the foresight becomes one of foreseeing the probability of an indecent image of a child and not merely the foresight of an indecent image.

This concern may have been resolved, at least in part, in the case of *R v Collier [2004] EWCA Crim 1411* where the Court of Appeal was once again asked to consider the *mens rea* requirement for these offences. Interestingly, this time the Court decided to link the *mens rea* to the statutory defences which, as will be seen, exist under this legislation. This approach has created a situation whereby there is not a single *mens rea* requirement for Sections 1 and 160 but, rather, a separate offence for certain types of *actus reus*. It will be noted below that there is a statutory defence within s.160(2)(b) and s.1(4)(b) that permits an offender to escape liability if he can show that he did not know, or have any cause to suspect, that the image was a child under 16. According to the Court in *Collier*, the effect of this is that the prosecution need only prove that the defendant possessed, made or distributed an image that was likely to be indecent, not that it was likely to be an indecent image of a *child*. The justification for this is that if the prosecution were required to show likelihood of a child, the statutory defence would never be triggered: a defendant would never have to prove an absence of knowledge because in those circumstances the prosecution could not come up to proof (at [29]).

Where *Collier* becomes more interesting is in respect of 'making' contrary to s.1(1)(a) where there is no related general defence. Here, the Court decided, albeit *in obiter*, that in the absence of the statutory defence the *mens rea* should require not only knowledge as to an indecent image, but also knowledge that this indecent image may be a child (at [29]). Whilst this may be welcome in terms of meeting the criticism rightly put forward by Ormerod, it does, as the Court itself notes, lead to a paradox:

> It follows (very ironically) that the prosecution have a heavier burden in the absence of a statutory defence.
>
> (at [30])

It would appear that the Court is undoubtedly correct in this observation: where a statutory defence applies the prosecution need only show one element of *mens rea* and yet where there is no defence the prosecution must prove two elements. As a justification for this paradox, the Court argues that this was because Parliament undoubtedly believed that someone who made an indecent image of a child would know, or suspect, the age of a child.

Whilst this may be true of situations where the activity involves the physical taking of a photograph (and even then there may be difficulties as to whether someone knows the precise age of a child, but it is perhaps easier to justify criminalising someone who fails to check) this is less certain where communication technologies are involved. If a person is sent an e-mail attachment, that person will not necessarily know whether the image contained is of a child until it is opened. It would seem appropriate, therefore, that only where an offender knows that the image is, or is likely to be, of a child that liability arises. It is likely that it will be comparatively rare that the prosecution will not be able to prove this in relation to offenders who have solicited, or sought, images because evidence of communication, through, for example, e-mails (which were used successfully as evidence in *Jayson [2003] 1 Cr App R 13, 212*), will exist.

Statutory defences

It has already been noted that there are a number of statutory defences contained within the offences. There are two groups of defences, those that were originally contained in the statutes and those defences that were recently added by the SOA 2003.

The original defences are where the defendant had a legitimate reason for the photographs (s.160(2)(a) and s.1(4)(a)) or they had not seen the photographs and did not know, or have any reason to suspect, that they contained an indecent image (s.160(2)(b) and s.1(4)(b)). Section 160 carries with it the additional defence of having not solicited the images and, having received them, not keeping them for an unreasonable time (s.160(2)(c)). The new defences introduced are that there is a need to make or possess the photograph for reasons concerning the prevention and detection of crime (s.160(1B) and s.1(1B)), or a limited defence to possessing images of, or taking photographs of, a child between the ages of 16 and 18 (s.160(1A) and s.1(1B)).

Reverse burden of proof

Whilst each defence operates slightly differently, they all have as a common feature the fact that they purport to place a reverse burden onto the defendant, that is to say, it is not for the prosecution to disprove the defence, but for the defendant to prove that they come within the defence. This is the opposite of the usual position within the criminal justice system and reverse burdens of proof are extremely controversial. It has been suggested that the reverse burden of proof is an extreme measure and more dangerous than a reduction in the standard of proof, arguing that instead of a person receiving the benefit of any doubt, they are convicted *'when it is a toss-up whether he is guilty or not'* (Williams, 1988).

The concept of reverse burden of proof has been controversial for some time and the courts have been entertained by trying to ascertain the extent to which reverse burdens are imposed by modern statutes. The latest, and most important, decisions in this area are those of the House of Lords in *R v Johnstone [2003] 1 WLR 1736* and *Attorney-General's Reference (No. 4 of 2002); Sheldrake v DPP [2004] UKHL 43*, together with the Court of Appeal decision in *Attorney-General's Reference (No. 1 of 2004) [2004] EWCA Crim 1025*, although the latter was, realistically, interpreting and applying the law as stated in *Johnstone* (see Gillespie, 2005a: 40).

It had been initially thought, following the decision in *R v Lambert [2002] AC 545* that reverse burdens of proof should normally be evidential in nature and not persuasive, and that they would be easier to justify if they did not relate to an essential ingredient of the crime (see Ferguson, 2004: 136). In order to explain the effect of this it should be noted that an evidential burden is where the prosecution still bear the burden of proof, i.e. they must prove that the defendant has a case to answer, but instead of having to disprove doubts merely raised by the defence, the burden shifts to the defence to adduce sufficient evidence to raise a doubt. Note that this is not saying that the defence must prove they are innocent, but they must prove a doubt (or flaw) in the prosecution case rather than merely raising the possibility of a doubt. A legal (or persuasive burden as it is often called) is different in that here the prosecution need not prove its case: it need only prove whatever matters are listed as its requirements and then the defence must prove to the balance of probabilities that they are not guilty.

It may be helpful to illustrate this through a related example. Let us take s.160(2)(a) which provides a defence where the defendant has a legitimate reason for possessing an indecent image of a child. Regardless of whether this is a persuasive or evidential burden, the prosecution need to prove the possession of an image and the fact that it is indecent. If the defence is evidential, then the defendant need only raise the possibility that they have a legitimate reason for possessing the image, and the prosecution will need to disprove this to the criminal standard (beyond all reasonable doubt). However, if it is a persuasive burden then the defendant needs to prove to the balance of probabilities that they had a legitimate reason for possessing the image. This burden is only triggered when the prosecution establishes a case to answer (i.e. possession of an indecent image) but it can be immediately seen from this example that the work the defendant must do with an evidential burden is significantly less than with a persuasive burden.

The House of Lords in *Johnstone* held that evidential burdens were not the only permissible form. The House held that even if a reverse burden of proof constitutes an essential part of the crime, proportionality can justify both legal and evidential burdens of proof where a pressing social need exists. The decision in *Sheldrake* has confirmed this approach and identified a situation when necessity cannot justify a legal burden. *Johnstone* was fiercely criticised as being unfair:

> *[the] principled approach . . . would have been to hold that the reverse onus may be justified if a prison sentence is not to be imposed; but that in principle no person should be deprived of liberty . . . unless the prosecution proves the case beyond reasonable doubt, and that burdens on the defence should be evidential only.*
>
> (Ashworth, 2004: 247)

This comment may be applied equally to *Sheldrake* and it is difficult to argue against, with Lord Nicholls acknowledging that reverse legal burdens can have the effect of allowing the tribunal of fact to convict someone notwithstanding an element of reasonable doubt in their minds (*[2003] 1 WLR 1736 at 1750*). It seems contrary to the rules of fairness, as traditionally understood, to allow someone to be sent to jail on the basis of a legal reverse burden of proof. Yet in both *Johnstone* and *Sheldrake* the offences were punishable by a significant period of imprisonment. A conviction under s. 1 or s. 160 could attract similar penalties, but arguably the consequences of conviction are even more serious because the offences carry a considerable stigma. The argument fashioned by Ashworth should be more compelling in these circumstances where the consequences are loss of liberty, employment and social interaction. Yet the Court of Appeal in *R v Collier [2004] EWCA Crim 1411*, citing *Attorney-General's Reference (No. 1 of 2004)* stated that in light of these authorities the statutory defences contained in ss. 1 and 160 impose a legal rather than evidential burden on the defendant.

Leaving aside Ashworth's argument about the propriety of the reverse persuasive burden, was the court in *Collier* correct to assume that these defences impose a persuasive, rather than evidential burden? The House of Lords in *Sheldrake* identified a number of factors in considering whether a reverse legal burden of proof is compatible with the European Convention on Human Rights. However, these factors can probably all be summarised by the general point made by Lord Bingham that the reasonableness of the reverse burden has to be considered ([2004] UKHL 43 at [41]). In reality, this is a combination of the necessity and proportionality required to justify the qualification to Article 6 approved of in *Salabiaku v France (1988) 13 EHRR 379*.

In deciding the reasonableness of the reverse burden, Lord Bingham identified a number of factors that could be relevant. Interestingly, one factor is that of international obligations. His Lordship, when referring to *Johnstone*, noted that an issue of particular importance to the House in that case was the international obligations surrounding trademark infringements ([2004] UKHL 43 at [41]). When Lord Bingham discusses the acquitted person within *Attorney-General's Reference (No. 4)*, he makes the point that there is no international obligation to combat membership of terrorist organisations and contrasts this with other obligations in connection with terrorism (at [47]). Within the field of abusive images of children there are international obligations, not least the European Framework Decision that the government has relied upon as the justification for the raising of the age of a child from 16 to 18 for abusive images (*Council Framework Decision 2004/68/JHA on Combating the Sexual Exploitation of Children and Child Pornography [2004] OJ L13, 20 January 2004: 44*). The Framework Decision includes a number of obligations on combating abusive images of children and, accordingly, it may seem that the indecent images legislation is more in line with

Johnstone than with *Attorney-General's Reference (No. 4)*.

However, international obligations by themselves cannot be the only factor and Lord Bingham discusses issues including the pressing social need justifying the burden ([2003] UKHL 43 at [40]), the breadth of the statutory provision (at [47]), whether the burden relates to issues that are within the defendant's knowledge (at [27]), and the ease by which the burden can be discharged (at [51]). Each of these factors will need to be considered, although many also relate to the decision of the House of Lords in *Johnstone*, which Lord Bingham is careful not to disagree with.

The least problematic area of the reverse burden of proof in respect of indecent images of children is the pressing social need. It has already been noted that the creation of indecent images of children is only possible by exploiting or abusing children and the trade in images (including the downloading or swapping of images) contributes to the demand for new images to be created, leading to further abuse (see above). The breadth of the provision may not necessarily be too troublesome either. Although commentators have, in the past, questioned the breadth of s.1 (e.g. Ormerod, 2003: 383), it is unlikely to be considered comparable to s.11 of the Terrorism Act 2000 which formed the basis of the indictment in *Attorney-General's Reference (No. 4)*. Lord Bingham noted in the case that somebody wholly innocent of criminal behaviour could be brought within the statutory provision, not least because it could cover situations when people joined a proscribed organisation before it was ever made illegal. As regards indecent images of children, however, the same argument cannot be made: innocent images are not brought within the provision, only those that are both indecent and of children are captured by the provision. If the legislation had adopted a reverse burden in respect of whether an image was indecent, it is quite possible that this would be comparable to *Attorney-General's Reference (No. 4)*, but the legislation does not require this and it is submitted that the provisions are sufficiently defined for their purpose.

The question is whether the issues constituting the defence fall within the defendant's knowledge and how easy it is to discharge the burden. Both points were considered explicitly in *Johnstone*, and Lord Bingham, in *Sheldrake*, implicitly approved of this being a factor in the decision. In *Johnstone*, Lord Nicholls, giving the leading speech, argued that the appellant's knowledge (or deemed knowledge) and the ability of the prosecution to ascertain facts known by the defendant should be highly relevant. It has been suggested that the knowledge aspect is the most important factor identified by the House of Lords but does this mean that a reverse burden should be regarded as acceptable just because the facts are within the accused's knowledge? (Ferguson, 2004: 138).

The Court of Appeal, in *Attorney-General's Reference (No. 1) [2004] EWCA Crim 1025*, considered knowledge to be important, but linked this to discharging the burden:

> *The easier it is for the accused to discharge the burden, the more likely it is that the reverse burden is justified. This will be the case where the facts are within the defendant's own knowledge. How difficult it would be for the prosecution to establish the facts is also indicative of whether a reverse legal burden is justified.*
>
> (at [52])

If these considerations are applied to indecent images of children it does not automatically follow that a defendant will be able to discharge any burden easily, not least because he may not have the required knowledge. It should be noted that, realistically, only two of these statutory defences are arguable. In respect of the requirement that a person has a legitimate reason for possessing, distributing or showing images, or that it was necessary to do so for the prevention of crime, it is unlikely that there would be any significant issue as to whether the reverse burden is legal or evidential, because the term 'legitimate reason' will undoubtedly be construed narrowly (see below). Where uncertainty may arise, however, is in respect of the defences applicable where a person has not seen the photographs and did not know, nor had any reason to suspect, that they were indecent, and where a person possesses unsolicited images and who does not keep them for an unreasonable length of time.

Legitimate reason

The first defence that needs to be examined is that the defendant had the right to possess, distribute or show the indecent image of a child (s.160(2)(a) and s.1(4)(a)). The term 'legitimate reason' is not defined within the Act and in *Atkins v DPP [2000] 2 Cr App R 248* the Divisional Court held that

whether an assertion will amount to a legitimate reason will be a matter of fact in each individual case and, accordingly, will be for a jury or magistrate to decide (p. 257). In the case of *Atkins* the Court confirmed, albeit almost certainly *in obiter*, that academic research could amount to a legitimate reason, but only where it was undertaken in a *bona fide* manner and would not work as a cover for sexual gratification.

It is worth noting that the defence of legitimate reason does not apply to 'taking' or 'making' and thus following the ruling in *Bowden* it would be of no assistance to a defendant that downloaded images from the Internet. The ruling in *Atkins* that *bona fide* research could be a legitimate reason does, however, further illustrate the difficulty posed by the ruling in *Bowden* as, in essence, this means that where two researchers examined the same image but in different formats (i.e. one holding the original photograph and the other having downloaded it from the Internet) a difference in liability would occur, with one being acquitted and the other convicted.

No knowledge of indecency

The second defence to examine is where a person has not seen the indecent image, and did not know, nor have any cause to suspect, that it was an indecent image (s.160(2)(b) and s.1(4)(b)). The wording of this statutory defence is slightly problematic in that in both statutes there is no express requirement that the indecent image be 'of a child', merely that it is not an 'indecent image'. This had previously been identified as an anomaly and it had been suggested that the defence must be construed so as to mean no knowledge or cause to suspect that it was an indecent image of a child, and not merely an indecent image (Ormerod, 2002a: 660). In *R v Collier [2004] EWCA Crim 1411* the Court of Appeal confirmed that this was indeed the position, arguing that Parliament must have intended the knowledge to be 'of a child'. Such a conclusion does not naturally follow, however, since Parliament expressly used the words 'of a child' in the immediately preceding and following defences, and thus it could be argued that the omission of those words was deliberate. However, *Collier* is undoubtedly correct in terms of fairness and so should be welcomed as a proposition.

The facts of *Collier* serve as an example of how this defence could work, and why that decision was correct. The defendant ordered CDs that he thought contained adult homosexual pornographic images. In fact, and unbeknown to him, the CDs contained four indecent images involving a child. The defendant contended that he had not seen these images and that he had purchased the CDs legitimately and without any cause to suspect that they contained indecent images of children. If the decision had been taken to take a literal interpretation to the wording of paragraph (b) then the defendant would be guilty of possessing indecent images of a child because there was no doubt that these images were indecent.

The decision that it requires knowledge did, however, provide this defendant with a defence because he did not know, or have cause to suspect, that they were on the CD. This line also appears in line with previous authorities on the *mens rea* of the offence, and had *Collier* not taken this approach then for cases such as that, it would in essence become a crime of strict liability which would not be appropriate. That is not to say that this will be an easy defence to operate, not least because of the reverse burden of proof, but also because the term 'or reason to suspect' will invite the prosecution to tender evidence, including circumstantial evidence, that a person may have had cause to suspect.

Unsolicited items

If an image is sent unsolicited to the defendant, it is a defence if the person did not keep the image for an unreasonable length of time (s.160(4)(c)). The statute does not define what 'unreasonable time' means but it is suggested that this must be an objective test that the relevant tribunal of fact can apply to the individual cases. There has been no reported appellate cases on this provision, in part because it is no doubt difficult to argue and also because prosecutorial discretion may mean that where any cases do arise they are not prosecuted.

Purpose of preventing or detecting crime

It was noted above that the statutory defences do not apply to 'making' indecent images of a child and this, in essence, caused a difficulty when it came to the Internet as it could lead to a situation where *bona fide* actions could, conceivably, lead to liability. In order to examine the difficulty let us take three examples:

Example 1 – Network Investigations
    D is a network administrator for a University. He receives a report from a member of staff (A) that she has seen another member of staff (B) accessing child pornography. In order to confirm this, D calls up B's history and when he looks at the recent sites, an indecent image of an 8-year-old girl appears on the screen.

Example 2 – Referrals
    D works for the NSPCC. X, a mother, found an indecent image of a child on a computer. Not knowing what to do, she forwards it onto the NSPCC who, when they confirm the image appears to be of a child and in line with their policies, forward it to the Child Exploitation and Online Protection Centre to investigate.

Example 3 – Prosecution
    D is a caseworker for the Crown Prosecution Service. He is currently assisting with the prosecution of X, someone who has downloaded indecent images of children. Duplicate images of this material must be made so that counsel, the judge and the jury can examine the material. D makes a series of copies of the images downloaded by printing them out on a colour laser printer. He then supplies these images to the relevant people at court.

Each of the situations above are arguably every-day occurrences and yet in each example had this occurred before the SOA 2003 then the liability could have accrued against D since on a literal interpretation of the law, an indecent photograph had been 'made' contrary to s.1, PoCA 1978. Perversely, in Examples 2 and 3, D would have a defence to the distribution that occurred after the making (legitimate reason) but this would not have acted as a defence to the initial making.

Prior to the SOA 2003 the only protection that D would have in each of these scenarios would be the likelihood that the Crown Prosecution Service would never consider it to be in the public interest to prosecute in such cases. However, s.46, SOA 2003 introduced a new statutory defence into s.1 (s.1(1B)), the essence of which states that where making is required for the 'prevention, detection or investigation of crime, or for the purposes of criminal proceedings, in any part of the world' no liability shall arise. Presumably it will be a matter of fact for the jury whether it was necessary to make the image for these purposes, and to that end, the police and CPS have developed a protocol that defines the circumstances when such necessity may be shown (the protocol known as *The Memorandum of Understanding between the CPS and the Association of Chief Police Officers concerning s.46*

Sexual Offences Act 2003 is available on the CPS website).

It should be remembered that this protocol exists outside of the Act and accordingly has no formal legal status: it is, in essence, merely an opinion of the police and CPS as to what the correct status of the law is. Whilst the protocol may be passed to those workers in Examples 2 and 3, it is unlikely it will come to the attention to the person in Example 1. That will not prevent the defendant in Example 1 pleading this defence and nor should it, and it will be for the jury to consider whether the actions of the defendant were necessary and *bona fide*. Excessive making (e.g. where, in Example 1, the network administrator looks at *every* image instead of calling the police after viewing one or two images) could, conceivably, be considered by the jury to be no longer necessary for a specified purpose and the defence may accordingly fail.

Marriage or other relationship

Perhaps the most bizarre statutory defence was also inserted by the 2003 Act, although this time into both PoCA 1978 (s.1(1A)) and CJA 1988 (s.160(1A)) statutes. The purpose of this defence is to militate slightly the raising of the age of 'a child' to 18 by providing that in limited circumstances it is a defence to possess, take or make an image of a 16 or 17 year-old child. It is contended, however, that all this section does is to reinforce the foolishness of the increase of the age and create an almost unworkable defence.

The defence applies to a limited form of actions:

- Possession of an indecent image of a child;
- Taking or making an indecent image of a child;
- Distributing or showing an indecent image of a child;
- Possessing an indecent image of a child with a view to distributing or showing,

but only in defined circumstances. The first circumstance is that the child must be aged 16 or 17; this defence does not operate in respect of children below the age of consent. The next circumstance is that the accused and the child must be either married or living together 'as partners in an enduring family relationship'. The term 'enduring family relationship' is not defined which is unhelpful, but the section makes it clear that the persons must be living together. This

potentially creates the situation where two 17-year-olds who have been boyfriend and girlfriend from the age of 14 and who are engaged to be married but do not live with each other, will not come within the defence, but two 17 year-olds who have been together for three months but who do live with each other could potentially come within the defence. It is difficult to see the logic behind this and it will undoubtedly cause unfairness.

Other conditions further limit the usefulness of this defence. Section 1A(3) states that the defence applies only where the image shows either the child alone or with the defendant, but not with anyone else. This subsection does not even limit the third person to someone under the age of 18. Accordingly, if A, a 17 year-old girl, had an intimate photograph taken of herself with B, a 19 year-old ex boyfriend, she could not show that picture to her new boyfriend as this would exceed the defence, meaning that A would be liable to a custodial sentence of up to ten years imprisonment. The third-party rule also demonstrates that the law is limiting photography in a way that it does not do with sexual activity. Three 17 year-olds can quite legitimately have group sexual activity but cannot photograph themselves doing so as this could amount to a breach of Section 1.

The absurdity of the defence is perhaps best reflected when one returns to the issue of the burden of proof. This defence purports to impose both a legal and evidential burden onto the defence whilst, at the same time, placing a legal burden onto the prosecution too. The defence burdens can be found in ss. 1(1A)(1) and (2) – '. . . *the defendant proves . . .*' which, following *Collier*, must be a legal burden; ss. 1(1A)(4) and (6) – '. . . *if sufficient evidence is adduced to raise an issue . . .*' which must mean an evidential burden. The prosecution burden can be found in s.1(1A)(4), (5) and (6) – '. . . *the defendant is not guilty of the offence unless it is proved . . .*' which can only mean a traditional legal burden of proof. It will be appreciated from the brief discussion of these issues previously in this chapter that reverse burdens of proof are complicated at the best of times, but it will be very interesting to see how a judge explains this provision, with all its conflicting traditional and reverse burdens, to a jury in such terms as to allow them to understand what their role is.

In summary, it is extremely difficult to see how this defence will operate. Whilst it appears to provide a solution to a bad law, all it actually does is create a bad solution to a bad law. Parliament's desire to interfere with the sexual autonomy of teenagers over the age of consent is difficult to understand and focusing its attention on the protection of marriage and the family home merely illustrates the unfairness of this measure, by suggesting that it is permissible for some 17 year-olds to be the subject of photographs but not others (see Gillespie, 2004a: 364). If children under the age of eighteen need to be protected then surely this must apply to all children and not just some? It is difficult to see how this defence can work in practice and it should serve as an additional reason to rethink the desire to raise the age of a child in these circumstances to 18.

Incitement

Operation Ore was the name given to the national law enforcement operation that arose out of the *Landslide Productions* operation conducted by law enforcement agents in the United States of America. *Operation Ore* was arguably the largest law enforcement operation of its time in the United Kingdom and involved upwards of 7,000 people being investigated in connection with indecent images of children.

A difficulty of *Operation Ore* was that of the considerable delay between when the data was gathered and passed to UK law enforcement officers and the dates when arrests were made. Indeed, there continues to be some controversy over this as it appears a number of perpetrators may still be outstanding. One difficulty this caused was that because the name 'Landslide Productions' was disclosed in connection with 'Operation Ore' it was thought that some offenders had sought to hide their computers from the authorities or some had purchased new computers. This meant that whilst police thought a person had been involved in purchasing indecent images of children, when they came to investigate the defendant's computer no images were present. What, if anything, can be done in these circumstances?

Obviously, without proof of any images then it would not be possible to show the offences of possession or 'making'. However, in *R (O'Shea) v Coventry Magistrates' Court [2004] EWHC 905*, the Divisional Court upheld a conviction for three counts of inciting the distribution of an indecent photograph of a child. To prove this it would not be necessary to show possession of any photographs but merely that a person encouraged another person to send him indecent images of children. The actual distribution can take place anywhere in the world because the incitement takes place where the person making the request is.

The decision in *O'Shea* is somewhat controversial because, as the Divisional Court noted it is 'trite law' to state that it is not possible to incite a machine ([2004] EWHC 905 at [32]). The Court, however, held that a human was incited here rather than a machine because a human operated the system. However, this argument has been criticised as being somewhat unconvincing and arguably widening the law of incitement beyond that which is appropriate (Ormerod, 2005: 352). The particular difficulty identified in respect of this case is that there is no evidence that the person responsible for the site was aware of the incitement by the defendant. Indeed, given the significant number of subscribers to the *Landslide Productions* site (numbering, at the very least, tens of thousands of subscribers), it is inconceivable that any human would be aware of the individual incitement. However, Ormerod concedes that the practical consequence of this decision is limited in that the facts would almost certainly lead to a conviction for attempting to incite (Ormerod, 2005: 353), but this certainly does not suggest the step taken by *O'Shea* is necessarily justified or helpful since it means, with inchoate liability, that the law can continue to be extended.

That said, it is clear that it remains the law and this means that where facts such as *O'Shea* arise there continues to be a legal solution. It would also provide a solution where a person sends an e-mail to another or goes onto a chatroom or bulletin board and requests indecent photographs to be sent to him. In all of those circumstances incitement could be found. In *R v Goldman [2001] EWCA Crim 1684*, the flexibility of the offence of incitement to this area was detailed. A company, based in Amsterdam, offered for sale a series of pornographic videos which, *prima facie*, appeared to include advertisements for indecent photographs of children. It was never, in fact, ascertained whether the advert was for children (because it was not relevant to the case). It should be noted that, whilst some of the descriptions implied young teenagers (e.g. Lolita pictures, young teens etc.), these terms are also used within the 'adult' industry even where the models are over the age of consent. However, at least one tape referred to 'illegal teens' which must, at the very least, provide *prima facie* evidence. The advertisement also stated they could supply 'custom-made' tapes and the defendant requested a tape containing images of pre-pubescent children. The distributors did not supply the tape and ultimately the letter came to the attention of the authorities.

The defence argued that it was not possible for the defendant to be guilty of incitement since the incitee would be committing an offence (in this case distribution of indecent photographs of a child). This was rejected by the Crown Court at first instance and subsequently upheld on appeal to the Court of Appeal. Potentially this could be important in circumstances where 'proactive' operations are used by law enforcement agencies, i.e. where the person asked is actually a member of the law enforcement community rather than a vendor. It has been noted that this could cause difficulties if the operation led to entrapment (Ormerod, 2005: 352), but such operations could be run without entrapment arising. The use of proactive police tactics will be considered elsewhere in this book (Chapter 6), but it is important to note that they could be used in these circumstances. For example, whilst it is unlikely that they would post an advert similar to that used in *Goldman*, but they could (where they identify the controller of a website distributing indecent images of a child) choose to 'take control' of a website in order to identify further perpetrators.

Encryption

It was noted in the first chapter that forensic computer examination can be an important tool when identifying whether it has been used for the criminal behaviour of a suspect. This is particularly true of the area of indecent photographs. Since the process of downloading is illegal, it does not matter whether the material is subsequently deleted.

However, increasingly, law enforcement officers have identified cases where a person has encrypted some or all of their computer (Home Office, 2006: 4). If the material is encrypted it becomes extremely difficult to forensically examine a computer. Whilst some encryption can be 'broken' the majority of it cannot. Even where 'breaking' is possible it can be extremely expensive and time consuming.

Part III of the *Regulation of Investigatory Powers Act 2000* (RIPA) provided a legislative framework under which law enforcement agencies could 'demand' the 'key' to encryption. Section 49 of RIPA allows a police officer to serve a 'disclosure notice' on someone that they reasonably believe to have a key. The effect of the notice is that it requires the person who has the key to either disclose it (s.50), or to disclose the encrypted information in an intelligible form (ss. 49, 50). The police are able to decide which form of disclosure they wish (subject to a necessity and proportionality test).

Knowingly failing to disclose the information required under s.49 amounts to a criminal offence (s.53) that is triable either-way and punishable by a maximum of two years' imprisonment. Part III of RIPA has only recently been brought into force following concern that terrorism and major criminal investigations have encountered encryption (Home Office, 2006). There is concern that Part III is of little use to investigations concerning indecent photographs of children.

The penalty for possession of indecent photographs is five years' imprisonment with the penalty for 'making' being ten years' imprisonment. It has already been noted that where communication technologies are involved this means realistically the more serious offence (s.1) will be committed. Why, therefore, would an offender disclose the key to his encrypted data if he knows that doing so could result in a sentence of up to ten years' imprisonment, yet refusing to comply would mean that a person would only face a penalty of two years' imprisonment. Also, an offence under s.1 or s.160 is subject to the notification requirements (Chapter 9) whereas a conviction under Part III does not.

The Home Office launched a public consultation suggesting that Part III of RIPA 2000 could be amended prior to coming into force. The effect of the proposed changes would be to increase the penalty for non-disclosure of the key in the following circumstances:

- Where a person has been previously convicted of an offence contrary to s.1, PoCA 1978 or s.160, CJA 1988.
- Where the device containing the protected information contains an indecent photograph of a child.
- The device containing the protected information was taken from someone who had possession of indecent photographs or other

apparatus or devices that contained indecent photographs of children.
- The court is satisfied that the protected information is likely to contain an indecent photograph of a child.

(Home Office, 2006: 6)

It should be noted that the circumstances above do not amount to a criminal offence, it would be the refusal to comply with the notice requirement that amounts to a criminal offence. Any legislative change would simply vary the penalty in the circumstances above.

The second and third possible circumstances exist because currently it is not unusual for suspects to be in possession of some unencrypted indecent photographs. The process of de-encrypting data, reviewing it and then re-encrypting the data can be somewhat time consuming. There have, therefore, been instances where although the bulk of a computer has been encrypted, there has been a small number of 'favourite' pictures unencrypted so that these can be viewed easily by the offender. In such circumstances it is currently possible to prosecute the offender (in respect of the unencrypted pictures), but this may not be representative of the offender's criminality and the sentencing options open to a court would be limited to that which can be proved (i.e. the judge could not take into account the encryption).

The final circumstance is perhaps the more likely. This would be where the prosecution would have to adduce sufficient evidence to show that it was likely the encrypted information contains indecent photographs of a child. This evidence may arise in a number of ways. It is possible that the offender has been identified as a result of payments to a commercial child pornography website or because another offender has been arrested and communications data suggests that the offender with the encrypted data has either supplied, or been supplied with, indecent photographs of children.

The results of the public consultation have not yet been released, but Part III was brought into force without amendment. The government has said it is committed to looking at this issue, but has not put forward a timescale. However, it appears relatively clear that legislation does need to be brought forward since Part III of RIPA 2000 will not by itself encourage people to de-encrypt their computer where the encrypted material contains indecent photographs of children.

Involvement in pornography

It was noted above that along with the offences contained within Sections 1 and 160, the SOA 2003 introduced three new offences governing involvement in pornography (ss. 48–50). These offences will also be examined in Chapter 7 as they are also relevant to the commercial sexual exploitation of children but their use should be briefly outlined here.

The offences all owe their origin to the detailed Home Office review of sex offences (Home Office, 2000), but in the review it was argued that there was a need for a set of new offences to tackle the commercial sexual exploitation of children, in particular the need for those who were involved in 'pornography for gain' (Home Office, 2000: 7.6.3). Although Sections 48 to 50 require an element of 'gain' when they relate to child prostitution, there is no such requirement when it relates to child pornography, the sole definition being that it relates to an indecent image (s.51(1)). The difficulty is that it undoubtedly blurs the boundary between these offences and s.1.

Realistically, where someone causes or incites a child to become involved in pornography (s.48), they must arguably also be committing an offence of either aiding and abetting the taking of an indecent photograph of a child (s.1(1)(a) PoCA 1978 when read in conjunction with the *Accessories and Abettors Act 1861*), or inciting a child to have their photograph taken and thus guilty of incitement (see 4.2.4 above). Similarly, 'controlling a child involved in pornography' (s.49) must also involve conduct that amounts to aiding and abetting the substantive offence under s.1 and the same is true of 'facilitating a child involved in pornography' (s.50). The explanatory notes to the SOA 2003 provided the example of:

A delivering B to a place where he will be used to make pornography . . .

Yet this is also the classic example of accessorial liability: this cannot be said to be anything other than aiding and abetting, or possibly procuring, an indecent photograph of a child. Accordingly, a person would be liable under s.1, PoCA 1978 in conjunction with the 1861 Act (above).

The offences created in ss. 48–50 carry a higher maximum sentence than s.1 (14 years imprisonment compared to 10), and this could probably be justified if they were restricted to commercial sexual exploitation. However, by not restricting the offences to commercial sexual exploitation it potentially creates some absurdities. If A, an adult, asks B to pose topless whilst he photographs her then this would amount to an offence under s.48, SOA 2003. Accordingly, A is liable to up to fourteen years' imprisonment and yet if he actually takes the photograph then he would be liable for the offence of taking an indecent photograph of a child (s.1(1)(a), PoCA 1978) which is punishable by a maximum sentence of ten years' imprisonment, four years less. In the absence of the creation of commercial child pornography offences it is difficult to see how and why ss. 48 to 50 should be used in preference to inchoate and accessorial liability under s.1, not least because ss. 48 to 50 do not (as yet) attract the notification requirements under the SOA 2003 (Gillespie, 2004a: 367).

CGI images.

Section 51(1) states:

> . . . *a person is involved in pornography if an indecent image of that person is recorded* . . .

This can be contrasted with the requirement under s.1, PoCA 1978 for an image to be a 'photograph'. 'Image' is further defined under the SOA 2003 as including *'an image produced by any means'* (s.79(4)) and this could therefore include cartoons, drawings, CGI images etc. Would this make any practical difference; in other words could ss. 48–50 be used to bring CGI images (for example) out of the arena of the obscenity legislation?

Section 48, SOA 2003 creates the offence of 'causing or inciting' a child to become involved in pornography. If we set aside inciting for the moment (as it is relatively difficult to see how one could incite a child to become involved in a CGI image rather than photography) we are left with

'cause' which bears an ordinary criminal meaning. When read in conjunction with s.51(1) this would appear to mean the offence becomes, *inter alia*, causing an indecent image, created by any means, of a child. Let us take an example:

> *A, a photographer, takes a photograph of B, a fourteen-year-old girl in a swimsuit. He then digitises the image and produces a CGI. He digitally removes the swimsuit and creates representations of B's breasts and nipples.*

It is quite possible that under these circumstances it can be said that A has caused B to be now involved in pornography, i.e. that an indecent image of B is recorded. However, this would appear to be restricted to where an image of a child has been recorded. Accordingly if A, when digitising the image, altered the appearance of B so that she was no longer recognisable then it would be difficult to see how a conviction could be sought. Whilst it is possible to attempt the impossible (s.1(2), *Criminal Attempts Act 1981*), it is unlikely to work here since this would be straining the law too far by criminalising fictitious representations of non-existent children.

This would also cause a difficulty, therefore, where it is not possible to identify whether the CGI image is a real child. Unfortunately, tracing children is a problematic exercise even where they are photographed, and the success rates of such tracings is not high (Holland, 2005: 78), although it should be noted that more resources are beginning to be dedicated to this task. Would the police have the time or resources to try and trace a CGI representation? It would seem unlikely and thus s.48 may be of limited practical use. Also, s.48 would probably not assist where the CGI image has been downloaded from the Internet since it would be difficult to say that the possessor has caused that child's image to be recorded: the creator of the image may have, but probably not the downloader.

CHAPTER 5

Grooming

Of all the dangers that children may experience online arguably that of grooming has received the most press attention. In this chapter an analysis will be made of what grooming is and what the limitations of the law may be.

Defining grooming

If one were to read only the media it would seem that grooming is a new phenomenon and yet we know that it is not. The process of grooming a child for sexual abuse is long-established and is, in essence, the main method through which children are abused. McLachlan, the former head of the Metropolitan Police's Paedophile Unit, argues that monsters do not get children, nice men do (Long, 2002: 6). By this he means that children will normally react to someone who acts badly towards them. It is relatively rare for an offender to use immediate physical coercion to force a child to submit to abuse because this is a high-risk strategy: there is a significant risk that the child will tell someone and thus the perpetrator will instead attempt to persuade the child to give what they perceive to be 'consent'[1] or seek some other form of emotional control over the child, so as to minimise the risk of detection (see, for example, Silverman and Wilson, 2002: 49–52). This behavioural control is sometimes known as 'grooming' and has been the principal method of facilitating abuse for a very long time. A typical example of how this process can work was presented by an offender:

> *I bribed my victims. I pleaded with them. But I also showed them affection and the attention they thought they were not getting anywhere else. Almost without exception every child I molested was lonely and longing for attention.*
>
> (in Tate, 1990: 6)

We are accustomed to the stories about abusers telling the victims not to say anything because they will not be believed, or it will result in them being taken into care etc. Various research studies have shown that this is exactly what is said, and that this is a perfect example of how to get an emotional control over the child (Howitt, 1995: 92). Similarly, an offender will frequently try to put the blame onto the child or, in their own eyes at least, make the child co-responsible, through statements such as, 'You like it' or 'I'm not really hurting you'. Although violence may not be an initial feature, once the grooming process has begun threats about the use of force, including the use of deadly force against either the child or a loved one (e.g. the mother) can become common as this reinforces the hold that an offender has over the child (Howitt, 1995: 92).

Howitt notes that the grooming process is cyclic (Howitt, 1995: 84), something that others argue is a commonly accepted proposition (Terry and Tallon, 2004: 21). The cycle of abuse is often related to Wolf's Offending Cycle (Silverman and Wilson, 2002: 58), and whilst the precise stages in the cycle often differ, Figure 5.1 shows my adaptation of a number of cycles to demonstrate one possible type.

It will be seen that this cycle has a number of stages within it, including a number of 'barriers'. Some people acknowledge that a barrier or wall exists within the cycle but do not believe that they are actual features, whereas other cycles explain their role is as important as any other stage within the cycle. Other cycles include specific reference to cognitive distortions, but Figure 5.1 does not because I believe that cognitive

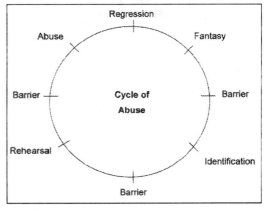

Figure 5.1 Cycle of abuse

distortion exists throughout the cycle and, as will be seen, it is directly linked to the barriers.

Each cycle has the same start point, which is that an offender suffers regression or negative thoughts about their life. Indeed, there are many varied internal and external factors that may lead to this regression, but they will all lead to the offender suffering a lack of self-worth (Terry and Tallon, 2004: 21). Eventually the offender will start to fantasise and then experience what some refer to as 'deviant fantasy', (ibid.) that is to say fantasising about inappropriate behaviour.[2] This will lead to the offender masturbating to orgasm to these fantasies which helps make the offender feel good. Some perpetrators will use abusive images of children to fuel this stage, especially where they have access to the Internet (Quayle and Taylor, 2002: 600–1). At this point the offender will normally discover the first barrier – they will realise that what they are doing is wrong, and will feel further negative thoughts because of their solution. Sometimes an individual will go no further than this but an offender will, through cognitive distortion, pass through the barrier (Silverman and Wilson, 2002: 58 and also see module 1 of the CROGA website).

The next stage in the cycle above is the identification of a victim, or potential victim. It needs to be understood from the outset that many offenders will take a long time trying to identify a victim (although as will be discussed below, when modern communication technologies become involved it is sometimes possible for this stage of the cycle to be accelerated), and sometimes the identification will be made through the adult, not the child. They may, for example, place an advert in a 'lonely hearts' column for a single mother. For some offenders, this identification stage will also involve befriending the victim's friends or family in order to become an accepted part of the victim's social life so that if the behaviour escalates it will not attract undue attention (Howitt, 1995: 84).

When a child is identified a further barrier is presented and sometimes this will mean that an offender will not go any further than being friends with the child (for an example of this, see for example the subject Q.X. in Quayle and Taylor, 2001: 599), but others will proceed through this barrier by means of cognitive distortions. It has been noted that a common distortion at this stage is to transfer the blame for the ensuing behaviour onto the child. Those who work with sex offenders note that this is a common strategy where they will seek to portray themselves as blameless or victims themselves (Tate, 1990: 105–7). Again, the use of abusive images of children may assist in this cognitive distortion because it allows abusers to justify their abuse on the basis that the existence of such material demonstrates, in the offender's eyes, that it is neither wrong nor abnormal (Quayle and Taylor, 2002: 866).

The next stage in the cycle is rehearsal, although not every cycle has this, with some professionals arguing that it is, in effect, a development of the identification stage. Others argue that it is sometimes used as a preparatory or 'dry run' of the abusive activity (Terry and Tallon, 2004: 21). It has been suggested that whilst this stage does exist, it is more often than not the start of the abuse-stage of the cycle in that it tends to involve direct contact with a victim, albeit in either an innocent way or at an experimentation stage (Howitt, 1995: 84).

The final stage in the cycle is where the actual abuse of the child takes place. This may be a final barrier for the offender to overcome, but it is more likely that the cognitive distortions of the offender lead to this being sidestepped. The abuse stage is where full sexual contact exists, although Howitt, citing Wyre, argues that there may be a spiral of sexual contact, i.e. the sexual conduct increases through the duration of the abuse (Howitt, 1995: 85). This is undoubtedly correct and the grooming is in respect not only of permitting the abuse, but of the type of abuse. Indeed, Howitt presents a case-study of 'Gary' who abused two children, and the case-study demonstrates how the sexual contact increased over time (Howitt, 1995: 87–9). Others confirm that the severity increases arguing that it is an inherent part of the grooming cycle (Terry and Tallon, 2004: 22–3).

The pattern of grooming is called a cycle because it is cyclic: i.e. when the abuse stage is reached it does not end, it continues. The initial part of this is that an offender who has abused may feel some negative thoughts or remorse for what has happened, but the cognitive distortions will then allow the offender to persuade themselves that it was consensual or, indeed, that the child instigated it. The cycle will continue into the fantasy when the offender recalls what happened and progresses again until repeated abuse occurs. The identification and rehearsal stages may be bypassed but are undoubtedly replaced by a stage where the offender has to continue ensuring that the child co-operates and does not disclose. Thus the grooming behaviour of rewards, presents, threats and distortions will continue. Some workers have suggested that the more pertinent question is how often the cycle continues (Silverman and Wilson, 2002: 58), and indeed with how many victims. Also, how the cycle is broken becomes one of the central questions to be addressed.

The cycle of abuse is undoubtedly individual to the offender and victim, and the speed of the cycle will depend on many factors. However, a full cycle could involve many months from start to finish, something demonstrated by Howitt in the case-study of 'Garry' who frequently discusses time lapses of weeks and even months (Howitt, 1995: 87–9). Internet grooming undoubtedly follows a similar pattern, but there is an argument that it can speed up the cycle. The words of one offender demonstrate how the relative anonymity of the Internet allows for the identification and sexual stages to be progressed in a more blatant and quicker way:

You can't go up to a boy in the street and say . . . do you fancy having sex . . . whereas you could online.
(Quayle and Taylor, 2001: 602)

The cycle of abuse has been adapted by one leading commentator to demonstrate its applicability to the online world. A portrayal of this adaptation is reproduced at Figure 5.2 and it can be immediately seen that there are less stages in this cycle, mainly because there is no express mention of barriers. In the explanation of the cycle, however, it recognises the need of an offender to use cognitive distortion to progress through the cycle.

This cycle starts at a slightly later point but presumably it must be taken as read that the entry point to this cycle portrays the same regression as within a traditional cycle, since something must cause the offender to desire to meet a child, albeit online. It was suggested that progression through the cycle need not be perfect, in that an offender may jump between various points before completing it (O'Connell, 2003: 7). An obvious example of this is that the 'risk assessment' stage of this cycle may occur several times and not just in the place indicated.

According to O'Connell, the first stage is the friendship forming stage. This is where an offender will identify a child and then begin to befriend them. O'Connell notes that at this stage

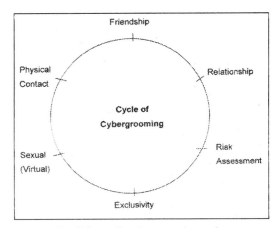

Figure 5.2 O'Connell's cybergrooming cycle

the behaviour is generally innocuous although an offender may ask for a (non-sexual) photograph to identify his or her profile and to contribute to the friendship building (O'Connell, 2003: 8–9). Related to the friendship stage but, according to O'Connell, a development of it, is the relationship stage. In this context relationship does not mean an intimate or sexual relationship but rather a 'special' friendship where the offender attempts to persuade the child that they are their 'best friend' (O'Connell, 2003: 9). This can include instances of persuading the child that the offender is the only one who knows what the child is going through, or treating the child as an adult, implying that others, especially the parent, does not (an example of how this can occur is presented in Long, 2002: 26–7). This is further developed into the 'exclusivity' stage, which is where the bond between the child and the offender is made stronger, so that the child comes to rely on the offender. Some commentators argue that in some situations the offender will prey upon vulnerable children, ensuring that any bond created between them will be cherished by the child and making it easier to control the child (Palmer, 2004: 26–7). If one were to relate these stages back to the traditional cycle of abuse it could be argued that they are a composite of the 'identification' and 'rehearsal' stages, but the advantage of the Internet and related mediums is that it enables a stronger bond to be formed because of the anonymity, not least because the offender could, at this stage, be posing as a child or a young person only a few years older than the victim (something which is not uncommon (Palmer, 2004: 27)).

The next stage in the cybergrooming cycle is the 'sexual stage', although this is not immediately about the perpetrator seeking the abuse of the child, but can be encouraging the child to discuss its sexual history, even if this is relatively minor, for example a kiss (O'Connell, 2003: 9). The sexual conversation increases and the child is encouraged to become more sexually explicit. If this is linked to the traditional cycle it can be seen that this is undoubtedly linked to the idea of fantasy because, although the cycle has a specific 'fantasy' stage, it is known that the whole cycle is bound up by fantasies until the perpetrator is able to put these fantasies into effect. The advantage of cybergrooming is that it can encourage the child to enter these fantasies in a proactive way. One method of heightening this fantasy is for the offender to pose as a child, thus encouraging child-to-child sexual experimentation, including cybersex (Quayle and Taylor, 2001: 601–3). O'Connell believes that the sexual stage is not a simple stage but a composite one, through which a series of micro-cycles may exist. She argues that there can be different types of behaviour, including:

- Child erotica and child pornography: image creation, exchange and distribution.
- Fantasy enactment.
- Fantasy enactment based on perception of mutuality.
- Fantasy enactment: overt coercion counterbalanced with intimacy.
- Cyber-rape fantasy enactment: overt coercion, control and aggression.

(O'Connell, 2003: 11–12)

The idea is that these levels arguably increase with severity. The first of these forms of behaviour, child pornography, will be discussed separately in this chapter because the law recognises that this is one of the most potent forms of grooming.

The fantasy enactment stages vary from the offender leading the action, through to both parties being involved, into the final two layers where the offender takes control. In the latter situations it would seem that there is an element of blackmail in the former and verbal abuse in the latter (O'Connell, 2003: 12). Where an offender has persuaded a child to forward a photograph of themselves, this can be a significant tool for persuasion as the offender can threaten to post the picture onto the wider Internet if the victim fails to comply (O'Connell, 2004: 18). Whilst it may be easy to say that all a child has to do is to shut down their computer or log-off the chatroom, this misses the point that such behaviour happens after the child and the offender have developed a relationship. It is clear that the child becomes confused and frightened by the activity and does not know who to tell, or is afraid to tell anyone. There is no reason to suggest that the grooming behaviour here would be any different to traditional grooming behaviour, i.e. it has been noted already that comments such as 'tell no-one, you will not be believed', or 'you will be taken into care' are not uncommon and are powerful; the fact that they occur over the Internet should not by itself necessarily mitigate them. By this stage the child is rarely in a public chatroom and has normally given the offender their personal e-mail address, Instant Messenger tag or even their telephone numbers. Accordingly, logging off is of little assistance as the offender can, if they so wish, cyberstalk the victim.

The final stage presented in the cybergrooming cycle is not one that is expressly mentioned by O'Connell, but is an adaptation by myself. We know from reported cases of Internet grooming that some offenders will restrict their behaviour to the online world and, accordingly, their cycle will bypass this stage. However, some offenders will seek to meet the child in the real world so as to abuse them. Typically, such offenders will have sexually groomed the children on the Internet first (Carr, 2003: 2–3), and it can be argued, therefore, that this is an acceptance that the offender will have travelled part-way through O'Connell's cycle. The offender will, before meeting the child, undertake an additional risk assessment stage to ascertain the safety of the meeting, and this will frequently include ensuring that the child is not storing any records of their conversations (Carr, 2003: 3), so as to minimise the chances of detection and disclosure.

Legal solutions

Having now identified what grooming behaviour is, or could be, it is now necessary to consider how the law can react to such behaviour. For the purposes of this chapter I will examine three spheres of law:

- 'Grooming' offence contained within s.15 of the 2003 Act.

- Showing sexual imagery to children.
- Risk of Sexual Harm Orders contained within Sections 123–9 of the 2003 Act.

Other offences can also tackle grooming situations, especially where there is no intention to meet (most notably s.14, SOA, 2003). This offence is discussed elsewhere in this book (Chapter 6), and accordingly it will not be rehearsed here. However, it is important to note that it is an important offence and extremely flexible, potentially allowing the law to act in situations where s.15 may fall down.

The 'grooming' offence: s.15

Section 15 of the 2003 Act introduces a new offence that has commonly been termed a 'grooming' or 'anti-grooming' offence. In fact, its description is 'Meeting a child following sexual grooming etc.' which is something slightly distinct. Whilst the 'etc.' seems a somewhat unusual inclusion within statutory language, it does suggest that the offence is not designed to tackle just grooming or, indeed, grooming *per se* as the term is prefixed by the word 'following'. This is an important point because the offence is not designed to tackle grooming but rather the effects of grooming. If reference is made to the cycles of abuse discussed previously in this chapter it will be easy to identify why this is the case. The majority of the stages of the cycle are somewhat transient and would be impossible to criminalise; the criminal law can only act in appropriate circumstances and generally speaking it will not cover liability that is too remote.

It must be recognised at the outset that this offence is somewhat controversial, partly because of the misunderstanding of what it was deemed to cover. The title 'grooming' is unfortunate and this has created situations where people have misunderstood what the law is supposed to achieve. In hindsight, even I have been guilty of this through referring to 'grooming' in published articles instead of saying it is to tackle the effects of, or the very late stages of, grooming. At the British Psychological Conference in 2004, a team of psychologists from Coventry University argued that the offence was harmful because it detracted attention from the fact that most children will be abused by someone they know (see Gillespie, 2004b: 586). It is beyond dispute that the majority of children are abused by someone they know and certainly the offence

contained under s.15 would be of limited use in these circumstances, but the point missed by the psychologists is that there have been cases of children being groomed over the Internet, including cases where the victim was abused after such approaches. Thus it could be questioned whether it is the offence that is at fault or its title? It must be its name, since the law is designed to prevent children from being abused and this cannot be an inappropriate aim for a law. Whilst the title of the offence may be somewhat clumsy, this should not detract from its purpose which is to tackle certain abusive behaviours. It is only one part of a wider process of tackling child abuse and the threat of abuse by someone known to the child is tackled in other ways.

Other commentators have criticised the offence for different reasons, most often arguing that it creates a thought crime or criminalises innocent behaviour (Khan, 2004). However, again this criticism arises out of a misunderstanding of not only what the offence is, but also what grooming is. If one refers back to the cycle of abuse, it can be seen that fantasy is a major element of this offence but it is simply not possible, nor desirable, to criminalise fantasy. This legislation is designed to tackle the very last stages of the grooming cycle. Ideally, it will operate just before the actual abuse of a child in the traditional cycle or, as will be seen, in the penultimate stage of O'Connell's cycle. The offence is not designed to tackle sexual behaviour over the Internet; it is designed to tackle behaviour where a person has groomed a child for sexual purposes and intends to meet them. The evidence required to prove this will be quite difficult to gather, something that critics of the provision note without any consideration of the fact that this is, in essence, mutually exclusive from their initial criticism which is that it is too easy to prosecute (Khan, 2004). It will be seen that intention is crucial to this offence and this is one of the primary safeguards of the offence.

The basic offence

Section 15 of the 2003 Act reads as follows:

A person aged 18 or over (A) commits an offence if:

  (a) having met or communicated with another person (B) on at least two earlier occasions, he –
      (i) intentionally meets B, or
      (ii) travels with the intention of meeting B in any part of the world.

(b) at the time, he intends to do anything to or in respect of B, during or after the meeting and in any part of the world, which if done will involve the commission by A of a relevant offence,

(c) B is under 16, and

(d) A does not reasonably believe that B is 16 or over.

The offence is serious in that it is punishable by a maximum sentence of ten years' imprisonment (s.15(4)) and is a sexual offence for the purposes of sentencing (see Chapter 9).

It is immediately clear that rather than criminalise the grooming process, i.e. the befriending, the offence instead hangs the criminal liability on the concept of meeting a child. This was a deliberate decision so that innocent behaviour or online sexual fantasy would not be criminalised *per se*. More than this, the offence requires that the meeting is for a sexual purpose. This restriction has raised some questions with some commentators, questioning whether the offence is too narrow:

A, 58, is a paedophile. He posts internet messages to B, believing her to be 15. She is X, an undercover woman police officer aged 32. No offence is committed.

(Ormerod, 2005: 636)

It is undoubtedly correct that no liability would arise under Section 15 as from the face of this example there is no evidence of any intention to meet, something necessary for the offence. Section 15 was not designed to tackle such behaviour but rather sets the nexus of liability at the solicitation of children for offline contact. However, it should be remembered that s.15 is not the only relevant offence. Depending on the nature of the communication it may be possible that other offences have been committed. If, for example, the communication involved pornography then s.12 may have been infringed (see below).

If the communication was to encourage the commission of a sexual act then it is possible that s.14 may be breached. A good example of this can be seen from the case of *R v Harrison [2005] EWCA Crim 3458* where s.14 was charged against a defendant who sought to 'groom' a child to perform a sex act on herself whilst on the telephone to the defendant. This falls outside of s.15 (as there was no intention to meet) but does fall within the remit of s.14 (arranging or facilitating the commission of a sex offence). It

will be seen below that the fact that it is an undercover police officer is no barrier by itself to its use. Accordingly, it can be seen that whilst Ormerod is correct to make this criticism about s.15 it does not follow that his example will necessarily be outside of the legal framework.

Actus reus

The *actus reus* of this offence has two stages; the intial act and the meeting. Each of these elements can be satisfied in two possible ways. The initial act is that there must be either a meeting or conversation on at least two earlier occasions. The reference to a meeting demonstrates from the outset that this offence, although designed by the *Task Force on Child Protection on the Internet*, is not technology specific – it is designed to apply equally to offline situations as online situations. Other jurisdictions have designed technological specific situations (this is most prominent in the USA; see, for example, the Main Criminal Code §11.259; see also Gillespie, 2001: 442–4), but the difficulty with this is that technology moves forward. If the legislation refers to the Internet, questions arise as to whether grooming via mobile telephones would be included, because is GPRS also the Internet? Also, who knows what the next generation of communication technology will bring, so it is sensible not to restrict statutory provisions to a set technology, not least because of the time it can take to amend legislation.

The requirement for two transactions is largely unproblematic because the behaviour that the offence is designed to prevent would not normally be completed within a single transaction. If reference is made to the cycles of abuse described at the beginning of this chapter, then it is apparent that there will be many small acts. The courts are, it is submitted, likely to construe communication in a way similar to the manner required by the *Protection From Harassment Act 1997* and accordingly a two-hour conversation within a chatroom may only count as a single transaction, but two separate e-mails may satisfy the requirement (see the discussion on *R v Kelly [2002] EWHC 1428* in Chapter 2).

It has been noted already that one criticism that has been levelled at this new offence is that it could criminalise innocent behaviour (see Khan, 2004; Ost, 2004: 151) and part of this argument is that the communication or meetings do not have to be sexual in nature. During the passage of the provision through Parliament, the opposition sought to amend the law to require at least one transaction to be sexual (*Hansard, HL Deb, vol 402, col 1261, 1 April 2003*). In the vast majority of situations this requirement would be unproblematic because as has been discussed already, a typical grooming behaviour would include a progression of sexual language, but the government rejected this proposal on the basis that this is only the preparatory stage of the offence, and no conviction can arise from just the communications. They also argued that introducing the need for at least one activity to be sexual could cause difficulty because it is not uncommon for someone grooming a child to talk about innocent activities such as football etc. (see *Hansard, HL Deb, vol 402, col 1262, 1 April 2003, Lord Falconer*). It has been noted that this would be very much the exception of the rule, since sexual contact is normally introduced, but an example where this may be relevant offline could be:

> *A works in a corner shop. B, a 10-year-old girl, frequently comes into the shop on her way home. After a few visits A starts to talk to B about who she is, what school she went to, what pop-groups she like etc. When she buys some sweets he always puts a few more in as 'treats'. After a few weeks, A invites B to meet him later on in a park to kiss and cuddle.*

Where intent can be shown (discussed below but almost certainly met within this example), then this may be an illustration where there has been behaviour without any express sexual conduct, but where there is a potential danger to the child. The Criminal Bar Association would probably argue that this is the type of case where child abduction could be pleaded (s.2, *Child Abduction Act 1984*) since taking a child somewhere can amount to abduction, although whether meeting a child at a pre-arranged place where the child travels independently would come within this legislation is open to question. For example, in *R v A* [2000] 1 Cr App R 418 the Court of Appeal gave the offence a wide definition arguing that the position was one of whether the child was under the lawful control of the parent, but with a pre-arranged meeting it may be difficult to show 'taking' (for further commentary on the 1984 Act see Gillespie, 2002: 415–17).

In any event, even if the 1984 Act applies it is submitted that it is not appropriate to these circumstances as it is not a 'sexual offence' for sentencing purposes and accordingly the ancillary public protection measures that arise

from a conviction would not be triggered (see Chapter 9). The mischief behind the 1984 Act is significantly different from that behind the s.15 offence and it has been argued that it is unhelpful for them to be treated in the same way (Ost, 2004: 151). This is a good point although the courts have traditionally given the 1984 Act a wider definition so as to encompass certain types of grooming behaviour. Perhaps one benefit of the passage of s.15 is that it may enable the 1984 Act to be restricted to its original purpose.

The second part of the *actus reus* concerns the meeting, s.15(1)(a) and makes it clear that the offender must either meet the child or travel with the intention of meeting the child. It is likely that this limb of the *actus reus* will be satisfied quite easily. Khan has suggested that the offence could endanger children because he argues that the police may need to allow an offender to meet with a child alone (Khan, 2004), but this misses the point that the second part of this limb is that a person travels to meet the child. Accordingly, if there is evidence to show an intention to meet, then there is no reason why the police cannot arrest the perpetrator when he enters the park etc. In at least one reported case prior to the introduction of the offence, the police disrupted a meeting by replacing the child and instead meeting the perpetrator themselves at the agreed location (Carr, 2003). Such behaviour easily answers the criticism of Khan and demonstrates that the offence can be versatile.

However, one small issue that may need to be discussed is that 'travelling' refers to A travelling to meet B and not B travelling to meet A. Thus if, for example, A sends B a train ticket allowing her to travel to meet him at his house, this would not *prima facie* meet the requirements of s.15 until the actual meeting takes place. It would obviously be not appropriate for the authorities to permit such a meeting if it came to their attention, but how would liability be construed? It could be argued that by arranging for B to travel to him, A has attempted to meet B, and the *Criminal Appeals Act 1981* permits liability to arise for attempted crimes. However, identifying what amounts to an attempt can be problematic.

Section 1(1) of the 1981 Act makes clear that an offender must take more than 'merely preparatory steps' to the commission of the offence, and by making these arrangements it may appear that this threshold has been passed, but in *R v Geddes [1996] Crim LR 895* the Court of Appeal adopted quite a strict line on what preparatory steps meant. In that case, the defendant was disturbed when he was found in the boys toilets at a school. He ran from the toilets and left a rucksack containing a bottle of cider, a large kitchen knife and a roll of masking tape. There was little doubt as to what his intention was, but the Court of Appeal quashed his conviction for attempted abduction arguing that all he had done was prepared himself to abduct a child, but he had not gone beyond mere preparation.

If we apply this reasoning to the example outlined above, can it be said that sending a train ticket to a child is beyond preparing to meet a child? If the conduct of *Geddes* was not beyond preparation then it could be argued that sending a ticket must only be preparation too, as there may be a number of reasons why it may not occur. However, one difference may be that in *Geddes*, the Court made an issue out of the fact that the appellant had not contacted or identified a child at the school ([1996] Crim LR 895 at [896]) whereas in the scenario described above there is, of course, such identification. On that basis it is to be hoped that the courts would consider the matter to be more than merely preparatory, permitting liability in these circumstances to exist. Scotland has its own version of this offence (s.1, *Protection of Children and Prevention of Sexual Offences (Scotland) Act 2005*) and it is notable that the Scottish Parliament decided to expressly cover the situation of B (the child) travelling to meet A (s.1(1)(a)(iii)) and it would have been preferable for s.15 to have done likewise but it is submitted that in its absence the law of attempts is likely to suffice.

Mens rea

The mental requirement for this offence is intention and, depending on the circumstances, this may be required twice. Intention is normally one of the most difficult forms of *mens rea* to establish, but its use was quite deliberate because the offence is designed to cover those who consciously seek to solicit children and the requirement for intention is an additional safeguard against the offence being applied to innocent behaviour.

It has been suggested that the police had raised concerns over the use of intention, with some arguing that it would make the offence 'unworkable' (Ost, 2004: 152), something that appears strange given that the *Home Secretary's Task Force on Child Protection on the Internet*, which

helped draft the offence, has senior members of the police attached to it. When it comes to proving intent it is likely that there will be considerable ways of proving intent. The content of the communications are likely to be of assistance, especially as noted above that in many situations the content of such material is likely to be sexual. The police are already used to the concept of forensically examining computers to recover e-mails and other computer data, and this is likely to find relevant material. It is important to note that in the grooming context there will be at least two opportunities to gather such evidence, because not only will it be the offender's computer that could contain information but also the child's, not least because many offenders will speak to others of a like-mind (Quayle and Taylor, 2001: 601) and thus it is quite possible that the adult will discuss how the grooming has progressed with another offender. This will certainly be admissible, not least because the requirement of the section is that A has the intention, not that A has communicated that intention to B.

Offline evidence will also be useful in showing the intention of an offender. Childnet International maintains a list of cases which involve children being groomed (Childnet, 2002), and existing cases have led to perpetrators being arrested in possession of PDAs or diaries, where they have booked a hotel where condoms were present, and in one incident where the offender was arrested in possession of comics, toys, condoms and lubricant jelly. It would not, it is submitted, be too difficult to place such evidence before a jury and invite them to consider what the intention of the offender was.

Sexual activity

The requisite intention that must be shown for the purposes of s.15 is that the offender intends to commit a 'relevant offence', which s.15(2)(b) defines widely to include any offence contained within Part 1 of the 2003 Act. This should mean that it will cover most sexual activity with a child, a deliberate decision because it is not the case that every offender will seek to have sexual intercourse with a child, so limiting the scope of the offence to penetrative offences would have been problematic.

It is known that some offenders will seek to groom children with the purpose of getting them to pose for child pornography (see Quayle and

Taylor, 2001: 606). Where there is no intention by A to meet B, but rather it is his intention to persuade the child to send digital pictures of themselves over the Internet, then it has been suggested that this may be outside of the law (Ost, 2004: 154). If there is no intention to meet then this is certainly outside the scope of s.15, but where a person invites a child to take a picture of themselves they are almost certainly inciting a child to take an indecent photograph of a child, or inciting the child to distribute an indecent image of a child. In both situations the adult will be liable, via inchoate liability, of an offence contained within the 1978 Act. However, even if there is an intention to meet for this purpose it is not immediately clear how s.15 would apply since the 1978 legislation is not mentioned within s.15(2)(b). It is possible that it could be argued that asking a child to pose for child pornography involves causing or inciting a child to engage in a sexual activity (contrary to s.10, SOA, 2003), and thus within s.15. The alternative would be to argue that involving a child in pornography is within Sections 48 to 50 of the 2003 Act (discussed in Chapter 4) all of which are within Part 1 of the Act and so also within s.15.

There are other sorts of behaviour that are involved within grooming that may not be covered by s.15, but it should be remembered that s.15 is only one offence, and it is not designed to be the sole weapon in the fight against grooming, but rather just one of a number of offences and accordingly any 'gaps' are likely to be filled elsewhere.

Global focus

The Internet and other communication technologies are, obviously, global resources, and one of the principal benefits of such technology is that someone in the UK could, for example, talk to someone else in the USA or Australia. This also, however, means that an offender could seek to groom a child within another country and there have already been reported cases of this occurring. Arguably, the most notable of these is probably when Toby Studabaker, a US Marine, met a 12-year-old UK girl on the Internet and groomed her, before flying to this country to meet her in person (see, for example, Paterson, 2003). The offence contained in s.15 seeks to tackle this global phenomenon, in part, by extending the nature of territoriality.

Traditionally, offences are only territorial in nature; that is to say that a person will only be

liable for acts committed within the territory of England and Wales. It is possible for Parliament to enact extraterritorially, i.e. to criminalise acts that occur anywhere in the world but this is not what Parliament has done with s.15. Instead, the offence extends territoriality by referring to a world-wide remit in two places. The first is in connection with the initial meetings or communications, where s.15(2)(a) states they can take place anywhere in the world, and expressly does not state that A or B has to be in England or Wales. Accordingly, any of the following three examples would be covered:

- A is in the UK and is talking to B who lives in Amsterdam.
- A is in Switzerland and is talking to B who lives in Manchester.
- A is in France and is talking to B who lives in Germany.

This extension is largely uncontroversial, with perhaps only the third example raising eyebrows. However, it will be seen below that there must still be a link to the United Kingdom and thus perhaps the justification of also involving the third example is the fact that it involves the UK being used to facilitate the abuse of children.

The second time when territoriality becomes relevant is in respect of what happens after this communication. It is clear that because the offence is not extraterritorial, any meeting between A and B should take place within this country, and thus in the third example above, if A and B decided to meet somewhere in the UK, liability could arise. Where, however, the prosecution seek to rely on the concept of travelling to meet the child (s.15(1)(a)(ii)), then s.15(1)(b) makes clear that the actual activity or meeting can take place elsewhere in the country, so long as the travelling takes place, in part, within the jurisdiction. This could prove useful as identified by the example below:

A meets B in a chatroom and talks to her over several weeks. B tells A that she is going to France on a school trip in one month's time. A states that he will be in France at the same time and suggests that they meet there and have sex. B agrees to this.

Prior to the implementation of the 2003 Act, if this came to the attention of the law enforcement community before A or B travelled then there is little that could be done other than to either prevent A from leaving the country (something that is not easily done unless the person is already a convicted sex offender, see Chapter 9), or notifying their opposite numbers who could prevent A from entering the country. However, using s.15 it would, subject to proving intent, be possible to arrest A when he attempts to board the ferry since by this stage he is undoubtedly travelling to meet B.

Proactive operations

In Chapter 6 the issue of proactive policing will be discussed. This is where the police use covert techniques, including posing as a child, to catch those who try to commit offences. It was noted that if the operations were planned carefully and in accordance with the legal rules then they can be a legitimate tactic to use. The *Home Secretary's Task Force on Child Protection on the Internet* recommended the offence under s.15 should be capable of being used in a proactive way. During the passage of the legislation, there was an attempt to expressly alter the definition of a child to include a police officer representing themselves as a child (*Hansard, HL Deb, vol 402, col 1266, 1 April 2003*), but it was withdrawn after the Lord Chancellor confirmed that it was unnecessary because the *Criminal Attempts Act 1981* would apply as this Act permits someone to attempt the impossible (s.1(2) CAA 1981), i.e. attempting to groom a child when 'the child' was, in fact, a police officer.

Showing sexual material to children

A common part of the grooming process can be to show children child pornography as this helps desensitise or 'normalise' sexual behaviour (Taylor and Quayle, 2003: 195). By showing pornography to a child, the offender is trying to persuade the child that sex is a normal activity, and thus to participate in activity with them. The offence contained within s.15 was not designed to tackle this behaviour, but instead it was left to other laws to deal with this.

The most obvious offence to use when it relates to an indecent image of a child is s.1 of the *Protection of Children Act 1978*, which was considered in Chapter 4. An offender who shows or distributes an indecent image of a child to a child will be in breach of this legislation. The courts have previously held that where the showing was part of a grooming process, the

offence is considered to be aggravated (Ost, 2004: 148) although it can be questioned whether s.1 is an appropriate offence to use as it does not highlight the grooming nature of the offence (Ost, 2004: 154). It is submitted that there is no reason why the offence, on the face of it, has to deal with such grooming, the offence covers the creation, showing and distribution of child pornography, and so it is the appropriate offence as this is the very behaviour being discussed. If the distribution or showing was to facilitate the grooming of a child then it is submitted that the courts are right to treat this as an aggravating factor and thus this behaviour is penalised.

The difficulty, before the 2003 Act came into force, however, was that showing pornography that did not amount to an indecent image of a child (e.g. adult pornography, Playboy magazines etc.) was not illegal regardless of the purpose of the showing. Parliament, in the 2003 Act, decided to legislate to cover such behaviour. It has created a separate offence, once again reinforcing the fact that s.15 is not 'the' grooming offence, but one resource in the fight against those who groom children. The new offence is contained within s.12 of the 2003 Act and is as follows:

(1)   A person aged 18 or over (A) commits an offence if:
   (a) for the purposes of obtaining sexual gratification, he intentionally causes another person (B) to watch a third person engaging in a sexual activity, or to look at an image of any person engaging in an activity,
   (b) the activity is sexual, and
   (c) either –
       (i)   B is under 16 and A does not reasonably believe that B is 16 or over, or
       (ii) B is under 13.

The offence is punishable by a maximum sentence of ten years' imprisonment (s.12(2)(b)) making it comparable to the offences contained under the 1978 legislation. The breadth of this offence is not apparent from the wording contained within s.12(1), however, and reference needs to be made to s.79(4) where the Act defines 'image' as:

'Image' means a moving or still image and includes an image produced by any means and, where the context permits, a three-dimensional image.

Interestingly, this is a much wider definition than that contained within the 1978 legislation which is concerned with the concept of a photograph. The 2003 legislation merely refers to an image and leaving aside the fact that it includes holograms(!), it must cover image formats other than a photograph. The dictionary defines 'image' as including, 'a representation of the external form of a person or thing in sculpture, painting, etc.' (Thompson, 1995: 677) and thus it must include a representation in any form, including cartoons etc. Obviously, this would be a very wide offence that could cause considerable difficulties, but the requirement within s.12(1) that the showing is for the purposes of sexual gratification is designed to prevent situations where gallery owners etc. are convicted if children see sexual imagery in a *bona fide* context.

The fact that s.12 includes a wider range of material has to be welcomed. It is known that some sex offenders will use adult pornography as an introduction to sexual behaviour, but also some will use drawings or cartoons involving children to help in the grooming process. The use of cartoons can be particularly useful as children are used to reading cartoons and enjoy them. Within countries where there has traditionally been a more liberal approach to child pornography, e.g. Japan, the prevalence of *Manga*-type cartoons is high and the importation of such material is increasing. Earlier in this chapter it was noted that such material is unlikely to be illegal *per se*, especially where only simple possession can be shown, but s.12 helps to remedy a potential flaw in the law by placing the emphasis not only on the material but the misuse of the material by showing it to children.

One potential issue that has been raised over the application of s.12 is whether it would apply where the intention is to groom a child rather than to obtain direct sexual gratification (see Ost, 2004: 154). The term 'sexual gratification' is not defined within the Act. The dictionary defines 'gratification' as 'indulging in, or yielding to, a desire' (Thompson, 1995: 593), and thus sexual gratification can be construed as indulging in activity for sexual purposes. 'Sexual' is discussed within the Act; indeed, it has its own section within the Act:

. . . [an] activity is sexual if a reasonable person would consider that:

    (a) whatever its circumstances or any person's purpose in relation to it, it is because of its nature sexual, or

    (b) because of its nature it may be sexual and because of its circumstances or the purpose of any person in relation to it (or both) it is sexual.

                                    (s.78, SOA, 2003)

It has been argued that this is not so much a definition but rather a process by which one can ascertain whether an activity is sexual or not (Temkin and Ashworth, 2004: 331). In essence, this section has adapted the two-part test adopted by the House of Lords in *R v Court [1989] AC 28*, a case where the notion of 'indecency' within the meaning of Sections 14 and 15 of the Sexual Offences Act 1956 was considered. The essence of the test is that 'indecent' (and now, 'sexual') can be classified in one of three ways:

- Those acts that are obviously sexual to a reasonable man (i.e. s.78(a)).
- Those acts that may be sexual depending on what the circumstances of the activity or purpose of the perpetrator is (i.e. s.78(b)).
- Those acts that on the face of it are not sexual (this category is present by implication and not mentioned in the section but it must be drawn by reference to what is not contained in paragraphs (a) and (b), see Temkin and Ashworth, 2003: 332).

It has been suggested that it would be appropriate for s.12 to make reference to sexual gratification or grooming (Ost, 2004: 154) but, of course, grooming itself is not defined and it has been noted already that it is difficult to precisely define. However, if we think about proving an intention to groom then it must be seriously questioned whether Ost is correct in believing that this is outside the remit of s.12. It is submitted that showing pornography to a child is unlikely to be ever considered an activity that is not on the face of it sexual, but neither is it an act that may be considered obviously sexual (as there may be legitimate reasons for providing sexual imagery to children, e.g. an art class, sex education class etc.). It is likely, therefore, that a jury would be called upon to consider whether, given the circumstances of the showing and/or purpose of the adult, the showing is sexual. Where there is evidence to show that the purpose of the adult is to groom a child for sexual purposes then it is unlikely that a jury would not consider this to be sexual within the meaning of s.78(b). Once that decision has been reached then it must follow that the showing is an indulgence for that purpose, thus satisfying the issue of 'sexual gratification' for the purposes of s.12. This argument gains support from the decision in *R v Abdullahi [2006] EWCA Crim 2060* where the Court of Appeal held that there was no requirement for temporal proximity:

> *There is . . . nothing in the language of s.12 to suggest that the offence can only be committed if the sexual gratification and the display of the images are simultaneous, or contemporaneous, or synchronised.*
>
> (at [17] per Sir Igor Judge P)

Allowing for non-contemporaneous intent makes it more likely that it can be used where grooming is used as part of the grooming process. It is not known whether this would include significant delays between showing and ultimate gratification but the Court of Appeal stated this would be a matter for the jury in deciding whether gratification was present (Ibid.).

Section 12 is likely to be useful and, in combination with s.15, it provides an excellent opportunity for the criminal law to tackle those offenders who groom children for abuse. This is not to detract from the warning issued by the academics from the University of Coventry noted earlier in this chapter about not ignoring the fact that the majority of abuse takes place by people known to the child, but this is a threat that is worth tackling and the combination of Sections 12 and 15 are worthwhile tools in the fight against child abuse.

The civil way: risk of sexual harm orders

The Home Office in 2001 announced that alongside the new criminal offences ultimately created by the 2003 Act, a new civil order would also be created. This order would be comparable to the existing civil protection orders first introduced by the *Crime and Disorder Act 1998* and which created the Anti-Social Behaviour Order (ASBO) and Sex Offender Order (SOO) (see ss. 1–4, CDA, 1998), the latter being incorporated into the new Sexual Offences Prevention Order (SOPO) contained within Sections 104–13 of the 2003 Act. Keeping its promise, s.123 of the 2003 Act creates a new order known as a Risk of Sexual Harm Order (RoSHO). This order was designed to complement the criminal law in tackling grooming behaviour although it is questionable whether this has necessarily

occurred. This book is primarily about the criminal law responses to the threats posed by modern communication technologies, but in this section I intend to give a brief overview of the orders.

The orders are undoubtedly controversial, with the principal ground of criticism being that it appears to permit someone to be labelled a 'paedophile' without being convicted of an offence (Lewis, 2004: 103). Certainly the RoSHO appears to bear all the hallmarks of the old SOO without the requirement for a conviction, something that is peculiar given that the justification for the SOO was the conviction of a serious offence.

Application

The applicant in any proceedings for a RoSHO will always be the chief officer of police (s.123(1) SOA 2003) and an application is to the Magistrates' Court (s.123(2)). The grounds for an application are that on at least two occasions (s.123(1)(a)) the offender has done something noted below, and that the chief officer has reasonable cause to believe an order is necessary (s.123(1)(b)). The acts are contained within sub-section (3) and are:

(a) engaging in a sexual activity involving a child or in the presence of a child;
(b) causing or inciting a child to watch a person engaging in sexual activity or to look at a moving or still image that is sexual;
(c) giving a child anything that relates to sexual activity or contains reference to such activity;
(d) communicating with a child, where any part of the communication is sexual.

If these acts are cross-referenced with the rest of this chapter it can be clearly seen that this test is designed to capture behaviour that could be used in the grooming process. A difficulty that does exist, and which the explanatory notes do at least acknowledge, is that some of these activities amount to crimes. Within the explanatory notes it is suggested that an offender may or may not have a previous conviction for a sexual offence (Home Office, 2003 §252) but it is submitted that this is flawed thinking. Where an offender has a previous conviction for a relevant sexual offence then the correct procedure would be to apply for a SOPO (discussed in Chapter 9) and not a RoSHO, as it will be seen that the former is the more versatile of the two.

Of more concern, however, is the fact that some of the grounds are covered by criminal offences. The first ground, engaging in a sexual activity, is a direct lift from s.11 of the 2003 Act, and the second ground, causing a child to watch sexual activity, is a repetition of s.12 discussed immediately above. The third ground, giving a child anything that relates to a sexual activity may be covered by ss. 11 and 12 or may, admittedly, be behaviour that is outside of these offences (the explanatory notes provide the example of an adult giving a child condoms or a sex toy (Home Office, 2003 §253) but equally it could, for example, be a sexually explicit toy). The fourth ground may appear to be the most obvious ground through which criminal behaviour may not be apparent, but it does depend on what the conversation is. If an offender has incited a child to do something sexual then again this would amount to a criminal offence contrary to Sections 8 or 10 of the Act.

The fact that the grounds cover behaviour that is within the criminal law does raise questions as to the purpose of the civil order. It will be remembered that an offender must have performed these activities *twice* to be eligible for an order, and yet a single activity discussed above would be sufficient to lead to criminal proceedings. It may be thought that the advantage of bringing a civil order instead of criminal proceedings may be that the standard of proof would be lower but this is not the case. In *R(on the application of McCann) v Crown Court at Manchester [2003] 1 AC 787*, the House of Lords confirmed that the standard of proof for an ASBO was the criminal standard and there is no reason to suggest that it will be any different for a RoSHO, not least because the latter is actually more draconian than the former. If, therefore, the authorities have proof beyond all reasonable doubt that an adult has twice undertaken an act that amounts to a criminal offence it is submitted that they should be instigating a prosecution for this and not rely on civil orders. To do anything else would seem to be a significant breach of the duty of care a child can expect from the authorities.

However, where the conduct does not amount to a breach of the criminal law, e.g. the third and fourth grounds (in part) then this order may be a useful addition to the armoury but the objections of Liberty etc. do have to be considered. Whilst a person who is subject to a RoSHO does not have to notify the police of their address and movements, this does not necessarily mean that their status will not be recorded, as they would undoubtedly be listed in intelligence systems and perhaps on registers maintained by social services or those who work with young children. The fact that a RoSHO has been made would undoubtedly show up on a Criminal Records Bureau check, although at what level this would be recorded is not known. Another difficulty with the RoSHO, in this context, is whether the proceedings will be held in public or not. A Home Office review that examined, in part, the issue of sex offender orders noted that sex offender order hearings are normally conducted in public (Home Office, 2001: 38). If hearings for RoSHOs are also heard in public this could create a situation where the press report the respondent's details, and thus the person is, as Liberty and others fear, labelled a paedophile without being convicted of any offence. The sociological implications of such labelling can be somewhat serious and this must be a factor in the justification for the orders. Given that a magistrate can only make an order if it is 'necessary to do so' (s.123(4) SOA, 2003) it is submitted that it is incumbent on the magistrates to consider the effect an order may have on an offender when deciding necessity.

Effect

Leaving aside the question as to whether such orders can be justified, what are the effects of a RoSHO? The first point to note is that, like SOPOs and ASBOs, they are injunction-like in form in that the order does not require or prevent any specific issues but they are instead an individual order drafted by, or for, the magistrates. Only prohibitions (and not requirements) can be placed on the order (s.123(5)(a)), e.g. it would be permissible to prevent someone from going to a park, but not to attend treatment. This is similar to that which occurs with SOPOs and ASBOs and inventive language normally allows the order to capture most behaviour. The order lasts for a period of not less than two years (s.123(5)(b)), which is less than the minimum for a SOPO but this perhaps reflects the fact that an offender will not have been convicted of any offence. However, it must be noted that this is the *minimum* duration and thus a court could, if it wishes, pass an indeterminate order or one that lasts for ten years. Whether this is appropriate given the absence of a conviction must be questioned and it is submitted that it would have been better for the order to last a *maximum* of two years so that there is automatic scrutiny of the necessity and proportionality of the orders.

The prohibitions on the face of the order are backed by criminal sanctions. Thus, although the order itself is a civil order, and made by the magistrates' Court sitting in its civil capacity, breaching the order is a criminal offence, and one punishable by up to five years' imprisonment (s.128(2)). This does bring about the interesting position whereby a person could be convicted in a criminal trial without ever committing a criminal act. For example:

> D has had a Risk of Sexual Harm Order made against him by Anywhere Magistrates' Court. The terms of the order prohibit him from entering the Public Park between 15:00 and 19:00 hours on any weekday, or between 08:00 and 19:00 on a weekend. D was arrested by Anywhere Police in the park at 16:15 on Wednesday afternoon.

In the example above D could be rightly convicted of breaching the RoSHO and yet all the person has done is to walk into a park, something not normally a criminal offence. Of course, the justification for this is that the offender poses a risk of harm to children but the fact that 'innocent' activities could, potentially, lead to an offender being imprisoned for up to five years does demonstrate the seriousness that magistrates must show for applications and the drafting of restrictions. Breach of a RoSHO is considered to be a sex offence for the purposes of the notification requirements etc. so long as the order is in force (s.129 SOA, 2003). Presumably this is because there is now a criminal record to

which the relevant registration flag can attach. However, where an offender is sentenced to a term of imprisonment then it would appear more appropriate to discharge the order (as it is unlikely an offender could do anything to breach the order whilst in prison) and to issue a SOPO if appropriate upon release. It will be seen in Chapter 9 that SOPOs are more versatile and it is submitted that the necessity and proportionality of a SOPO are easier to establish where a person has already committed a relevant offence.

In summary, therefore, the RoSHO is highly controversial and it will be interesting to see how many are made. When ASBOs and SOOs were first introduced it took many years before the authorities were prepared to apply for them, and for courts to grant them. Given the controversy that exists with these orders it may be that this approach is repeated. In any event it is to be hoped that the authorities use alternative powers, especially prosecution where they can, as a conviction will nearly always be better than a RoSHO.

Notes

1   It is not suggested that a child is giving true consent to any sexual activity, and by this I mean that the perpetrator, through a process of cognitive distortions, believes that the child is consenting (see Howitt 1995: 93–94).

2   The CROGA website (www.croga.org) was developed by the COPINE team and is designed to help people who download or access inappropriate images on the Internet. One of its resources (Escalation of Fantasy) discusses the use of fantasy and the various types of problematic or deviant fantasies (see http://www.croga.org/selfhelp_module_3.php).

CHAPTER 6

Child Procurement

A threat to child protection on the Internet that gets perhaps less attention than many others is undoubtedly child procurement. This is in part because it is difficult to differentiate it from other forms of abusive behaviour that can be experienced on and offline. Child procurement can be considered to be the act of seeking to obtain a child for sexual purposes. Where it differs from 'grooming' (Chapter 5) is that the approach is usually made to other adults rather than to the child itself. Also, there is frequently no issue about a person seeking the 'consent' of the child. It differs from prostitution for similar reasons; the approach is usually made to someone other than the child and payment is normally made to someone other than the child.

There may be a number of reasons why a person seeks to procure a child. The first is that they may wish to undertake sexual activity with the child. The second is that they may wish to watch the child or children perform a sexual act. The third possibility is that they wish to photograph the child and, by doing so, create abusive images of children. All forms of behaviour are sexually abusive and linked by the common purpose of procuring the child.

History of procurement

Like most of the threats that are discussed in this book, child procurement is neither a new phenomenon nor is it restricted to online abuse. In 1996, Dennis Hundermark, a South African citizen, was one of the first to be convicted of a procurement offence. Hundermark did not use the Internet but instead walked into a Soho sex shop and asked the owner whether it was possible for him to obtain a toddler for sex. The Soho shop reported the matter to the police and the newly created Paedophile Unit of the Metropolitan Police who arrested Hundermark.[1]

The first Internet related case was not, however, that far away. In 1999, Kenneth Lockley, a computer software designer, was arrested and charged for the online equivalent of Hundermark's actions. Lockley approached an agency on the Internet requesting a small child (Bennetto, 1999: 2). The agency was operated by the FBI in America and they passed the details to the Metropolitan's Paedophile Unit who continued the 'sting' operation. The police arranged to meet Lockley in a hotel where he believed that he was going to have sex with a nine-year-old girl, and where he was tape recorded as confirming that he wanted the 'transaction' to proceed. He was arrested and charged.

It was not possible to charge either Hundermark or Lockley with a substantive child sex offence because the law of attempts requires a close proximity between the offender's actions and the result (see *R v Geddes [1996] Crim LR 895* and also see Gillespie, 2001, for further discussion on the law of attempt). Instead, Hundermark and Lockley were charged with an old offence that was originally conceived for prostitution, *attempting to incite someone to procure a girl under the age of 21 for sexual purposes* contrary to s.23 of the Sexual Offences Act 1956. The attempt aspect was required because in neither case was there ever a child; the police had adopted a proactive approach to these crimes and pretended that there was a child. As a matter of law it is perfectly possible to attempt to commit the impossible (s.1(2), *Criminal Appeals Act 1981*) and thus by charging an attempt the defendants could properly be charged with a crime. The incitement is required because it was not the defendant who would procure the child but the police officer, acting as the agent or facilitator. Again, this is not necessarily difficult because as a matter of common law it is an offence to incite a person to commit an offence (Ormerod, 2005: 350 *et seq.*).

The substantive crime, therefore, was *procuring a girl under the age of 21 for sexual purposes*, which dates back to the 1950s. The offence did not carry notification requirements (discussed in Chapter 9), something the judge in the Lockley case was unhappy about (Verkaik, 2000: 11). Dennis Hundermark was sentenced to sixteen months' imprisonment and Kenneth Lockley to eighteen months' imprisonment. Neither was given the maximum sentence because they pleaded guilty to the charges (see Chapter 8 for a discussion on sentencing but it should be noted that the legal position is that the maximum sentence should be reserved for the most serious example of the offence and where there is a 'not guilty' plea) but in each case, the sentence caused a furore in the press.[2]

Another high-profile example of procurement took place shortly before the *Sexual Offences Act 2003* was passed by Parliament. This time the incident involved a 19-year-old trainee teacher known as Luke Sadowski. Like Lockley, Sadowski was caught after contacting an online 'agency' which was, in fact, an undercover US 'sting' website. The matter was passed over to the Metropolitan Police (Thompson, 2003: 14) who continued the operation. When arrested, Sadowski was carrying a teddy-bear, a condom and an imitation firearm. Despite the presence of the soft toy and condom it was not possible to charge Sadowski with any substantive offence (and this is reinforced by the fact that in *Geddes* (op. cit.), the defendant was carrying similar items), and so the only recourse was, yet again, to procuring a girl under 21. The judiciary and media were again highly critical of the law not least because, as DCI Sarti (as he then was) of the Metropolitan Police Paedophile Unit commented, he was *'a real and significant threat to children'* (Clough, 2003: 8).

Procuring boys

Potentially, a major loophole existed in the law in respect of this behaviour. Section 23 of the 1956 Act was, like most of the 1956 Act, gender-specific. The offence was not procuring a child under the age of 21 but procuring a *girl* under the age of 21. Unsurprisingly, a defendant appeared that would test the effectiveness of the law.

Victor van de Walle, a Belgian national, was arrested and charged following another 'sting' operation by the Paedophile Unit of the Metropolitan Police after entering the UK in order to have sex with a young boy.[3] The particulars of the offence were very similar to the cases noted above, but the difficulty that arose here was what to charge the defendant with. Section 23 obviously could not apply and neither could the proximity nexus required by the *Criminal Attempts Act 1981* be shown. The culmination of the difficulties was to charge van de Walle with *attempting to incite an undercover police officer to procure a boy under the age of 16 with*

an act of indecency. The substantive element of this crime was the 'act of indecency' (s.1, *Indecency with Children Act 1960*) leaving inchoate liability for 'attempt', 'incite' and accessorial liability for 'procuring'.

Van de Walle pleaded guilty to this offence and was sentenced to two years' imprisonment, the court basing its sentence on the equivalence of the s.23 charge. However, considerable doubt must exist as to the proprietary of this offence and whether the defendant pleaded guilty to an offence not known to law. The issues of 'attempt' and 'incite' are not controversial for the reasons discussed above, but there are doubts as to whether this liability is too remote for liability to arise. It has been noted already that procurement is required because it is not the offender who will obtain the child but another, and thus the liability of any inciter will be to persuade someone to become an accessory to a crime, rather than a criminal. It has been argued such liability is too remote:

> *It is not an offence to attempt or, it is submitted, to incite or to conspire to do an act which would involve no more than secondary liability for the offence if it were committed.*
> (Ormerod, 2005: 200)

This has to be the position here. Mr van de Walle was not inciting the undercover police officer to commit the substantive offence of indecency with a child, but to become an accessory to this crime. This position can be contrasted with Hundermark, Lockley and Sadowski where the substantive element was procuring a girl under the age of 21, i.e. the procurement was not accessorial liability but substantive liability, and thus the incitement was to become a principal and not an accomplice. The reasoning of the above was adopted by the Crown Court in *R v Bodin* [1976] *Crim LR* 176 where a judge at first instance accepted a submission of no case to answer where the two defendants incited P to procure an assault by G on V. The reasoning of the judge was that at the time of the incitement there was no accessorial liability in respect of P since procuring an assault is not a crime until the substantive crime has taken place, by which time the incitement was complete ([1976] *Crim LR* 176 at [178]). In other words, the judge was stating that there is no crime of being an accessory before the fact (the substantive crime).

It has to be said that the remoteness argument is not universally supported with some leading commentators arguing that the justification for denying liability in these circumstances is not particularly convincing (Simester and Sullivan, 2003: 266). They argue that perhaps the principal justification for the ruling is remoteness, i.e. that inciting someone to become an accessory is too remote from any actual crime, and that the criminal law is often reluctant to stray too far from the nexus of harm. They then seek to dismiss this argument by arguing that there is no requirement for any substantive act to take place in a traditional incitement case. In other words, if X incites Y to shoot Z, it does not matter whether Y does shoot Z, or indeed, whether Y had any intention to shoot Z. X would be guilty of the crime. Why, they ask, should it be any different for accessorial liability?

If Ormerod and *Bodin* are correct then van de Walle was charged with an offence not known to law. The fact that the Crown Court in van de Walle accepted the indictment and plea cannot, by itself, be considered evidence that the argument is false because there is no indication that the trial judge had his attention drawn to the argument put forward in *Bodin*. However, the case of van de Walle must help demonstrate a justification for Simester and Sullivan's argument. It is quite illogical for identical behaviour to lead to criminal liability only where the victim is a girl. It has been argued that *Bodin* is a first-instance decision and should not be followed (Simester and Sullivan, 2003: 266). Whilst this is undoubtedly correct from the perspective of a literal application of the legal doctrine of precedent, the fact that it has stood for over 20 years without being overruled does, perhaps, suggest that a court would be slow to depart from this rule.

Revising the law

The conviction of Luke Sadowski caused concern, especially when the trial-judge, HHJ Gerald Gordon, stated that the law was inadequate at dealing with such behaviour. The issue of child procurement had been discussed by the *Home Secretary's Task Force on Child Protection on the Internet* who recommended new legislation to ensure that the law was capable of acting against the behaviour noted above. The government responded in the Sexual Offences Act 2003, which contains a number of solutions, one of which is a new offence, eventually enacted as s.14 of the

Sexual Offences Act 2003, *arranging or facilitating the commission of a child sex offence*.

Section 14 provides:

(1) A person commits an offence if –
    (a) he intentionally arranges or facilitates something that he intends to do, intends another person to do, or believes that another person will do, in any part of the world, and
    (b) doing it will involve the commission of an offence under any of sections 9 to 13.

This offence is punishable by up to 14 years imprisonment (s.14(4)), a significant improvement on the two years imprisonment for s.23 offences. At the outset it should be realised that it will still be necessary to charge an incitement to commit this offence in a procurement case. It would not be the would-be abuser who would arrange or facilitate the abuse, but the 'agent'. Where the operation involves the use of an undercover police officer then it would also be necessary to use an attempt, so as to circumvent the fact that the crime would be impossible to commit (in that a police officer who has no intention of marking such arrangements).

The principal advantage of this section is that, like with s.23, the liability which would appear to be accessorial in nature – arranging or facilitating – becomes substantive, thus meaning that the principle in *Bodin* would not apply because it is trite law that it is possible to attempt to incite a person to commit a substantive offence.

'Arranging' and 'facilitating' will, it is submitted, almost certainly be given a broad meaning and this could mean that true accessorial liability could be covered within this section too. Let us take an example:

A asks B to find him a 9 year-old girl to have sex with. B approaches C who agrees to supply him with a girl.

A would be guilty of inciting B to arrange or facilitate the sexual abuse of a child, which demonstrates that the new offence should cover the situations that occurred with Hundermark, Lockley and Sadowski. What of the liability of B and C? It could be argued that it is C who has procured the child and not B, and perhaps it would be more appropriate to charge him with being an accessory to the procurement. However, this is not necessary because both B and C can be said to have either 'arranged' or 'facilitated' the abuse. The abuse of the child cannot take place without B or C and both must have, at the very least, facilitated (which the Concise Oxford English Dictionary defines as '*making easy or less difficult or more easily achieved*.') the abuse and, arguably, B has arranged it. In other words, it is unlikely that it will be necessary to consider the secondary liability of accomplices, as 'facilitated' is likely to cover most situations where someone is an accessory. (The usual forms of accessorial liability are aiding, abetting, counselling and procuring (see s.8, Accessories and Abettors Act 1861 as amended by the Criminal Justice Act 1977). Whilst each has a separate definition the terms also all overlap (see Ormerod, 2005: 170–1) but each is about helping the principal to do his task, and this must be considered facilitation if the ordinary meaning of the word is to apply).

This offence, in common with most other offences under the 2003 Act, is gender neutral and thus it does not matter whether the person seeks either a male or female child, thus rendering any argument surrounding the applicability of the law to male children a moot point. One peculiar aspect of the offence is its breadth. The offence is restricted to conduct within Sections 9 to 13 which encompasses:

- Sexual activity with a child (s.9)
- Causing or inciting a child to engage in sexual activity (s.10)
- Engaging in sexual activity in the presence of a child (s.11)
- Causing a child to watch a sexual act (s.12)
- Child sex offences committed by children (s.13)

On the face of this section it would appear, therefore, that offences such as rape are not within the offence. This is even more perplexing given that s.5 of the 2003 Act created an offence of statutory rape where a person penetrates the vagina, anus or mouth of a child under 13. In all of the cases discussed above the perpetrator wanted to have sexual intercourse with a young child so would have been guilty, had it occurred, of the rape of a child under 13. It seems somewhat anomalous that Parliament, when creating the offence to deal with the cases above, should miss out the offence that they would be guilty of. That said, the offence should still apply because sexual activity with a child includes any sexual touching and s.9 expressly mentions penetration (s.9(2)). Also, the offence under s.9 does appear to apply to child victims under 13

(s.9(1)(c) even though there is a specific offence that was designed for victims under 13, see s.7), and so it is likely that procuring a child for any contact offence could come within the scope of s.14.

It should be noted that the courts have held that where a charge is laid under s.14 it is necessary for the prosecution to state what the relevant crime is (*R v Harrison [2005] EWCA Crim 3458 at [13]*)) i.e. they must say which of the offences, listed above, the person was trying to arrange or facilitate.

Legitimate facilitation

Concern was raised during the passage of the Sexual Offences Act 2003 that s.14 could criminalise doctors or sex-education workers. This argument is based on the fact that doctors and sex education workers could provide contraceptives to children under the age of 16. A literal interpretation of s.14 could mean that this is construed as facilitating illegal sexual activity, given that the provision of contraceptives is, presumably, because the child wishes to have sexual activity with another, irrespective of its illegality.

In fact, the law would not have applied here because of a legal principle dating back to the landmark case of *Gillick v West Norfolk and Wisbech Area Health Authority [1986] AC 112*. This case was not a criminal case but rather a judicial review questioning the legality of a Department of Health memorandum purporting to allow doctors to prescribe the contraceptive pill to children under 16 without parental consent. Mrs Gillick, the applicant, sought leave to challenge this memorandum arguing it was illegal. One issue that the House of Lords were asked to consider was whether the actions of a doctor following this memorandum would be committing a crime, on the basis that it could be argued they were aiding or abetting illegal sexual activity. It has been argued that the reasoning of the House of Lords was that there would be no intention because the doctor's intent is to help protect the child rather than facilitate sexual intercourse (Ormerod, 2005: 180), although it has been doubted whether this judicial reasoning is necessarily accurate (Ormerod, 2005: 98).

Regardless of the precise reasons for the decision, it has been long-accepted as providing a defence to a doctor in such circumstances and similar reasoning would have applied to s.14. However, Parliament decided to clarify the law and sub-section (2) provides a defence where a person arranges or facilitates something that he believes another will do, but that he will not do, and he does so for the purposes of protecting the child. Protection is defined as:

(a) protecting the child from sexually transmitted infection
(b) protecting the physical safety of the child
(c) preventing the child from becoming pregnant
(d) promoting the child's emotional well-being by the giving of advice

(s.14(3) SOA 2003)

and not where the person would obtain sexual gratification from it. Accordingly, the provision of *bona fide* advice or services to protect the child from, for example, an STI or pregnancy, would not lead to criminal liability. However, where the action is not *bona fide* (e.g. someone supplies condoms to two children so that they can have sexual intercourse safely whilst he watches them), then the defence will be of no assistance.

It is submitted that this defence was largely unnecessary because of the ruling in *Gillick* but clarity in the law can be sometimes welcomed, and so long as the courts do not interpret this provision wider than that contained within *Gillick* it is likely that this defence will be appropriate.

Territoriality

It is important to note that s.14 states that the conduct can take place anywhere in the world (s.14(1)(a) SOA 2003). The law in England and Wales normally adopts what is known as a territorial approach to criminal liability, i.e. the alleged activity must occur within England or Wales. However, Parliament reserves the right to legislate in an extraterritorial manner, rendering actions illegal wherever they are committed. Within the area of sex offending the most obvious example of extraterritorial liability was Part 2 of the Sex Offenders Act 1997. The effect of this offence was that a British citizen who committed certain sex offences whilst abroad could be tried upon his or her return to England, subject to appropriate evidence being introduced.

The offence created in s.14, however, is not truly territorial since the facilitation or arrangement must take place in this country (or, presumably, some part of the facilitation must take place within the jurisdiction), but the objective of the facilitation can take place anywhere in the world. An example will help illustrate this:

> *A is travelling to the USA on business. Whilst in the UK he uses the Internet to identify a procurement agency based in America. He contacts them and asks them to arrange a nine year-old girl for sex. The UK police intercept this communication.*

In this example, A could be charged under s.14 as he has incited another to arrange or facilitate the sexual abuse of a child. An element of the arranging has taken place in this country and this will be sufficient for s.14, even though it is intended to abuse the child abroad. This is obviously a useful extension of liability, especially given how often the Internet is used to book travel. It should be noted that where the substantive offence takes place but is discovered after the subject returns then the offender would be liable for a substantive 'sex tourist' charge (s.72, SOA 2003), but this does not rule out s.14 also being charged since they are technically two separate courses of events; the first is the arranging the commission of an offence and the second is actually committing the offence.

Procuring children for pornography

It was noted at the beginning of this chapter that one reason why an offender may wish to procure a child would be to involve that child in pornography. Chapter 4 discussed much of the law relating to indecent images of children, but does the procurement element change anything? Where the pornography is going to involve the activity of a person other than the child (i.e. someone penetrating the child, or the child penetrating someone else), then it is likely that this conduct would come within one of the situations discussed above, because the person who is procuring the child for the pornography must also be facilitating the activities of the other. What about where there is only the child however, and the activity is solely the child being photographed?

Section 14 has a limited sphere of influence and is restricted to that behaviour which is listed within Sections 9 to 13. None of these sections refer to child pornography *per se* although it could be argued that s.10, causing or inciting a child to engage in sexual activity, could be caught. This offence is triggered where someone intentionally causes or incites a person under the age of 16 to do something sexual (s.10(1)). 'Sexual' is defined later in the Act as follows:

. . . any activity is sexual if a reasonable person would consider that –
  (a) whatever its circumstances or any person's purpose in relation to it, it is because of its nature sexual, or
  (g) because of its nature it may be sexual and because of its circumstances or the purpose of any person in relation to it (or both) it is sexual

(s.78, SOA 2003)

This definition is useful for the purposes of the activity under discussion. Some photography of a child will be inherently sexual (thus coming within the provisions of paragraph a), for example where the child is told to touch itself, or use a sex-toy. Other photographs may not be inherently sexual (a child in underwear, nudist shots etc.), but would become sexual because of the circumstances surrounding the taking of the photographs (i.e. that they are not innocent shots but ones being taken for the purposes of sexual gratification of either the photographer or others). With these images it is submitted that Section 14 would probably still apply because a reasonable person would consider them to be sexual and thus within the remit of s.10 and, accordingly, s.14.

An alternative to this somewhat convoluted approach would be to rely on other offences within the Sexual Offences Act 2003 that relate to child pornography. It will be remembered from earlier in the book that three new offences are created by the Act (ss. 48–51, SOA 2003 and see Chapter 4) and one of these offences may be relevant, not least because it is similar in structure to s.14. Section 50, arranging or facilitating child pornography, creates an offence for a person to facilitate or arrange the involvement of a person under the age of 18 for the purposes of child pornography. It is difficult to see how someone could procure a child for the purposes of child pornography without also being in the position of facilitating the involvement of a child in pornography. Where there is no child, or the person was not successful in procuring a child for these purposes, then, as with s.14, it is likely that there would be a need for the person to be charged with an attempt.

There are two significant differences between Sections 14 and 50, one of which is arguably useful and the other is undoubtedly a hindrance. Section 14 only applies where a child is under the age of 16 whereas s.50 applies to children under 18. The reason for this discrepancy is because of the controversial change to the meaning of 'a child' for the purposes of child pornography (s.45(2) SOA 2003), but this would mean that an attempt by someone to procure a 17-year-old in order to take pornographic pictures of her could be prosecuted. The second difference is that whilst someone who is convicted of s.14 is subject to the notification requirements (see Chapter 9), a person convicted under s.50 is not. This is because Parliament for some reason did not prescribe Sections 48 to 50 as notifiable offences for these purposes. The reasoning behind this will be discussed elsewhere but it can be seen from the behaviour discussed here that it could cause a difficulty. Accordingly, prosecutors must take care over the decision to charge an offender under this provision as it may be that this could cause law enforcement officers some difficulty in the management of offenders.

Collectives

This chapter has discussed child procurement and it is opportune to discuss the issue of collectives here. In using this term I mean to discuss the position whereby more than one person is involved in the procurement or abuse of children. The collective is contained within this chapter because of all the forms of exploitation discussed in this book it is probably closest to procurement which is, in essence, the obtaining of a child for sexual purposes.

Two aspects of collectives need to be considered. The first is where the collective plans the procurement of a child and the second is when they are considered complicit within the abuse undertaken by one or more persons.

Conspiracy

The first issue to examine is where a collective plans to procure a child for sexual purposes. This issue was raised in the public consciousness during the winter of 2006 where three men (David Beavan, Alan Hedgcock and Robert Mayers) became the first people in England and Wales to be convicted of a 'cyber-conspiracy', that is, a conspiracy that took place over the Internet.

The men were convicted of planning to abduct two young teenage sisters and to rape them. It was also alleged that two of the men conspired to kill the girls but it should be noted that the jury acquitted the defendants of this charge. What was interesting about this case was that there was no evidence that the people involved had ever met each other offline; they 'met' online only after one of the men stated that he had identified the two girls and fantasised about raping them. However, it has been noted in several places in this book that the English law works on the premise that what is illegal offline is illegal online so what was the legal position?

Since the plan was not put into effect all that could be alleged was a conspiracy, i.e. two or more persons agreeing to commit a crime. The law of conspiracy is relatively confusing in that there are both statutory and common law conspiracies (Ormerod, 2005: 360). The latter includes a conspiracy to outrage public decency and conspiracy to corrupt public morals, both of which have an application in the field of sex crimes, but have traditionally been used in the arena of prostitution (Ormerod, 2005: 390–2). The more usual approach is a statutory conspiracy, which is defined as:

Subject to the following provisions of this Part of this Act, if a person agrees with any other person or persons that a course of conduct shall be pursued which, if the agreement is carried out in accordance with their intentions, either –

(a)   will necessarily amount to or involve the commission of any offence or offences by one or more of the parties to the agreement, or

(b)   would do so but for the existence of facts which render the commission of the offence or any of the offences impossible,

he is guilty of conspiracy to commit the offence or offences in question.

(s.1, Criminal Law Act 1977)

It can be seen, therefore, that the essential agreements are an agreement to pursue a course of conduct, and that this course of conduct will involve a criminal offence being committed or, would do so if it were not for the fact that the offence is impossible. The issue of impossibility has been discussed before (see Chapter 5) but is unlikely to have much implication here.

A conspiracy must obviously involve more than one person (and indeed there are rules as to who may be a party, see below), but it is also important to note that it is a 'continuing' offence so that other members may join the conspiracy if invited to do so. Within the online world this could be important where initial members may conceive a plot and others may join in. Although it is a continuing offence, it is not possible to 'withdraw' from a conspiracy: once the agreement has been made the offence is satisfied. It is, of course, possible to withdraw from any implementation of the offence.

Parties

Perhaps the most important part of a conspiracy concerns those who are a party to the conspiracy. The statute provides strict rules on who can, and perhaps more importantly, cannot be a party to a conspiracy. However, before considering these rules it should be noted that it is not necessary to identify the other party, i.e. it can be a conspiracy with a person 'unknown' (*R v Phillips (1987) 86 Cr App R 18*) which can be important in the context of communication technologies. Whilst it is necessary to be able to prove that another party exists it is quite conceivable to imagine a situation whereby forensic examination of a computer identifies an instant-messenger account, chatroom transcript or e-mail address that cannot be easily traced. The rule that the party need not be identified will assist in such cases.

The two principal rules relating to parties that cannot be part of a conspiracy are contained within Section 2, CLA 1977. The first relevant rule is that a husband and wife cannot be sole conspirators (s.2(2)). It should be noted, however, that the key word in the last sentence is 'sole'. Where there are at least three conspirators, two of which are husband and wife, then a conspiracy can still exist (*R v Chrastny [1992] 1 All ER 189*) because the conspiracy will exist on different planes. An illustration may assist:

X and Y are married. They agree to procure a child, V. No conspiracy can exist because of s.2(2). X and Y meet Z who also wishes to procure the child. A conspiracy can now exist because X can conspire with Z, Y can conspire with Z and Z can conspire with X and Y.

The second most notable rule is that where the only other party is the victim then no conspiracy will exist (s.2(2)). The CLA 1977 does not define 'victim' and it has been suggested the definition should be:

A person is a victim of an offence when the offence is held to exist for his protection with the effect that he is not a party to that offence when it is committed by another with his full knowledge and co-operation.

(Ormerod, 2005: 395)

This is a valuable definition and recognises that knowledge and co-operation can be immaterial to crimes. Within the arena of sex crimes against children, however, it means that it is not possible to conspire to commit a sex crime with the victim itself. That is not to say that liability does not accrue under such circumstances but it cannot, in law, amount to a conspiracy. It is for this reason that conspiracy was not considered in respect of grooming (Chapter 5) and neither will it be considered in respect of prostitution (Chapter 7).

It should also be noted that the fact that an alleged conspirator is acquitted by the court does not mean that all alleged conspirators will be acquitted (s.5(8), CLA 1977). This applies even where there are only two co-conspirators so long as the prosecution can still prove that a conspiracy still existed with at least one other person (*R v Anthony [1965] QB 189*). It should be remembered that an acquittal does not mean that a crime did not occur; simply that the prosecution were not able to prove it. Accordingly, there may be other evidence that can be adduced in respect of the other conspirator.

The agreement

It has been noted that the essence of conspiracy is an agreement. Clearly this is not meant in the sense of a legally binding contract but they must at least reach a decision that they agree to commit a crime (Ormerod, 2005: 363). The key distinction that must be drawn in respect of this decision is between an agreement and a negotiation (*R v Walker [1962] Crim LR 458*) i.e. the parties must not be simply discussing the terms under which they would agree to commit the crime.

This could be considered an important aspect in this context. Ormerod questions when such agreement can be concluded and provides the following example:

If A agrees to sell B certain goods, known to both to be stolen, at 'a price to be agreed by us'

(Ormerod, 2005: 363)

Within our context this could be an agreement between A and B for them to have sexual intercourse with a girl who is not yet identified.

Ormerod argues that a conspiracy is effective at this point (and it is submitted this is correct), because the parties have agreed to do something illegal, it is merely ancillary details that have not yet been concluded.

Jurisdiction

It has been noted in a number of places within this book that cyberspace goes beyond the normal territorial provisions operated by the law. It is certainly conceivable that a conspiracy could traverse geographical boundaries and certainly the 'w0nderland club' case demonstrates that this can occur where members were from all over the world.

The law relating to international conspiracies was updated by the *Criminal Justice (Terrorism and Conspiracy) Act 1998* and this allowed a conspiracy to occur in respect of acts committed outside of England and Wales so long as the crime that would be committed amounts to an offence in both England and Wales and the country where it is to be committed (s.1A, CLA 1977). In respect of child sex offences this is unlikely to be problematic since most countries have laws relating to the sexual abuse of children. Indeed, this was expressly considered to be relevant when this offence was passed since one of its purposes was to consolidate a previous statute that extended conspiracy solely for sex offending (s.1, *Sexual Offences (Conspiracy and Incitement) Act 1996*, see Hirst, 2003: 142). The 1996 Act was introduced to tackle so-called 'sex tourism' (Hirst, 2003: 140), i.e. the conduct whereby a British citizen would arrange to travel abroad to sexually abuse a child. Concern was raised that UK citizens were not being prosecuted in the country where the offence took place. As a result of the 1998 Act it is possible for A, a citizen of the UK, to conspire with B, a citizen of a country outside of England and Wales, to rape a child in the country where B is resident.[4]

Intention to carry out the agreement

Conspiracy is not a crime of strict liability in that it does require a *mens rea* although it has been noted that it is difficult to differentiate between the *actus reus* and *mens rea* (Ormerod, 2005: 374). However, for the purposes of this book the requirement can be summarised as an intention to agree and an intention to carry out the agreement (ibid.).

Intention to agree

One of the reasons for the confusion between the *actus reus* and *mens rea* is that this part could simply be considered to be part of the requirement of an 'agreement'. Clearly what this requirement means is that a person must be aware that they were entering into an agreement with the other party rather than discussing issues in general terms.

Intention to carry out the agreement

Arguably this is one of the more complicated aspects of the law. A conspiracy is a form of inchoate liability and thus clearly it does not need to be carried out in order to attract criminal liability but neither is it sufficient for an agreement to be made if nobody actually believes that it will be implemented. Some confusion existed over what this meant in practice (Ormerod, 2003: 375) with the House of Lords in *R v Anderson [1986] AC 27* appearing to imply that it was not actually necessary to intend to carry out the agreement. This, however, appeared to be contrary to the previous common law and, potentially, the CLA 1977 and in *R v Siracusa (1990) 90 Cr App R 340* the Court of Appeal suggested the House was wrong and had meant to say that intention to 'play some part in' the crime. They also held that this intention could be shown through not stopping the unlawful activity. It is doubtful that a failure to prevent a crime can be an appropriate test, however, (Ormerod, 2005: 376), since a conspiracy is an inchoate offence, i.e. one that is complete *before* a crime takes place. It has been suggested that the more accurate position is that it must be contemplated that the commission of the offence will occur by one or more of the parties (Ormerod, 2005: 377).

Complicity

It has been noted that a conspiracy is an example of inchoate liability, i.e. it is liability that exists before a substantive crime occurs. However, if they are implemented it does not necessarily follow that everyone will be considered to be principals in the crime since the role they are all to play may differ. This is particularly true in communication technologies where it is possible that the parties to a crime may not even necessarily meet up.

An example of this can be found from the 'w0nderland club'. This was an online collective that existed primarily to trade child pornography. However, it is believed that some members of the club would also become involved in the virtual abuse or exploitation of a child (Corbin, 2001). What was alleged to happen was that a member of the club would state that he had access to a child. Others within the club would then log-on to the site at a predetermined time. A webcam was set up and the child would be abused in front of the camera, the result being broadcast to the other members. The members could also talk to the abuser and suggest ways in which the child could be abused.

This behaviour is arguably not that different from child procurement in that people are 'seeking' the exploitation of a child but it is as part of a collective instead of an individual. However, although the behaviour may not be too different it is unlikely that s.14, SOA 2003 would assist. It will be remembered (6.2 above) that the offence is arranging or facilitating the commission of a crime. It could be argued that a person who makes suggestions as to how a child could be abused is 'arranging' the commission of a child sex offence but this perhaps depends on how the word 'commission' is construed. Arguably, the different modes of abusing a child will not necessarily amount to individual crimes, but rather the totality of the acts will be considered a crime with the most serious offences being charged in respect of it. Even if s.14 could be used in respect of those who made suggestions to the principal abuser it is unlikely that those who were simply watching the broadcast or who were encouraging the offender without making suggestions would come within the remit of s.14.

That is not to say that there is no liability in these circumstances. The most likely result would be to rely on the rules of complicity, i.e. that section of the law that governs those who assist or encourage another's criminality. For our purposes, the most relevant form of liability will be that known as accessories and is contained in s.8, *Accessories and Abettors Act 1861* (as amended) which states:

> *Whosoever shall aid, abet, counsel or procure the commission of any indictable offence . . . shall be liable to be tried, indicted and punished as a principal offender.*

The latter words simply mean that a person who is an accessory will be tried and punished in the same way that the person who commits the actual substantive offence (known as the principal). Let us take an example:

A assists B to have sexual intercourse with V, a girl aged 12, by bringing V to B's house.

Here A will be guilty of the offence of rape of a girl under 13 (s.5, SOA 2003). This is a crime punishable by up to life imprisonment. B, as an accessory, will be tried as though he was also accused of an offence under s.5 but instead of the *actus reus* being that A raped V, the *actus reus* is that he was an accomplice to the rape. However, if he is convicted then he will be liable to the same punishment, i.e. a maximum sentence of life imprisonment.

Definitions

It is clear from s.8 that the forms of accessorial conduct are 'aid', 'abet', 'counsel' and 'procure' but what do these terms mean? In *Attorney-General's Reference (No 1 of 1975) [1975] 2 All ER 684* the Court of Appeal stated that since four terms were prescribed by the Act the presumption must be that each has its own definition. Notwithstanding this, however, it will be seen that there is some overlap between the terms and it is perfectly possible to charge an offender using all four words and the person may be convicted if evidence is adduced that one type of behaviour is satisfied (Ormerod, 2005: 171). This perhaps reinforces the fact that the terms overlap.

The basic definitions of the terms are as follows:

- *Aiding*. This, along with abetting, is perhaps the more common form of complicity. Indeed it has been suggested that the two terms describe a simple act (Ormerod, 2005: 171). If it is to have a distinct definition it is to assist the principal.
- *Abetting*. The ordinary meaning of abetting is to incite or encourage the offender. It is for this reason that it is sometimes said that it is difficult to distinguish between this and aiding as encouraging may often be said to be assisting.
- *Counselling*. This terms means to advise or solicit but confusingly it also means to encourage. Accordingly, the difference between this and abetting is not always easy to identify although in *National Coal Board v Gamble [1959] 1 QB 11* it was suggested that abetting may require physical presence whereas counselling does not.
- *Procuring*. This means to 'produce by endeavour' (*Attorney-General's Reference (No 1 of*

1975) (op. cit.) and see Ormerod, 2005: 174). The meaning of procuring has been discussed throughout this chapter but it should be noted that 'procure' here means the commission of an offence rather than the procuring of a child.

Presence

To return to the focus of cyberspace one issue that may be raised is whether presence is required. If we return to the example of the 'w0nderland club' discussed above it was seen that this involved a member of an organisation 'broadcasting' the abuse of a child whilst others watched the footage. It was noted that there were two types of persons watching. The first simply watched and the second offered suggestions as to how to abuse a child. In neither case, therefore, would these other members be present but this would be irrelevant since there is nothing within the 1861 Act which requires presence.

However is there any difference in their liability? Those who suggest ideas are, at the very least, assisting (or more likely) procuring the crime committed and accordingly there is no real difficulty with complicity here. Even if the person who is committing the substantive offence does not follow the suggestion, the person making it would be guilty of inciting the other to commit an offence. The more complicated position is those who do not make any suggestions but simply watch the action. Can they be considered an accomplice without making any suggestion?

In *R v Coney (1882) 8 QBD 534* it was suggested that mere presence at a scene cannot amount by itself to encouraging the conduct and, therefore, accessorial liability. Presence can easily be translated to cyberspace with presence meaning the online presence within a chatroom or other online real-time communication system. However, an online presence is arguably different to merely being present at a scene of a crime in the offline world. It would usually be difficult to 'stumble' across such broadcasts and this means that the persons viewing the site are likely to have 'joined' the site at a predetermined time etc. In *Wilcox v Jeffrey [1951] 1 All ER 464* a conviction for encouragement was sustained on the basis that voluntary presence is *prima facie* evidence for encouragement and when taken with other facts, in this case the fact that they had purchased tickets to an illegal concert, it could be concluded that presence was sufficient. A similar position could be reached in the online world where a person voluntarily joins a website at a predetermined time knowing that a child will be abused 'live' at that time. Accordingly, it is submitted that they could be liable for accessorial conduct.

What of the unlikely situation where a person does stumble on to such abuse but decides to stay and watch the 'broadcast'? This is slightly different from *Wilcox v Jeffrey* in that there is no pre-determined knowledge from which encouragement could be drawn. The disturbing case of *R v Clarkson [1971] 3 All ER 344* would be not dissimilar. In this case two soldiers returning to their barracks entered a room where a young woman was being raped by several soldiers. They stood and watched the rape taking place although there was no evidence that they did anything that could be considered to be actively encouraging the rape. Their conviction for being an accessory to rape was quashed on the basis that there was no proof that they had encouraged the offence. Arguably, the same could be true in the circumstances noted above. If a person does view this footage without there being any predetermined knowledge of it and without there being evidence to suggest they encouraged the offender it may be difficult to secure a conviction for complicity. However, that is not to say that such a person would escape all liability since the broadcast would almost certainly constitute an 'indecent image' of a child and accordingly, if the video was stored in the cache, even temporarily, a conviction for indecent photographs may be possible (see Chapter 4).

Relationship with principal

The final relevant aspect of complicity to note[5] is the relationship with the principal, i.e. does there need to be a principal in order for accessorial liability to exist? The simple answer is 'yes' although it is not necessary for the principal to be identified (see, for example, *DPP v K and B [1997] 1 Cr App R 36*). It has been noted in respect of conspiracy this could be quite important in the online world where it may not be possible to identify the person who committed the offence. Similarly, it does not matter whether the principal is acquitted (*R v Huges (1860) Bell CC 242*) or if he is, for some reason, immune from prosecution (*R v Austin [1981] 1 All ER 374*).

What is the position where the principal is in another country? If the principal is not within the United Kingdom (or subject to its laws through extraterritoriality), then he is not subject to the laws of England and Wales and accordingly there can be no principal offender. In these circumstances can there be secondary liability? It has been suggested not (Hirst, 2003: 129), presumably on the basis that this position can be distinguished to those discussed immediately above. Where a principal offender cannot be identified this does not mean that the offence did not occur. The crime occurred but unfortunately it was not possible to identify who committed it. A person can continue to be a secondary party, however since they are an accessory to a crime that was committed. It may seem that a different position is reached whereby the principal is acquitted but again this need not be the case. An acquittal does not mean that a person did not do the act that he has been accused of; it may mean that the prosecution could not prove that he did that act. The acquittal may occur not because there is doubt as to whether the crime occurred but over who committed it. Again, if a jury can be satisfied that a crime *did* occur then there can be secondary liability.

The difficulty that exists where the principal is abroad is there is no crime within the meaning of English law. It is not the case that an offender has committed a crime outside of the English territory: behaviour only becomes a crime (i.e. action or omission contrary to the relevant criminal law of a country) when it is within English territory or its extraterritorial jurisdiction (see Hirst, 2003: vii). Since there is no crime it follows that there cannot be any secondary liability of assisting someone to commit the crime. Where, as discussed above, this means that someone logs onto a chatroom or Internet site to watch live streamed abuse, but without inciting any actions, then no liability would arise even though they may be intending to encourage the behaviour. This is because intending to encourage is probably insufficient for incitement without there being words or actions that can be construed as inciting the person to perform an illegal act. Encouraging a crime will ordinarily amount to complicity but where there is no crime (through lack of jurisdiction) then a person cannot be so liable (although, as discussed above, if any of the imagery of the stream is stored in the computer, even on the cache, then liability may arise for making indecent images of children contrary to s.1, *Protection of Children Act 1978*).

Proactive operations

At the beginning of this chapter a number of case-examples were presented that illustrated procurement. In all of these it will be recalled that the defendant did not actually manage to procure a child because they were identified by the police prior to this step and the police used proactive techniques to gather the evidence and convict them. 'Proactive operations' in this sense means that the police are not simply reacting to crime (i.e. detecting and investigating a crime after it has occurred) but instead are trying to frustrate the efforts of those who seek to undertake a criminal enterprise. Colloquially it is sometimes given the term 'sting operations'.

The history of 'sting operations' within the police service has a long history (Ashworth and Redmayne, 2005: 260), and is now a central part of intelligence-led policing. Modern 'sting' operations will take two forms; either a static operation that may be ongoing or for a finite period of time, or a dynamic operation. Static operations tend to occur where there is intelligence that a type of crime is being committed but the information is less certain as to who may be committing the crime.

A static operation will ordinarily involve setting a 'sting' and seeing who tries to commit the relevant offence. Classic examples in the 'offline' world are specially-adapted cars which trap people inside who try to steal them, or in 2007, special tents in Glastonbury were set up, complete with CCTV cameras etc., to catch those who sought to steal items from other peoples' tents. Within the 'online' world the police have created websites that purport to advertise child pornography but, when a 'purchase' is attempted, the site simply records the IP address of the offender and alerts the relevant law enforcement community (Sher, 2007: 62; Krone, 2005: 4).

Dynamic operations tend to be in relation to specific 'targets' or individuals that intelligence have identified. Within the 'offline' world they will not infrequently be used in the fight against drugs and a covert police officer or informant (more properly known as a Covert Human Intelligence Source) will be used to gather information. The police have, in the past, been allowed to 'carry on' the criminal enterprise in order to gather sufficient information to identify and prosecute the major individuals within an organisation, often known as the use of 'participating informants' (see Clark, 2004: 612).

Dynamic operations can also be used in the 'online' world too. A good example of this is the operation in respect of Luke Sadowski discussed at the beginning of this chapter. The police 'posed' as someone who was able to procure children in order to gain sufficient information to identify and arrest the individual, in this case Sadowski, a person who was seeking a very young child to have sex with.

What are the proprieties of 'sting' operations? Many people perhaps do not give them a second thought but proactive tactics are controversial. Indeed, the Sadowski case itself was the cause of some mutterings in respect of the tactics. One commentator noted how the Internet now meant that a person could be convicted of a crime '*before they have done anything wrong*' (Ingrams, 2003: 30). This emotive comment appears to neglect the fact that inchoate liability has existed for many years and does raise questions as to what the police are supposed to do when they have information that a person wishes to procure a child? Are they supposed to wait until a child has been harmed before arresting the offender?

Nevertheless, although it may seem that the answer is therefore comparatively simple, there remain doubts as to the propriety of 'sting' operations with at least one commentator noting that they have been used in the past to oppress minorities, principally the gay community (Paris, 2003: 24). Paris does, at least, note that there is a line to be drawn in covert policing tactics, conceding that operations may be necessary but the key is whether the police are enticing someone to commit a crime or whether they are simply detecting a person who is freely attempting to commit a crime. Sadowski is undoubtedly an example of the latter: the police did not 'seek out' Sadowski, he came to them, albeit not knowing their real identity, and thus the police, through deceptive tactics, allowed Sadowski to demonstrate that he wanted to commit a crime. One argument justifying such activities is the suggestion that if the police did not do this then the person may be able to find another 'person' who is willing to fulfil the act with the result (at least in this context) that an actual child has been harmed.

There is an undoubted sense of unease over the use of 'sting' operations in general. One commentator has suggested:

> . . . behind [the] doctrine is an underlying anxiety, not articulated by the courts, about what might happen if the

state were permitted to induce into crime those not ordinarily confronting it as a plausible possibility and the kinds of people that might be ensnared as a consequence.
(Squires, 2006: 373)

This is an interesting comment and it perhaps reflects some of what Ingrams was concerned with above. Whilst 'sting' operations undoubtedly can be beneficial in certain circumstances there is the concern that they could be used to 'coerce' or 'induce' ordinarily law-abiding citizens into committing a crime. It is perhaps easier to see this in the offline rather than online world. A 'honeytrap' that consists of an unlocked car with valuable items in it will be more tempting to ordinary citizens than an online advertisement to supply young children for sex. Does this mean that the concerns alter depending on the type of operation? Possibly, but the concerns probably remain: if a proactive operation is to be used, in this context online, it is perhaps important that it continues to be targeted at those who are exhibiting inappropriate behaviour.

If this 'line' that Paris is concerned with exists, and certainly most commentators would agree that it must, with proactive operations being permissible in certain contexts, how does one draw the line and where? The leading case in this area in England and Wales is *Attorney-General's Reference (No 3 of 2000); R v Looseley [2001] 1 Cr App R 360* (hereafter referred to as '*Looseley*' for ease of writing). This case was two separate conjoined appeals heard by the House of Lords, and called upon their Lordships to decide whether there was a line to be drawn and what the remedy would be where the police exceeded the boundaries of the law. Where permissible conduct has been exceeded it is common to refer to the doctrine of 'entrapment', the term given to the circumstances when the law enforcement community has ensnared someone, implying they would not ordinarily commit this offence. Traditionally in English law entrapment was not a defence but simply went towards sentencing (*R v Sang [1980] AC 402*), but this view has gradually changed with the House of Lords in *Looseley* deciding that where a person has been entrapped then the usual remedy would be for the prosecution to be stayed as an abuse of process. A stay does not formally lead to an acquittal of the defendant but the prosecution is halted and may not commence again without leave of the court (which is unlikely to occur). Accordingly, at least one commentator has suggested that entrapment,

through the abuse of process doctrine, has become a defence in all but name (Ormerod, 2002a: 304).

The decision in *Looseley* expressly addresses the issue of 'sting' operations, as has been noted:

Nothing in Looseley casts doubt on the propriety of 'sting' operations which are properly authorised and well run . . . So long as the undercover officers conduct themselves as an ordinary person would do in the given situation . . . there is no objection.
(Ashworth, 2002: 173)

The concept of acting like an 'ordinary person' is somewhat controversial since ordinary people do not commit crimes, especially of the sort we are discussing in this book. That said, in the 'offline' world it can be seen how this test may work. In *Nottingham City Council v Amin [2000] 1 WLR 1071* the Divisional Court was called upon to rule on a case where two special constables, in plain clothes, 'flagged' down a taxi and asked the driver to convey them somewhere. The taxi was unlicensed and when the 'fare' was accepted the driver was told he would be reported for breaching taxi regulations. When prosecuted, the driver claimed he had been the subject of entrapment but this was rejected by the Divisional Court, in part because it was said that the police acted in the same way as an ordinary member of the public and accordingly it could not be said that they 'created' a crime.

It is perhaps this distinction between the 'creation' of crime and allowing someone the 'opportunity' of committing the crime that is the line between lawful and unlawful conduct, but the distinction between these two forms of conduct has been considered 'highly problematic' (Squires, 2006: 353). In part, this is because wherever there is a 'sting' operation it could be argued that the police have 'caused' a crime to be created in that *but for* the action of the police a crime would not have been committed. However, the House of Lords meant more than this and were concerned realistically with the inducement of people who would not ordinarily have committed an offence. Certainly the courts appear to be affronted by the 'luring' or 'inducement' of the commissioning of an offence (Squires, 2006: 361), perhaps reinforcing the fact that the police ought to be tackling those who seek to commit a crime rather than creating new offenders.

This is an important point and is particularly relevant within the operation of the online world in this context. A person who looks at (lawful) adult pornography should not be offered the opportunity to purchase (illegal) child pornography. There is no defined nexus between adult and child pornography and without any intelligence to suggest that a person is interested in purchasing child pornography it is submitted that such an approach may go too far: it can be said that the law enforcement community would be coercing, or at the very least incentivising, the illegal conduct. However, where the converse occurs: i.e. someone deliberately seeks out illegal material or seeks to contact a person for the solicitation of a child, then it would be easier to justify undertaking proactive operations against such persons. The key is perhaps voluntariness, something that has been commented upon:

> The criminal law aims to restrict punishment 'to those who have voluntarily broken the law' and who can thus be regarded as bringing punishment on themselves by their own conduct.
>
> (Squires, 2006: 371 citing Hart)

Within our context this may be an extremely pertinent point. If the law enforcement community allows those who voluntarily seek to break the law an opportunity to identify themselves then this could be justified notwithstanding the fact that Ingrams argues that they have not yet done anything (substantively) wrong. The argument would be that the law is both preventative and about protecting the vulnerable. Where this voluntary arrangement breaks down, however then the courts should be slow to accept evidence.

The use of proactive operations has become increasingly important in the fight against child exploitation facilitated through communication technologies (Krone, 2005: 4, 6). This has increased in recent years with the establishment of the Virtual Global Task Force which has, itself, established some proactive static operations allowing a whole new dimension in the fight online to be established. So long as the rules are followed then it is submitted that this is appropriate and that proactive operations allow the police to identify individuals who pose a danger to children prior to them gaining access to a live child and exploiting them.

Notes

1 See Sex Case Fuels Law Change Plea (1996) *The Guardian*, 17 September.
2 See, for example, Anger Over Paedophile Sentence (1996) *The Times*, 17 September, and Prison for Internet Paedophile (2000) *The Guardian*, 23 May.
3 (2003) *The Independent*, 18 January.
4 If there is no agreement but the British national was attempting to persuade a foreign national to become involved in a sexual offence abroad then this may amount to an incitement and thus contrary to s.2, *The Sexual Offences (Conspiracy and Incitement) Act 1996*, see Hirst, 2003: 141.
5 For a fuller discussion on the general law of complicity see Ormerod, 2005: 164–214.

CHAPTER 7

Prostitution

The use of the Internet and other information communication technologies to facilitate prostitution may come as a surprise to some but it does exist and is arguably one of the faster growing forms of exploitative behaviour against children. In this chapter we will explore how modern communication technologies are allowing for the exploitation of children and how the law has reacted to this. The second part of this chapter will consider a rather more disturbing trend, that being the growth of self-exploitation through the Internet.

Terminology

As with other aspects of this book the use of words can be problematic in this area. The term 'prostitute' is generally considered to be unhelpful because it carries with it connotations of being a 'whore' (see, for example, the wording used in a thesaurus). There are undoubtedly negative connotations to the use of the word 'prostitute' although a considerable debate has arisen over what other terms could be used.

Where the issue concerns adults it is not unusual to hear references to the 'sex work industry' or 'sex workers'. This is, in part, a reaction to the negative connotations of the word 'prostitute' but also because some advocates for sex workers wish prostitution to be seen not as a seedy and illegal business but a legitimate service industry. Certainly it is easy to see why such campaigns arise since the sex industry has become increasingly popular in recent years with significant numbers admitting to visiting a massage parlour or brothel. Whilst much of the sex industry is illegal, there is a belief that this allows for sex workers to be exploited by 'pimps' and other unscrupulous controllers, whereas if it were legitimatised it would allow for more appropriate controls to be brought forward. However, it is important to note that such opinions are not universally shared with many believing that the sex industry is intrinsically wrong and is a manifestation of masculine power normalising a power imbalance whereby females may be exploited for the needs of man (see, for example, Dworkin, 2004).

The debate over the legitimacy of the sex industry can be set aside for this chapter since this book is focused solely on children. Whatever the debate over the correct term used for adults who work in the 'sex industry', it would be simply inappropriate to use the term 'sex worker' to describe a child or young person working as a prostitute. The media appear, over the years, to have an obsession with child prostitutes but they rarely portray the true characteristics of those who are involved (Goddard et al., 2005: 276). Whilst there may be a small number of mature young people who exercise some choice to enter the industry it is accepted by the vast majority of commentators that young people enter prostitution without any choice in the matter (Cusick, 2002: 236). Much of the literature suggests that victims should not be considered as prostitutes but rather as victims of child sexual exploitation (Pearce 2006: 190; Brown 2006: 295), but this is not universal, with some observers suggesting that focusing on the idea of a controlling 'pimp' abusing a child ignores the wider social and economic reasons that may result from a young person entering prostitution (Phoenix, 2003: 156).

The law has traditionally not engaged in this debate and has recently arrived at a statutory definition that is to be used by the law. Section 51(2) Sexual Offences Act 2003 (SOA) defines a 'prostitute' as:

> . . . a person (A) who, on at least one occasion and whether or not compelled to do so, offers or provides sexual services to another person in return for payment or a promise of payment to A or a third person; and 'prostitution' is to be interpreted accordingly.

This definition is expressly related to children and thus the law has, for the first time, used the terms 'child prostitute' and 'child prostitution' even though the terms are considered to be inappropriate by many working with them. It is regrettable that the law has adopted this approach but it is directly analogous to how it reacted to the use of terms such as 'pornography' (see Chapter 3 and Gillespie, 2005a: 285).

Within this chapter the term 'young person involved in prostitution' will be used which is the term used by other commentators (e.g. Phoenix, 2003), and also by the government in its other policies (see, for example, DoH, 2000). The use of the term is, it is submitted, neutral in that it shows that unfortunately some young people are involved in prostitution but without suggesting that they are necessarily complicit within it.

Identification

Whilst nobody would seriously question whether young people are involved in prostitution it is not actually very easy to state how many young people do work within prostitution. Commentators have noted that it is very difficult to quantify the scale of the problem because it is 'essentially a clandestine activity' (Ayre and Barrett, 2000: 50) and is thus hidden away from society as a whole and those in authority who work to support those who are exploited.

The stereotypical perception of prostitution is that of a woman standing on a street corner or in a 'red light district' of a particular town. Whilst some young prostitutes are involved with street prostitution the reality is that most is hidden away in flats, private residences and massage parlours (Brown and Melrose, 2003). Where this occurs it can, as will be seen, be easily facilitated through the use of modern communication technologies. However, this does mean it is difficult to identify how many children are being exploited through prostitution. It is known that between 1989 and 1995 some 4,000 young people under the age of 18 were convicted or cautioned for offences relating to prostitution (Ayre and Barrett, 2000: 50). Since 2000 there has been a policy not to prosecute children (Gillespie, 2007a) a policy that must be considered welcome. However, it does mean these 'official' figures become of little use in identifying the children.

It is known that those who are involved in prostitution consider themselves to be rejected by society (Ayre and Barrett, 2000: 49), and they will frequently shun those agencies that exist to assist them (Cusick, 2002: 232), meaning that relying on official figures can be difficult. The studies therefore produce quite varied figures with research estimates ranging from 2,000 young people per year (Cusick, 2002: 233), to 5,000 per year (Barrett and Melrose, 2003). Whatever the true figure is it is clear that it is a not insignificant number and that this can also set the pattern for future life, with studies showing that many adults involved as prostitutes began prostitution whilst under the age of 18.

Forms of exploitation

Having decided that there are young people involved in prostitution in the United Kingdom it is then necessary to consider what forms of exploitation they suffer. This book is concerned with the exploitation of children facilitated by ICT and so not all forms of exploitation will be discussed in this chapter being outside this focus. The three key forms relevant to this chapter are, it is submitted:

• Facilitating off-line prostitution.
• Sex lines.
• Online sexual activity.

To this list could perhaps be added the facilitation of trafficking but this will be discussed briefly later in this chapter because the behaviour is distinctly different from that set out here.

Facilitating off-line prostitution

Whilst it has been noted that a majority of child prostitution is likely to take place off the streets this does not mean that it is not contact abuse. The vast majority of prostitution is contact abuse, i.e. the person who pays for the sexual service will be in direct contact with the young person involved in prostitution. How does this contact occur?

The Internet has permitted a number of websites to be created that advertise the services of prostitutes and other sex workers. Some of the sites that are listed are merely a list of massage parlours, some of which will be legitimate, but in other cases it is known that the parlours are merely a (relatively limited) cover for advertising a brothel. Other sites offer escort services and these tend to try to avoid criminal liability by including a message on the site that states one is paying purely for the company of a man or woman and that if anything else is agreed this is a purely private arrangement between consenting adults. The justification for this approach is that where both parties are adults, prostitution itself, i.e. the payment of money for a sexual service, is not illegal but rather it is ancillary issues (e.g. soliciting, running a brothel or living off the earnings of a prostitute) that is illegal. Accordingly, man X could decide to pay woman Y £250 for sexual intercourse and this would not be illegal (for a useful summary of the limits of soliciting see Selfe and Burke, 2001: 245–50).

The Internet does not always hide the meaning of its advertising and some sites are more candid in that they expressly state that they exist to advertise and discuss prostitution. Some of these sites operate on a local basis and there have, for example, been examples of local 'cooperatives' setting up their own sites. Other examples appear to demonstrate individual adults setting up a website advertising their services. This does raise some interesting issues because some argue that this provides the sex worker with the opportunity to act independently (Soothill, 2004). The argument in support of this contention is that the worker does not need to pay somebody to advertise or control her activities. However this, it is submitted, is slightly naïve. Whilst learning the basics of web-design is not difficult, the issue of web-hosting is slightly more complicated and it can put some people off. In any event it is not clear that it is an individual who is designing the website and it could just as easily be the 'controlling influence'. Support for this latter contention is the fact that many 'individual' sites look almost identical which suggests that an element of organisation still exists. Arguably, the demographics of the sex workers themselves also demonstrate this, with many sites showing a large number of young, eastern-European ladies. This, it is thought, is more indicative of organised prostitution rather than a large number of such women deciding independently to come to the same area of England and set up their own websites.

Not all sites are necessarily local or individual sites and there are two prominent national sites that exist to facilitate prostitution. The prominent nature of these sites does give rise to an ethical dilemma in terms of their names. Should I, as an author, use their names? Doing so would, at least, ensure that there is clarity as to which sites I mean and how they operate. However, there is the counter-argument that naming them could be considered to be somehow unintentionally condoning their activities, something that I do not. On that basis, it may seem more prudent not to use their names (although arguably they are not illegal in their own right) although this justification is slightly undermined in that it is obviously necessary to describe the sites making it relatively obvious what the sites are.

The two sites (referred to inventively as Site A and Site B here) have existed on the Internet for a number of years with site B being in existence for eight years at the time of writing. There is no easy way of discovering whether they are operated by the same person but it is clear that they are linked in the sense that each provides a weblink to the other. It should be noted that such behaviour is not, of course, extraordinary in that many sites are linked to both sites in much the same way as ordinary websites are. Site A is, in effect, a directory of prostitutes, sex workers and brothels. The site allows 'hosting' space which will allow individual members to advertise on the site and they also provide a series of links to other websites. They have an extensive search algorithm that allows users to search for a particular preference of service, person or location. They make an ambitious claim that they are able to find a sex worker within 30 miles of any location in England and Wales.

Site B is, to an extent, a natural extension of site A in that it is in essence a guide to the use of prostitutes. At one level it is an extension of site A in that it allows people to search by location, person or service, but the principal concept behind site B is that it allows (and indeed encourages) those who use the prostitute to write a 'field report' on their experience. A field report is a review of the services offered by the prostitute and includes, for example, the price, duration and description of the services offered (the services often being coded allowing for a further search to be conducted), together with a critique of what occurred and a suggestion as to whether they would recommend others to contact this person.

Ostensibly, both sites A and B together with the vast majority of 'local' sites, specifically address the issue of age and suggest that only adult sex workers are used. Indeed, site B provides a link to the 'Crimestoppers' website (the national charity that was set up to allow members of the public to anonymously pass information about crime to the police, being sometimes offered cash rewards for doing so), together with a message saying, 'You the punters, CAN make a difference . . .' Whilst this would appear to be commendable, is it at all realistic?

It is known that massage parlours etc. also purport to state that all of their workers are aged over 18, yet it is also known that this is the very place where a significant amount of child prostitution is based. Many of the girls on the websites that are set up to advertise prostitutes list a number of girls aged 18–20. Of course, to an extent this can be a 'trick' in that it is known that youth brings a price premium and thus some sites will deliberately lower the age of the worker. However, it would also be extremely naïve to suggest that the variation of age does not go the other way by ensuring that agencies purport to advertise lawful girls. Soothill, in an informative article, provides an example where an agency referred to a girl as aged 16 and provided a testimonial to this effect. When, on a discussion board (which was linked to this site) the question was raised whether the correct (lawful) age for a sex worker was 16 or 18 the agency quickly changed their description of the girl to say that she was 18 (Soothill, 2004). Whilst it is possible that the true age of the girl was 18 it is equally possible that the original age was correct and the agency was simply attempting to ensure that their worker was of legal age.

Given that the involvement of children and young persons in prostitution is a reality it would be extremely naïve to suggest that no child involved in prostitution will be found on the Internet. Research does suggest that this happens with one commentator presenting the case-study of 'Natalie' who was included on a website for child prostitutes (Palmer, 2004: 16–17). This is perhaps unusual in that it was a site expressly set up for child prostitutes, but other examples have shown that they exist on normal advertising sites too. The legality of sites that either advertise children or permit advertisements for children to be hosted will be discussed below.

Sex lines

Sex work need not always be direct contact; a significant proportion of sex work takes place in more indirect ways, e.g. through chat-lines. Whether this amounts to 'prostitution' is a topic of debate but it is submitted that for our purposes it does meet the definition put forward in the SOA 2003 in that it is a sexual service for payment. There seems little doubt that it is a 'sexual' service because nothing in the Act requires sexual services to be direct and, in any event, the definition of 'sexual' provided by s.78, SOA 2003 would ensure that a sex line would come within the provisions.

Sex lines are certainly not hi-tech but are a (relatively) recent phenomenon. The sex line can take a number of forms:

- Caller engages in a two-way conversation with a live operator.
- Caller engages in a two-way conversation with two live operators.
- Caller listens to provocative discussion and description of adult fantasies.
- Caller listens to a fully recorded fantasy message narrated by a sexy (female) voice.
- Automated dating system whereby callers can listen to 'adverts' posted by other callers
(Lane, 2001: 159)

It can be seen, therefore, that the system operates on the basis of either live interaction or a person listening to someone talking about sexual activities, with the caller receiving sexual gratification from this. Sex lines have been popular over the past 20 or so years but have not been in existence for much more because the technology requires an operator to (usually) have access to a number of telephone lines and the technology to harness large numbers of telephone calls. Where something other than a premium telephone line is used (see below) there would also be the complication of identifying how someone would be paid for the service. Historically, premium lines were used only for pre-recorded messages rather than live interaction since the costs (upwards of £2–3 per minute) are heavily regulated and also because they would often not cover the salary of an operator.

The greater commercial profit is in interactive sex services: i.e. where a caller can speak to an operator and they participate in a two (or more)-way sexual conversation. The experience can be extremely graphic for both sides of the conversation, although some debate exists about whether operators are truly participating or whether it is simply a 'script' or 'role' through which they participate in a detached manner (Lane, 2001: 164–5).

The Internet can facilitate sex lines in two distinct ways. The first is through an advertising opportunity. E-mails can be sent, either directed or, more likely, SPAM, to try and encourage callers. These messages tend to appeal to the stereotypes of sexuality within society:

Tammie here, my girlfriend and I are **strippers** *[sic] actually we are first year college students, but we strip at* *night for extra money. We do good because guys like our Tight Asses and our Big Tits. We just bought a computer and thought we would send a couple of emails out just to see if this thing really works, we are sooo bored at college – we are just sitting in our dorm room doing nothing if you want to call and talk, we love to talk about how naughty we can get at work.*

Hope you call!

(Lane, 2001: 158)

This message is typical of an unsolicited (SPAM) e-mail and plays to many of the stereotypes of society. It involves a young nubile lady who has a girlfriend (thus linking into the male fantasy of lesbianism) and who is in college (reinforcing youth). It includes a basic (stereotypical) description of their bodies and suggests that when they are bored they like to be 'naughty' and thus be sexually suggestive. Other e-mails concentrate on other stereotypes and fetishes: the Internet has allowed a considerable amount of 'nonmainstream' sexual desires to find an outlet. E-mails can be sent out to appeal to the various desires (e.g. 'fat' women, gay or bisexual, bondage, domination, sado-masochism etc.) (Lane, 2001: 161), and this can also be taken into the illicit desires such as paedophilia etc., whereby people wish to be sexually explicit with young girls etc. Of course, on a telephone it is not necessarily easy to identify the age of a child and thus some will be young girls over the age of consent pretending to be youthful, but similarly it is known that some young teenagers involved in prostitution have also become involved in this activity.

The second way that the Internet has become involved is in usurping the telephone call. Whilst some callers still want the vocal interaction that is brought through a telephone call others are less bothered. For as long as there have been chatrooms (and Internet Relay Chat arguably predated the World Wide Web), there has been 'cyber-sex'. Cyber-sex can take a number of different forms but is commonly where two people describe a sexual activity that they want to do with the other person and sometimes inviting them to masturbate themselves whilst participating in the chat. The anonymity of the Internet means that the two people undertaking the cyber-sex can pretend to be anyone and anecdotal evidence suggests that this means the two people who are engaging in 'cyber-sex' quite often have no idea who the other person is, including their gender.

This latter form of contact is less likely to be relevant to the topic of this book since although it is undoubtedly the case that teenagers do undertake cyber-sex, there is no real evidence to suggest that they do so for reward. In reality, it is more likely that when a commercial site creates a text-based 'cyber-sex' forum involving children that the persons undertaking the chat will be actors pretending to be children. However, that is not to say that children will never be involved because thanks to technological advancement it is possible to combine a 'text' service with a webcam. In this way, one (or both) parties will 'see' the person they are communicating with via a webcam. Accordingly, a child could be asked to participate in a 'cyber-sex' session including a webcam and the 'correspondent' could see that she is a young girl and conduct the 'cyber-sex' session accordingly, including asking the child to touch herself in front of the webcam so that he can see what is happening. This behaviour is, however, perhaps better thought of as an online activity rather than a sex line.

Online sexual activity

Although the Internet may seem to be a relatively new innovation, the speed of change has escalated dramatically over the past few years. Broadband has now provided transfer speeds that were completely unimaginable even four or five years ago. Broadband is now the most popular form of connecting to the Internet and it has now spread to mobile telephones where this high-speed access is sought. The speed of connections and increase in bandwith means that it is now possible to be in instant communication with someone and to watch in real-time extremely detailed imagery. This technology is being used in many legitimate contexts with 'video-conferencing' becoming increasingly popular to allow multi-national companies to communicate without the expense of travel. Within the entertainment media this growth of speed has revolutionised the way that we deal with media. It is now possible to download an entire music album within minutes and organisations such as the BBC will broadcast live coverage of events that we can watch live and in high definition.

The 'adult industry' has not, unsurprisingly, been slow to use this technology and indeed arguably it has been pushing some of the technological advancements in this area. Sex sites such as *Playboy* and other less reputable sites now advertise hardcore videos that can be downloaded and viewed in high-definition. The quality of the video is beyond that which we could have imagined only a few years ago and broadband connections means that someone can download as much as they wish without the embarrassment of having to enter a shop to purchase the material.

Some websites have taken this video technology one step further and allow the opportunity to view live, real-time pornography. This can, in some situations, be a broadcast from a webcam but other sites are now increasingly allowing for an interactive broadcast. This is where a person, for a set sum of money, will be given access to a web-channel whereby he can watch a live-sex show and interact with the performers, suggesting possible acts. This technology exists and several websites allow this to occur, as it is often seen as being financially lucrative.

Unfortunately, this technology, as has been seen already in this book, can be abused and in the context of prostitution could create a situation whereby a young person involved in prostitution is forced to perform in front of a webcam or other broadcasting technology and 'perform' for the benefit of those subscribing to the content. Some commentators have already noted the existence of this sort of behaviour, with a central organising character arranging with a variety of people to log onto a particular site in order to view or contribute to the online abuse of the child (Palmer, 2004: 28).

This sort of behaviour also identifies the difficulty in defining the different types of exploitative behaviour that occurs. It will be remembered that earlier in this book similar behaviour was discussed in the context of child procurement (Chapter 6). It is difficult to understand the distinction that may exist between this behaviour and procurement. If there is any difference between them, and this is anything but certain, it could be through the motivation of the abuser. The online abuse of children was discussed in Chapter 6 because the 'w0nderland club' participated in such acts, but motivation arguably linked all those involved in the abuse. The broadcaster and the members watching were linked by the desire to obtain sexual gratification through the abuse. It could be argued that in the context of prostitution, the motivation of the broadcaster is commercial

rather than sexual. This argument receives some support, albeit implicitly, when it is noted that some pornographers distribute child pornography not because they are sexually interested but because they see it as a way of making significant sums of money (Tate, 1990). It is a sad reality of society that such people undoubtedly exist and in the same way some of them will see the broadcast of children being abused, or abusing themselves, to be another way of earning money.

Legal solutions to child exploitation through prostitution

It has already been noted that the scope of this book is limited to involvement with ICT and accordingly issues such as the legality of street prostitution fall outside this area, as do arguments as to the legality of those young people who are involved in prostitution themselves (for a discussion on this see Gillespie, 2007, Phoenix, 2002, 2003). The legality of the operators of the sites discussed above (e.g. site A and site B) will also not be discussed other than where it relates to the issue of child prostitution. Whilst there is an argument that sites that concentrate solely on adult prostitution may be illegal (see *Shaw v DPP [1962] AC 220* where the publisher of a prostitutes directory was convicted of the common law offence of conspiracy to corrupt public morals, although whether the same decision would be reached today is perhaps debatable), it is not appropriate to discuss this.

When concentrating on the issue of child prostitution it is important to note that the SOA 2003 reformed this area of law in a significant way. Perhaps one of the first points to note is that the reforms in the SOA 2003 mean that the age of consent for commercial sexual exploitation becomes 18 and not the normal age of consent (16). By doing this, Parliament has laid down a clear marker that they believe that the sexual exploitation of children is a crime of child abuse and that they link the offence to the age of majority not consent. This is certainly an improvement from the previous law that used to relate to the age of consent (e.g. s.28, *Sexual Offences Act 1956*) and must be welcomed as a step forward. That said, the law does still distinguish between the ages when it comes to the way in which an offender will be tried and sentenced.

Paying for the sexual services of a child

The first crime to examine is that contained within s.47, SOA 2003 which states:

(1) A person (A) commits an offence if –
 (a) he intentionally obtains for himself the sexual services of another person (B)
 (b) before obtaining those services, he has made or promised payment for those services to B or a third person, or knows that another person has made or promised such a payment, and
 (c) either –
  (i) B is under 18, and A does not reasonably believe that B is 18 or over, or
  (ii) B is under 13.

Sub-section (2) defines 'payment' in wide terms to include not only positive pecuniary transactions but the remission of a debt or services and the provision of discounts. Thus whilst there must undoubtedly still be a commercial element to the transaction, the offence has not restricted itself to money which would have been a significant loophole. Sub-sections (3)–(5) set out the mode of trial and penalty for these offences, which can be summarised as:

- B is under 13. Triable only on indictment and punishable by a maximum sentence of life imprisonment.
- B is under 16. Where the offence is penetrative (either to or by B) then triable only on indictment and punishable by a maximum of fourteen years imprisonment, otherwise triable either-way but punishable by a maximum of fourteen years' imprisonment.
- B is under 18. Triable either-way and punishable by a maximum of seven years' imprisonment.

The penalties and modes of trial are comparable to the other child sexual offences contained in earlier sections of the Act. It could be questioned why, when the child is under the age of 16, this offence exists? Sub-section (1) requires sexual services which must mean some sort of sexual activity. This activity could involve A committing an act on B, or B committing an act either alone, towards B or towards another. The act must be sexual, so would it not be more appropriate to

bring a substantive child sex offence against the perpetrator instead of using s.47? The emphasis of s.47 appears to be commercial exploitation rather than sexual abuse and yet paying for sex with a child must be considered the sexual abuse of a child and not a mere commercial transaction. There could be a danger that s.47 minimises the abuse point, labelling the offender a prostitute or sex worker and not the victim of sexual abuse. There has been a concerted effort over recent years to ensure that child prostitutes are treated as victims not criminals, but this offence could be taken to draw away from this somewhat.

One method of differentiating between the offence under s.47 and the substantive abuse offences would be through sentencing. The *Sentencing Guidelines Council* (SGC) in the definitive sentencing guideline have stated that the penalty for an offence under s.47 should, where it is in respect of a child between 13 and 16 (where the child is under 13 the 'substantive' child sex offences should ordinarily be charged) be greater than that which would be given for sexual activity with a child (SGC, 2007: 116). The *Sentencing Advisory Panel* (SAP) had suggested a notional increase of 25 per cent (SAP, 2004: 13–14) but the guideline does not expressly state this although the suggested 'starting points' for sentences do bear resemblance to this percentile increase. However, this does not really answer the question as to whether it would be appropriate to ordinarily charge this offence. The maximum sentence under s.47 is comparable to that of the substantive offences and accordingly there is no reason why the substantive offence could not be charged, with the judge simply increasing the sentence to take account of the commercial exploitation.

Where the offence can be useful is in respect of children between the ages of 16 and 18. It has been noted already that there is no offence of prostitution *per se* and this means that it is not illegal for person X to pay person Y to perform a sexual act. Section 4 of the 2003 Act creates an offence of causing or inciting a person to engage in sexual activity, which is defined widely and could, therefore, include performing a sex act to be broadcast over the Internet etc., but this section requires that B does not consent. The issue of proving consent has always been one of the most controversial and complicated aspects of the law. Where a person is involved in prostitution it may be even more difficult to persuade a jury of an absence of consent, notwithstanding the fact that the 2003 Act creates a series of evidential presumptions governing when a person does not consent (ss. 75–76, SOA 2003). Parliament has, quite correctly, decided that children should not be sexually exploited and this must mean that this part of s.47 is to be welcomed.

Causing or inciting child prostitution

Sections 48 to 50 create three new offences that relate to child prostitution and are designed to tackle those who 'assist' a child in prostitution. The offences have all been discussed in an earlier chapter of this book (Chapter 4) because they all apply to pornography too. However, the offences also apply to child prostitution and, accordingly, it is necessary to briefly consider them again.

Section 48 creates the offence of causing or inciting a person under the age of 18 to become a prostitute in any part of the world. The definition of 'prostitute' was discussed earlier and it will be remembered that it is, in essence, a person who provides a sexual service in return for payment or the promise of payment (s.51(2), SOA 2003). The term 'cause' used in s.48 is not defined in the Act but it has been suggested that since it is a common legal term it simply means any causative action (Rook and Ward, 2004: 2.81) i.e. it will be a matter of fact for the jury to decide whether the defendant was the cause of B becoming a prostitute. An interesting issue is the fact that the Act is silent as to whether the defendant has to be *the* cause or simply *a* cause. In order for this offence to protect those who are exploited it is to be hoped that the courts interpret the legislation in such a way that it covers those who have more than a minimal causative effect on the victim. It is important to note that the phrasing of the Act is that A causes or incites the victim to *become* a prostitute and accordingly if a person is already a prostitute then it is not possible for liability to arise. That said, a person is not a prostitute for the rest of their life and accordingly a former prostitute can be caused or incited to return to prostitution. Where there is a dispute as to whether the child was a prostitute before the actions of the defendant the matter will inevitably be left to the jury.

Controlling a child prostitute

Section 49 creates an offence where someone controls the activities of a child prostitute. It is important to note that s.49 is triggered by a person controlling *any* of the activities of a prostitute and not just the actual prostitution. The explanatory notes accompanying the Act state that it could be used where a person states that a prostitute should use a particular room or charge a particular price (see para 96 of the explanatory notes to the Act).

Within an online context this could, presumably, also include the owners of a website that a child prostitute uses to advertise. It has been noted already that some prostitutes advertise on websites, and this can include websites that offer young prostitutes. The owner, or webmaster, of these sites must, it is submitted, be considered to be 'in control' of one aspect of the activities of a prostitute, that being advertising. An important aspect of this offence will be the mental element and s.49(1)(b) makes it clear that where the prostitute is over the age of 13 but under 18, the defendant must 'reasonably believe' that the prostitute was over the age of 18. Reasonable belief must mean that the defendant must be able to show the logic behind his belief, and take steps to validate that judgment. Within the online context this may be possible by requiring, for example, a credit card, although this is hardly a fool-proof measure. Merely asking a prostitute to certify that they are aged 18 by, for example, e-mail is unlikely to satisfy the reasonable belief.

Arranging or facilitating child prostitution

The last of the three offences and arguably the most flexible is that contained within s.50 which makes it an offence to arrange or facilitate child prostitution. The term 'facilitate' is not defined within the Act and accordingly it must be given its ordinary definition. The dictionary defines the term as '*to make easy or less difficult or more easily achieved*' (Thompson, 1995: 482). Thus anyone who helps a prostitute would, *prima facie*, be covered by this offence.

The explanatory notes to the Act provide examples of delivering B to a particular location or allowing premises to be used for these purposes (para 97). Within the online context anyone who helps a child prostitute to arrange contact with a customer could come within this provision, thus someone who hosts a website or assists a child prostitute in creating an advert may be covered. Similarly, someone who broadcasts the sexual acts of a child could commit this offence, whereas the person(s) who pay to watch the broadcast may be liable under s.47.

Sentencing flaw

Sections 48 to 50 are crimes of sexual exploitation and thus it is likely that for similar reasons as outlined in the discussion on s.47, the sentence may be increased as a result of the commercial exploitation of children. Where these offences differ from s.47, however, is in respect of notification. If someone is convicted of an offence under Sections 48 to 50 they are not required to notify their details to the police (see Chapter 9). The effect of this will be discussed elsewhere in this book but potentially this could lead to a situation where the law enforcement agencies will have to be careful as to whether they use these offences or alternative ones. The logic behind this can be seen from a case study.

The case study arises from Nathan Eyre who, on 16 September 2004, was sentenced to consecutive sentences of five and three years' imprisonment in respect of sexual offences relating to a boy he had met on the Internet and groomed for abuse (see (2004) *The Times*, 17 September). The first point to note is that despite the fact that every media outlet referred to the fact that Eyre groomed the victim (and thus it can be implied that this was mentioned in court), the 'grooming offence' put forward in s.15 of the 2003 Act would not be appropriate. The purpose of that offence is not to deal with substantive sexual liability but, rather, to act as a preparatory offence that can make culpable the behaviour leading up to the abuse of children (see Gillespie, 2004b: 586). It was always the intention of the *Home Secretary's Task Force on Child Protection on the Internet*, which helped formulate the offence, and Parliament itself, that where substantive offences take place alternative liability would be sought (unless it is appropriate to also charge the offence to acknowledge long-scale preparatory behaviour).

The principal offence that Eyre was convicted of was living off the earnings of a prostitute contrary to s.30, Sexual Offences Act 1956 and yet in reality this prostitute was a fourteen-year-old boy and thus this was complicity in respect of child abuse and not mere prostitution. Eyre would make contact with the various people who wanted to 'buy' the boy for sexual purposes and would then encourage the boy to partake in the activities. Thus Eyre would, at the very least, now be considered to be liable under Sections 48 or 49 of the 2003 Act. The liability of such offences is now increased in comparison to the old offences

and yet the difficulty is that, for reasons known only to Parliament, these offences do not require the offender to notify the police of their whereabouts.

There can be no doubt that Eyre is a danger to children – he carefully groomed this child in order to sexually exploit him. The fact that Eyre groomed the child for abuse by someone else does not make him any less dangerous and yet if this had been the case then Eyre would almost certainly have been required to notify. If a situation as this arises again then the solution may be to rely on substantive child sex offences. Section 14 of the 2003 Act creates the offence of arranging or facilitating the commission of a sexual offence and it would seem highly likely that the activities of Eyre would come within this offence. A sexual offence within the meaning of s.14 is somewhat restricted (being an offence within Sections 9–13 of the 2003 Act) but s.9 relates to sexual activity with a child, and the end result of Eyre's actions was that someone did have sexual activity with a child, so s.14 would be satisfied.

An alternative to the use of s.14 would be to use s.10. This creates an offence for a person to *intentionally cause or incite another person (B) to engage in a [sexual] activity*. It is not particularly clear where the distinction lies between Sections 10 and 14 since a person who causes or incites must also arguably be arranging or facilitating (the one significant difference being that s.14 permits the behaviour to be anywhere in the world, something that s.10 does not expressly mention). It could be argued that Eyre, by 'selling' the child victim to the other sex offenders will be guilty of either causing that sexual activity or, depending on whether he sought to persuade the child to become involved, inciting the victim to participate in the behaviour. The offence under s.10 is also punishable by a maximum sentence of 14 years imprisonment, but where the activity involves the penetration of or by B then the mode of trial changes to one of indictment-only (see s.10(2), SOA 2003).

If these crimes were used in a future case then it would ensure that perpetrators such as Nathan Eyre would be required to notify his whereabouts. However, the sting in this is that Sections 10 and 14 relate to children under 16 and not children under 18. Whilst, therefore, in a situation such as within this case study this will not be problematic, what would the result have been if the child was actually 16? In this case the only liability that could arise would be Sections 48 to 50.

It is submitted that Sections 48 to 50 are, for children under 16, somewhat irrelevant. The behaviour caught by these sections could quite easily be captured by substantive sex offences, including the use of Sections 10 and 14. It will be seen in Chapter 8 that sexual exploitation should be considered an aggravating factor in any event and given that the maximum sentences for Sections 10, 14 and 48 to 50 are the same it should be possible to cater for this behaviour. Where Sections 48 to 50 do have to be used is in relation to prostitution but it is submitted that in these instances then thought must be given as to whether sex offender notification requirements should arise here. It would appear somewhat illogical that the person who pays to have sex with a child prostitute should be considered a danger to the community (s.47 being an offence attracting the notification requirements) yet the person who controls the prostitute and who arranges the meetings should not. This is something that Parliament needs to reflect on.

Self-exploitation

So far the discussion in this chapter has been focused on the issue of those who exploit children for gain. However, in this section a modern and somewhat worrying trend will be discussed, which is where people are starting to be responsible for their own exploitation. It will be seen that there is some disagreement as to what this behaviour entails and how it should be classified but it will be discussed in this chapter because it seems the more appropriate place for it.

This form of self-exploitation is a creature of the modern technological revolution and for our purposes can be classified in two related forms. The first is the phenomenon known as 'camgirls' which uses webcams to portray the lives of a subject. The second, and related, form is a simple web-space whereby digital photographs are placed on the site, again usually to attract interest etc. There have recently been further developments of this style whereby mobile telephones are starting to be used as well. Third generation mobile telephones (video-equipped mobile telephones) are being used to share video footage of a person, usually for money.

Controversy exists over this behaviour with some suggesting that it allows women to take control of pornography (White, 2003: 8), and allowing them to reap the rewards of their behaviour rather than allowing others to profit. Others disagree, however, and suggest that it is simply reinforcing the exploitative nature of pornography. However, it is quite clear that for a significant number it can be an extremely lucrative form of behaviour (Lane, 2001: 252). Probably the first person to truly exploit this behaviour was Jennifer Ringley who, in 1996, created 'Jennicam'. Controversy exists over whether Jennicam was the first explicit webcam but to an extent this is irrelevant since it undoubtedly became the best known and led to an explosion of copy-cat productions.

'Jennicam' was created in 1996 when the technology was quite crude and the images produced from the early Jennicam is certainly of significantly poorer quality than that which can be broadcast using current tools. It is also worth pausing to note that a reason why this is lucrative is because it is cheap to operate. Webcams are extremely inexpensive and now ordinarily come bundled with a computer. The cost of broadband has now reduced significantly and the production of a site with a large bandwith is not expensive. Jennicam operated on a simple premise: the webcam was always left on and people could log onto the site and see what Jenni was up to. This would include her studying, working on the computer, sleeping but, perhaps most notably, occasional nudity (Lane, 2001: 253). It was perhaps this that led to the popularity of the site although Jennifer Ringley was adamant that this was not its primary purpose but was, instead, about documenting life (White, 2003: 14).

Whatever the original purpose of 'Jennicam' it did not take long for people to realise that webcams could be used specifically for the purpose of broadcasting pornography. Today it is easy to find any number of sites where, for a membership subscription, people can view live pornography. It has already been noted that a debate exists as to whether this is allowing women to take control or not, but for the purposes of this chapter we can set this to one side because it is not just adults who are creating such sites but also teenagers. Indeed, the term 'camgirl' has increasingly been seen as a way of describing teenagers exhibiting themselves via a webcam (White, 2003: 15).

The first point to note is that many teenagers operate webcams, often coupled with 'blogs' and it has been suggested that this is no different to the phenomenon of a teenager keeping a diary (Mieszkowski, 2001) and it has also been noted that *'most teenage sites show surprisingly little skin'* (Emmett, 2001). It is important to place this behaviour into context. Although, as will be seen, there is a trend for some girls to exploit themselves, it should not be thought that the concept of a webcam site is necessarily bad: there are many that exist and they can be largely harmless or even a sociological development tool.

However some teenagers are also aware of the fact that teenage sexuality intrigues many, especially on the Internet. Some sites operate so-called 'wish-lists' whereby a person creates a list of goods that they would like (akin to a wedding list service) at online stores and this allows people to purchase gifts that can then be sent to the operator. It cannot be said that the teenagers are necessarily being naïve over what they are doing since some appear to be fully aware of what they are doing; a notable example being a fifteen-year-old girl who called her site, 'Underage piece of ass' (Emmett, 2001).

Typical sites will simply be sexually provocative rather than explicit with many involving teenagers posing in their bra or a bikini: the suggestion being that they remain in control and that what a person sees is no different to that which a person could see on a beach (Rowan, 2002). Whilst this may be true the concern is that there is a cycle of exploitation and that teenagers will travel down this path relatively easily believing that they are safe because of the apparent anonymity of the Internet. There would appear to be similar cognitive distortions in this area as are exhibited in 'grooming' and it does mean that some teenagers are undoubtedly placing themselves in danger.

Financial reward is sought in two principal ways. The first is through the 'wish-lists', with people purchasing sometimes expensive gifts for the girls. The second method is traffic throughput. Many sites have 'banner ads' which display advertising to each person who looks at the site. Many will also include 'referral ads' whereby money is collected every time that a person is referred from one site to another. The difficulty with this approach is that it is heavily reliant on the traffic flow. Whilst a large number of people are visiting the website, the amount of money that can be earned can be considerable. When the visitor numbers begin to drop off, however, so does the amount of money.

The difficulty for teenagers is that they feel a sense of purpose in what they are doing and they can receive considerable financial reward. However, some then feel obliged to go a step further to reward those who provide financial gifts to them, or need to do something to keep the flow of traffic through the site:

> *I need some money and would really like to do this for a living. I'm always offered money to go on cam ... so I might as well take advantage.*
> ('Kerry' quoted by Rowan, 2002: 15)

The girls are quite clear what this means:

> *Showing a bit of skin does guarantee more hits ... showing a bit of cleavage does catch people's attention.*
> ('Livian' quoted by Emmett, 2001: 8)

The difficulty is that there is a danger that a spiral is created whereby to continue receiving the presents and the money it is necessary to keep posting stronger material in order to ensure visitors return:

> *I've tried having just a normal teen site before, but the only way to make any profit is to cater to the people who are looking for porn. Showing more skin on your webcam gets more people to visit.*
> ('Kate' quoted by Rowan, 2002: 16)

Whilst 'Kate' is above the age of consent she freely admits that she has told people that she is as young as 15 and yet still they purchase gifts such as lingerie. Where people send lingerie they will then suggest that the girl goes on webcam to show what it looks like. The temptation for the girl is to do this since the person bought it yet this can be the start of a normalisation process whereby the girls decide that acting sexually in front of a webcam can be perfectly normal. Others believe there is security in doing things before a webcam because of the perceived anonymity of the Internet:

> *After all, isn't it potentially safer to show a little skin on a webcam than pretty much anywhere else? ... It's even safer than if some young gal [sic] decided to wear something revealing on a beach or on a street ...*
> (Mieszkowski, 2001)

Yet the Internet is not necessarily a safe place, as other chapters in this book have identified. Whilst one may feel anonymous on the Internet it is quite possible to be traced on the Internet, especially where companies are delivering goods to an identifiable address. There have been instances of 'camgirls' being approached by people who have found out their addresses and tried to act inappropriately to the girls (Emmett, 2001; Rowan, 2002).

This form of self-exploitation is not something that the law, and certainly not the criminal law, should intervene in. However, it is a cause of concern that some young people are willing to exploit themselves in this way without a real understanding of the potential dangers that can arise. It is not, of course, just the physical danger of someone meeting a 'camgirl', but also the danger that whilst online a girl decides to go 'too far' and later regrets it. If webcam images are broadcast they can be easily captured, saved and distributed. It has been noted elsewhere in this book that once a pornographic image is posted onto the Internet it is virtually impossible for it to be ever removed. Where a camgirl goes 'too far' there is a danger that an (identifiable) photograph of her will circulate the Internet for many years, potentially causing extreme embarrassment for a very long time. A programme of education will need to be put in place to try to inform teenagers of the risks that is posed by this form of exploitation.

CHAPTER 8

Sentencing

Perhaps the most controversial aspect of the criminal justice system is that of sentencing and this is particularly true where the offence for which a person is to be sentenced is a sex offence. The media and various campaign groups have distinctive views on how a sentencing should be carried out and this undoubtedly impacts on public perceptions and policy. This chapter will examine how a person could be sentenced for the crimes set out in the preceding chapters. It will not be possible to provide a comprehensive analysis of sentencing theory and policy because this is something that can (and indeed has) been the subject of a book by itself. Instead, this chapter will concentrate on some of the core themes relevant to the sentencing of sex offenders and, in particular, those convicted of an offence facilitated by information and communication technologies.

The sentencing framework

Recent years have shown an almost unparalleled tension existing between the judiciary and the government, with the principal battle ground being the way that sentencing occurs. Perhaps the most illuminating of these skirmishes was that which erupted over the sentencing of Craig Sweeney, who had been convicted of the abduction and rape of a three-year-old girl. Sweeney was given an indeterminate sentence, but with a minimum period of imprisonment of just five years. The judge had, in fact, stated that he did not know whether Sweeney would ever be released but this comment was not widely reported whereas the reaction of the Home Secretary, John Reid, was. Mr Reid suggested that the judge had passed an 'unduly lenient' sentence and made it quite clear he did not approve (Gillespie, 2006c: 1153).

After several days of anger it became apparent that the judge had passed a perfectly legitimate sentence and, in fact, the only sentence that could have been passed by law. How did this furore erupt and what does a judge need to do when passing sentence?

The purpose of sentencing

The purpose of sentencing has been the topic of debate for many years, with many lawyers and academics debating whether there is a theoretical basis for the sentencing of an offender. The clearest example of a theoretical underpinning to sentencing was probably the *Criminal Justice Act 1991* which was considered to be the 'apotheosis of the proportionality (or 'just deserts') approach to sentencing' (Koffman, 2006: 281). The 'just deserts' theory is based on the premise that a sentence should be proportionate to the wrongdoing (Ashworth and Redmayne, 2005: 26) and thus where a 'wrong' is particularly bad then sentences beyond that which would ordinarily be permitted can be imposed. It is commonly thought that sentencing has, since the CJA 1991, retreated from the desert theory, in part because identifying seriousness is not an easy task, especially where there is a guilty plea (see Koffman, 2006: 290–4 for a useful history of the difficulties encountered by the CJA 1991 approach).

The new sentencing framework is to be found in the *Criminal Justice Act 2003* and it is commonly accepted that this Act does not have at its centre the just deserts theory. Indeed, trying to identify what, if any, theory lies at the heart of the CJA 2003 is particularly problematic (see Taylor et al., 2004: 175). However, the CJA 2003 does, for the first, time explain what the purpose of sentencing should be. It does not do so in a theoretical way but in a pragmatic way set out in statute:

Any court dealing with an offender in respect of his offence must have regard to the following purposes of sentencing:

(a) the punishment of offenders
(b) the reduction of crime (including its reduction by deterrence)
(c) the reform and rehabilitation of offenders
(d) the protection of the public
(e) the making of reparation by offenders to persons affected by their offences.

(s.142(1) CJA 203)

These purposes do not fit into any single description of sentencing theory and indeed they have been criticised as being a 'bran tub' of policies and theories without any real thought (Dennis, 2002: 688). Even a casual understanding of sentencing theory would appear to confirm this criticism with it allegedly 'balancing' desert, restorative and retributive models of sentencing. It has been suggested that this makes it virtually impossible to implement, not least because some of these theories contradict each other and one prediction was that 'nobody [will] refer to it, because it is of little theoretical value and has no practical relevance' (Taylor et al., 2004: 176). In reality, this prediction appears to be accurate because the courts have rarely referred to s.142 and have certainly never explained it. Perhaps the most detailed reference was when the Court listed the provisions set out above and stated:

> *Unless imprisonment is necessary for the protection of the public the court should always give consideration to the question of whether the aims of rehabilitation and thus the reduction of crime cannot better be achieved by a fine or community sentence rather than by imprisonment and whether punishment cannot adequately be achieved by such a sentence ... Particular care should be exercised before imposing a custodial sentence on a first offender.*
> (R v Seed; R v Stark [2007] EWCA Crim 254 per Lord Phillips CJ)

This is an interesting comment because it suggests that a hierarchy of sentences does exist and, in this way, it is very similar to the CJA 1991 which, perhaps most notably, created a hierarchical pyramid of sentencing. Where the Acts differ, however, is in their approach to public protection. It is clear from the comment of the Lord Chief Justice above and indeed the whole rationale of the Act (see below) that the protection of the public is a primary aim of the CJA 2003 (hence its mention in s.142(1)(d)), whereas it was considered a secondary matter for the CJA 1991 (Koffman, 2006: 285). This rationale was subsequently watered down in its later years, particularly after the Labour government was elected in 1997 with several notable pieces of legislation altering the sentencing framework where the public were deemed to be at risk.

Protecting the public

It is clear from the above that the protection of the public is a key theme within the CJA 2003 and according to the Lord Chief Justice this decision arguably acts as a key division between sentencing. Where the public are in need of protection then imprisonment would appear to be the starting point (*Seed; Stark*, op. cit.) whereas where this is not necessary then non-custodial sentences become the starting point. The threshold for custody when the protection of the public is not required will be discussed below but what does protecting the public mean?

One of the most controversial aspects of the CJA 2003 was the way that it handles 'dangerous offenders' (see Chapter 5, Part 12, CJA 2003). Strong action is taken in respect of people they consider dangerous, with the government arguing that it is necessary in order to protect the public. An offender can only be considered dangerous if he commits a relevant offence, i.e. one listed within Schedule 15 of the Act.

Specified offences

Schedule 15 lists over 200 separate offences and virtually every sex offence is contained within it. Certainly every sexual offence discussed in this book is contained within Schedule 15 so it is relevant for our purposes. The concept of relevant offences is then sub-divided into two categories.

The first class is 'specified offences' and these refer to offences that have a maximum sentence of less than ten years' imprisonment (s.224, CJA 2003). For our purposes there are only two offences that have been discussed in this book, namely:

- Indecent photographs of a child (s.160, CJA 1988) (Chapter 4).
- Paying for the sexual services of a 16 or 17 year old child (s.47(5) SOA 2003) (Chapter 7).

The second classification is the 'serious specified offence' and this is a relevant offence that is punishable either by life imprisonment or for a period of at least ten years' imprisonment (s.224(2) CJA 2003). For our purposes all of the other sexual offences listed in this book are serious specified offences. In terms of offences contained within Chapter 2, it should be noted that Sections 18, 20 and 47, *Offences Against the Person Act 1861* are specified (Section 18 being a serious specified offence), although it is less certain that these provisions will be of any real significance in the context of cyber-bullying because of the criteria involved in triggering the provisions (see below).

Sentencing action

The distinction between these classifications is seen from the type of action a court must take when it is decided that it is necessary to protect the public from serious harm. Where it is a serious specified offence and the offence is punishable by a maximum sentence of life imprisonment then a judge should ordinarily consider whether this should be the appropriate sentence (s.225(2) CJA 2003). This is the first time that the courts have been placed under a statutory duty to consider a discretionary life sentence (at other times they have been told to impose a mandatory life sentence) but it is notable that they are not required to pass the sentence but merely to consider whether it is the appropriate sentence. If the offence is punishable by life imprisonment but the court is not satisfied that a life sentence should be imposed or if the offence is punishable by a term of imprisonment for ten years or more then where the finding of risk is made then the court *must* impose a sentence of imprisonment for public protection (s.225(3) CJA 2003).

A sentence of imprisonment for public protection (IPP) is an indefinite sentence, i.e. a person is not released automatically after a set period of time (see below) but may be released only when the parole board is satisfied that they are suitable for release. Controversially, this means that the sentence could result in someone serving a sentence for longer than the period imposed by statute: if the parole board do not believe that a person is eligible for release then they may be kept in gaol, notwithstanding the fact that they will be detained beyond the term which the statute provides.

Where the offence for which the offender is being sentenced for is a specified offence (rather than a serious specified offence), then, when a finding of risk is made, the judge *must* impose an 'extended sentence of imprisonment' (s.227(1) CJA 2003), which means a (determinate) sentence of imprisonment together with an additional term which an offender spends on licence (see below). The extended sentence can be for any period that the court so orders but the extended licence may not be more than five years for a violent offence or eight years for a sexual offence (s.227(4)). In any event, the total extended sentence of imprisonment (i.e. both parts combined) may not be higher than the length of the sentence prescribed by Parliament (s.227(5)). In other

words, if we take as an example s.160, CJA 1988, this is punishable by a maximum sentence of five years' imprisonment. Accordingly, a judge could pass an extended sentence of four years, consisting of one year incarceration and three years on licence, but could not pass a sentence of two years incarceration and four years on licence as the total sentence (six years) would be beyond the statutory maximum.

The mechanics of these sentences will be discussed below but it can be seen that they are interesting in that they are examples of circumstances where a custodial sentence has to be imposed. Sections 225 and 227 are written in mandatory language (a court *must* impose the sentence) although a degree of discretion exists in that it is for a judge to decide whether the risk posed is sufficient to trigger these sections. It does demonstrate why, however, the Lord Chief Justice was careful to distinguish public protection from the ordinary sentencing process (*R v Seed; R v Stark [2007] EWCA Crim 254*) because clearly in those circumstances the custodial threshold is always passed.

Criteria

It can be seen therefore that the decision as to whether it is necessary to protect the public is an important one. What is the criteria for the imposition of these sentences? The Act uses the same test for each of the different types of protection (i.e. life imprisonment, IPP, extended sentence) which can be summarised as:

> ... the court is of the opinion that there is a significant risk to members of the public of serious harm occasioned by the commission by him of further specified offences.
> (s.225(1)(b) CJA 2003)

Central to this definition are the terms 'significant risk' and 'serious harm'. It is also worth noting that the danger is of committing further specified offences and not necessarily the same offence as he has been convicted of. Schedule 15 lists over 200 separate criminal offences which does perhaps broaden the concept of risk. Where a person has a previous conviction for a relevant offence then there is a presumption that the risk is present unless the court concludes it would be unreasonable not to so conclude (s.229(3), CJA 2003).

Guidance on what the terms 'significant risk' and 'serious harm' meant was provided in the case of *R v Lang et al. [2005] EWCA Crim 2864*. The court noted that the risk was in terms of two matters. The first was that the offender would commit a future relevant offence (and in *R v Johnson [2006] EWCA Crim 2486* the Court of Appeal expanded on this point by noting that even where the presumption applies (above) the court must still consider whether there was a risk that the offender would commit a future offence), and the second factor was whether the public (or a member of the public) would be caused serious harm by this re-offending ([2005] EWCA Crim 2864 at [7]). This is an important point as it emphasises that it is not sufficient that there is a future risk of re-offending but, rather, that the public must be protected from serious harm. It has been questioned whether all of the offences contained in Schedule 15 (which includes voyeurism) would necessarily meet this criteria (Thomas, 2006a: 179), but that will be a matter for the courts.

The term 'serious harm' is defined in the Act as including 'death or serious injury, whether physical or psychological' (s.224(3) CJA 2003) and this phrase has been used in other legislative instruments which can assist in the construction of this term. Perhaps the most relevant example for our purposes was its use in s.5A, *Sex Offenders Act 1997* which allowed a court to impose a restraining order (injunction) on a convicted defendant controlling what they could do. In *R v Beaney [2004] EWCA Crim 449* the Court of Appeal held that downloading indecent images of children could cause serious psychological injury to those who were portrayed in the images (see Gillespie, 2004d). This was an important decision and will be discussed in more detail elsewhere in this book (Chapter 9), but it is important in this context because it demonstrates that the meaning of 'serious harm' can be quite wide. Many sexual offences, particularly those in respect of children, can cause psychological distress to the victim and accordingly it does demonstrate that the criteria for these offences could be met reasonably frequently.

An interesting point about these concerns about risk is how this is to be presented to the judge? It has been suggested that evidence of the likely impact an offence may have on a victim may need to be presented to a judge (Thomas, 2007: 181) but who has this responsibility? It could be argued that the prosecution should adduce such evidence, but in England and Wales the prosecution are traditionally considered to be independent in relation to sentencing: it is not for them to 'push' for a particular sentence (see Paragraph 11.8, *Written Standards Applicable to Criminal Cases*), although they do have a responsibility to ensure details of the defendant's background and information is presented.

In terms of whether the defendant poses a risk of future re-offending this is something that can be presented in pre-sentence reports (PSR), prepared by the National Offender Management Service (NOMS). Where a court is considering classifying a person as 'dangerous' a court should ask for a PSR (s.156(3) CJA 2003), but doubt exists whether this always occurs, not least because a failure to do so does not invalidate a sentence (Ashworth, 2005: 349). However, even if a PSR is requested this will only answer part of the question as to whether an offender will re-offend, and not necessarily what the consequences of such re-offending is. Thomas appears to be implying that this kind of evidence should be put before the judiciary but it is difficult to see how this could occur. Also it is submitted that the judiciary are able to take 'judicial notice' of the cumulative evidence they gather through sitting on sex offences etc. Certainly the decision in *Beaney* (op. cit.) does suggest that they are aware of the psychological effects of some crimes.

Guidance

Perhaps one of the more significant changes in recent years is the way that the courts are given 'guidance' over their sentences. Traditionally, sentencing has been considered to be purely a matter for the judiciary and was treated as an essential part of their independence. Guidance was provided by the judiciary themselves through judgments of the Court of Appeal, with some of the judgments being given 'guideline' status which meant the Court explained how 'typical' offenders may be dealt with. At the turn of the century it was decided that this was no longer sufficient and a new creature was created, the *Sentencing Advisory Panel* (SAP).

The SAP was, as its name suggests, simply an advisory body that existed to assist the judiciary. Its members included members of the judiciary, practitioners and academics. The chair is now Andrew Ashworth. The SAP came into existence by statute (*Crime and Disorder Act 1998*) and would, upon the invitation of the Court of Appeal, produce advice on possible guidelines for offenders. The SAP would issue a public consultation document and then formulate its views which were then handed to the Court of Appeal. The Court was obliged to consider the guidelines but was not bound by them and could depart from them if they so wished. A good example of doing so was in connection with the original guideline on sentencing relating to indecent photographs of children, see Gillespie, 2003.

This procedure worked reasonably well (Thomas, 2002: 486), but it did not ease the political controversy surrounding sentencing and ultimately the government wished to play an increasing role in the setting of sentences. The CJA 2003 kept the SAP as a body but introduced a new layer into the guidelines system through the creation of the *Sentencing Guidelines Council* (SGC). However, it had been suggested by two formal reviews of the sentencing and the criminal justice system that guidelines had to go beyond sentencing for specific crimes towards more general guidance on sentencing *per se* and indeed procedural matters such as allocation, i.e. whether a matter should be heard in the Magistrates' Court or Crown Court (see Taylor et al., 2004: 199).

Rather than widen the remit of the SAP it was decided to create the SGC as a new body. The Council, like the SAP, would include people other than members of the judiciary and significant controversy existed over what role the government should play. After much debate in the House of Lords it was eventually decided that the government could nominate a person who can attend meetings of the Council and present views but who would not be a formal part of the Council or, therefore, eligible to vote (s.167(9) CJA 2003). The Council is chaired by the Lord Chief Justice (s.169(1)(a)) and a majority of its members are members of the judiciary (seven members of the judiciary (eight including the Lord Chief Justice) compared to four non-judicial members) and accordingly there is, at the very least, the appearance of judicial independence remaining intact. The SAP continues to exist but instead of now providing advice direct to the Court of Appeal it is now sent to the Council who will produce the definitive guidance.

At the time of the first guideline the tension between the government, Parliament and the judiciary was reignited when a question was raised as to whether the Council must consult Parliament before issuing a guideline. The statute is silent as to this, merely stating that proposals (known as 'draft guidelines') must be sent to:

- The Secretary of State (meaning the Home Secretary).
- Such persons as the Lord Chancellor considers appropriate.
- Such other persons as the Council considers appropriate.

(s.170(8), CJA 2003)

It will be remembered that before this stage has been received a full public consultation will have occurred through the SAP, but despite this it was ultimately decided that Parliament should be added to the list of consultees, although it was never resolved whether this was because either the Lord Chancellor, the SGC or both considered 'it appropriate' to do so. Ultimately, this means that the position is as follows.

Stage 1: The SGC or SAP decides that guidance is required, or existing guidelines need to be updated.

Stage 2: The SAP produce a consultation paper which is sent to a number of statutory and non-statutory bodies and put out for general consultation.

Stage 3: The SAP produce formal advice and send this to the SGC.

Stage 4: The SGC formulate a draft guideline on the basis of this advice.

Stage 5: The draft guideline is sent to the Home Secretary, Lord Chancellor, Parliament and any one else they think they should consult (e.g. the police and, occasionally, charitable bodies such as the NSPCC etc.).

Stage 6: The SGC formulates the final guideline after taking into account the responses to this consultation.

It can be seen, therefore, that this is certainly not a streamlined procedure and where there is political controversy over what is being suggested the position can become incredibly complicated. A classic example of this is the guidance in respect of the sexual offences. It has been noted already in this book that the SOA 2003 dramatically altered the law in respect of sexual offences and it came into force on 1 May 2004. On 7 June 2006 the SGC published a draft guideline on the SOA 2003. This was an interesting guideline in that there had not been a formal consultation by the SAP although some of its previous advice (most notably on rape and offences involving child pornography) were taken into account.

Before the guideline was produced it was obvious that some time was taken preparing it, but by June 2006 the draft guideline had been produced. The guideline was made final on 30 April 2007, some ten months after the publication of the draft guideline. This can be contrasted with, for example, guidelines on domestic violence which went from draft guideline to final guideline in just over 6 months, with a similar timeline being taken up with the guideline on the reduction in sentence for a guilty plea (see below) taking less than three months. Part of the delay was undoubtedly taken up with the fact that there are a lot of crimes within the SOA 2003, but it is also understood that some of the delay is as a result of awaiting feedback from the Home Office and (to a lesser extent) Parliament. It is important that guidelines are produced in a timely fashion.

What is the status of a definitive guideline? A court must 'have regard' to a definitive guideline (s.172, SOA 2003), but does this mean they are bound by them? This issue has been addressed by the courts, perhaps most notably in *Attorney-General's Reference (Nos 14 and 15 of 2006) [2006] EWCA Crim 1335*, an extremely controversial case which again led to disagreements between the judiciary and the government. Webster was convicted of raping a six-month old baby whilst French, his girlfriend, filmed the incident. The trial judge felt obliged to give a one-third discount to the sentence because of the SGC guideline that indicated that a 'red-handed' defendant (i.e. one who had no option but to plead guilty) still must receive the discount. The Court of Appeal specifically addressed this guideline:

> Guidelines do no more than provide guidance . . . There may well be circumstances which justify [departing from the guidance] . . . We have difficulty, however, in seeing how section 172 [of the CJA 2003] can be said to be complied with if a judge deliberately or inadvertently flouts the guideline . . .
>
> ([2006] EWCA Crim 1335 at [52] per Lord Phillips CJ)

In other words the Court is saying that guidelines only provide guidance and so there is room to manoeuvre but not where the intended actions of the judge would completely contradict the guidelines. Thomas, the leading academic author on sentencing, notes that the effect of this is that

'it is not open to the Court [of Appeal] to overrule the Council, or to qualify the guideline' (Thomas, 2006b: 948) before stating that the only way the guideline can be altered is if the mechanism above is followed. This is undoubtedly an extremely burdensome procedure and it is notable that the government is currently looking at providing ways to give discretion back to judges. This is somewhat ironic given one of the purposes of the SGC was to remove discretion from individual judges. It perhaps serves as a useful lesson that sentencing is not easy and has often been described as more of an art than a science, i.e. it is not possible to always get consistency and, perhaps more importantly, if the rules are tinkered with in respect of one case the potential repercussions reverberate far beyond the individual decision.

Types of sentence

Before examining how sentencing could occur for the types of crimes that have been discussed here it is worth pausing to consider the types of sentence that can now be imposed and what the criteria for such sentences are. It has been noted already that the CJA 1991 adopted a definite sentencing pyramid but it has been suggested that the CJA 2003 effectively mirrors this through the creation of a 'penal ladder' (Ashworth, 2004: 382). The penal ladder is, in essence, a way of describing the way in which a sentence escalates according to the circumstances of the case.

Discharges

The lowest penalty a court can order is a discharge. There are, in fact, two types of discharges known as *conditional discharges* and *absolute discharges*, the latter being the more lenient of the two. An absolute discharge requires nothing of an offender and so is, in effect, a conviction without punishment (Ashworth, 2004: 295). The conditional discharge differs in that it does not impose any immediate punishment on an offender but it carries with it a condition that an offender does not commit any further criminal offences for a period of time fixed by the court, which can be a maximum of up to three years (s.12(1)(b) *Powers of Criminal Courts (Sentencing) Act 2000*).

Where an offender has been conditionally discharged and they breach this discharge (by committing another offence), then the offender is liable to be not only sentenced for the crime that they committed which led to the discharge being breached but the offender can be re-sentenced for the original offence (s.13, PCC(S)A 2000).

A discharge (including a conditional discharge) is not ordinarily considered to be a 'conviction' for most purposes (s.14, PCC(S)A 2000). There are exceptions to this, particularly in respect of the recruitment and vetting of staff, but these are generally quite limited. Prior to the SOA 2003 there was confusion as to whether a person discharged for a qualifying sex offence was subject to the notification requirements (for details on the effect of this see below). The language of the SOA 1997, which established the notification requirements, referred to a conviction and accordingly if a discharge was not a 'conviction' then this would mean that a person discharged would not be subject to the requirements (see Gillespie, 2002b). The Court of Appeal in *R v Longworth [2004] EWCA Crim 2145* argued that this was wrong and that Parliament had clearly intended discharges to be within the notification requirements. Whilst this was undoubtedly true it did not alter the fact that this was not supported by the wording of the statutes, and the House of Lords ([2006] UKHL 1) ultimately agreed that those discharged under the 1997 legislation were not subject to the notification requirements.

Ultimately, the decision in *Longworth* was historical (although see Gillespie, 2004c who suggests that it may have some practical consequences) because the SOA 2003 altered the law to ensure that those who are conditionally discharged for a sex offence are subject to the notification requirements (s.134, SOA 2003). However, it should be noted that where an offender is given an absolute discharge rather than a conditional discharge that person is *not* subject to notification requirements. The courts have been warned, however, that they should not use absolute discharges to circumvent the notification requirements (see, for example, *R v O'Carroll (Application for Amendment) [2003] EWCA Crim 53*).

Financial penalties

Next on the ladder of penalties is the financial penalty ('fine'). The courts have used fines for a considerable period of time and it is realistically a purely punitive measure in that it cannot have any purpose other than to punish an offender. It is not infrequently combined with a compensation order which, of course, allows a victim to be compensated for the harm caused by the offender, but their use is somewhat controversial.

In the arena of sex offences it has to be recognised that realistically a fine will be of limited use. Within the definitive guideline on sex offences a fine was suggested as a starting point for only one offence (sexual activity in a public lavatory (s.71, SOA 2003) see SAP 2007: 95) although admittedly it considered its use appropriate for some other offences where mitigation can be shown. However, it is submitted that it would be extremely unlikely for a fine to be imposed for a sexual offence as contained in this book.

Community sentences

The diet of community sentences has always been complicated (Ashworth, 2000: 278–93) and the CJA 2003 has attempted, to some degree, to simplify this by introducing a single order known as the 'community order' (s.177, CJA 2003). Whether it can be said to simplify the system, however, is highly debatable since the single order can have a series of requirements imposed on them, those being:

(a) an unpaid work requirement
(b) an activity requirement
(c) a programme requirement
(d) a prohibited activity requirement
(e) a curfew requirement
(f) an exclusion requirement
(g) a residence requirement
(h) a mental health treatment requirement
(i) a drug rehabilitation requirement
(j) an alcohol treatment requirement
(k) a supervision requirement
(l) in a case where the offender is aged under 25, an attendance centre requirement.

Most of these requirements were already permissible under the old regime but the principal change is making them all express and allowing them to be used in any combination. In essence, the requirements are designed to allow a court to combine punitive, rehabilitative and preventative requirements thus leading to an appropriate sentence.

Particular requirements

Whilst it is not necessary to consider all of the factors above, the most relevant for the purposes of sex offenders will be discussed.

Unpaid work requirement

Section 199 of the CJA 2003 discusses the unpaid work requirement and sub-section (2) states that the requirement is for not less than 40 and no more than 300 hours work. Interestingly, sub-section (5) states that whilst it is possible to make consecutive orders, the total amount of unpaid work is not to be greater than 300 hours. Section 200(1) states that it is the probation officer who is responsible for allocating the work and how frequently the work will be undertaken but s.200(2) states that the work should normally be completed within twelve months of the order.

Activity requirement

Section 201 discusses the activity requirement and it requires a person to present themself to a place, or places, where the activity will occur. Section 201(2) expressly states that the activities can include activities relating to reparation, including meetings between victims and offenders, but the activities are not designed to be restricted in this way and it could also include employment activities etc. (Taylor et al., 2004: 220). Section 201(5) limits the number of days an offender can be required to participate in an activity to an aggregate of 60.

Programme requirement

Section 202 states that a court can order a person to participate in a programme. This is a particularly useful provision in the context of sex offenders as s.202(1) defines a programme as 'an accredited programme specified in the order' and this must include sex offender treatment programmes. The success, or otherwise, of sex offender programmes has been a matter of some debate (see, for example, Silverman and Wilson, 2002: 54–100 and 2002: 65–85), although there does appear to be some evidence to suggest that it can help prevent reoffending (Grubin, 1998). Section 202(3)(b) states that the Secretary of State will authorise a body to be the accrediting body who will have the right to accredit individual programmes and this will, accordingly, ensure that only appropriate courses are certified for these purposes.

Prohibited activity

Section 203 states that a court may require an offender not to do an activity on either the day or days specified or during a period specified. Sub-section (2) states that the court can only make this order after consultation with a probation officer, although it is important to note that there is no suggestion that the court is bound to follow the advice of the officer, the only requirement is to discuss the proposed order with the officer. Taylor et al. argue that this is a wide order that could prevent someone from attending, for example, a football match (Taylor et al., 2004: 220).

It is unlikely, however, that a court would necessarily have to use this section in the context of a sex offender since it is possible, upon the time of conviction, to make a Sex Offence Prevention Order (s.104, SOA 2003 and see Chapter 9) and, as will be seen, this is perhaps more versatile. That said, however, it may be that where the court was thinking about passing a community order it may decide that it is more proportionate to use this requirement rather than an additional power.

Exclusion requirement

Section 205 governs the exclusion requirement and sub-section (1) defines this as 'prohibiting the offender from entering a place specified in the order for a period so specified'. Sub-section (2) states that the period cannot be more than two years and sub-section (3) states that it is possible to exclude someone from a place on certain specified dates rather than for a whole period of time (i.e. 3, 6 and 9 March rather than 3 to 9 March).

Again, whether this will be used for sex offenders is more open to question as the Sex Offence Prevention Order can also prohibit an offender from entering a location and, as will be seen, the duration is not limited to two years and so it may be more appropriate.

Residence requirement

Section 206 provides the court with the opportunity to require a person to reside at a particular location, but s.206(4) states that a court can only require the person to stay in a hostel or other institution when this has been recommended by the probation board. This could, conceivably, be a useful order in terms of sex offending, especially where there has been an impact on the family. Presumably the court could decide that whilst a person is being subject to treatment they should not live in the family home and using an exclusionary requirement it could prevent the offender from being at the family premises.

Breach of a community order

Having a flexible diet of community orders is one thing, and placing requirements onto an offender may seem appropriate but what happens if the offender does not abide by them? The CJA 2003 introduces new measures to deal with the breach of a community order, the details being provided by schedule 8 of the Act.

The initial breach is dealt with administratively in terms of the relevant probation order issuing a written warning to the offender (Taylor et al., 2004: 225). If there is a second breach within twelve months then the matter must be brought back to the court where there are three options:

> (i) *Vary the order by making it more onerous.*
> (ii) *Revoke the order and sentence the offender in any way it could at the time of the original sentence.*
> (iii) *Where the matter was not capable of being dealt with by imprisonment, sentencing the offender by a term of imprisonment of not more than 51 weeks.*
>
> (s.226)

The latter is very interesting and certainly a more draconian approach than with the previous community orders but is somewhat irrelevant to sex offenders where every offence is imprisonable. Of course an interesting argument would be in connection with the sentencing guidelines. It may be that a sex offender commits an offence to an extent that would not normally be imprisonable, e.g. downloading a moderate amount of indecent images of children classified at levels 1 and 2 (see below). If, under these circumstances, the court had provided a community order then, presumably, after breach of this order the court may decide to pass a custodial sentence. This could be justified either because the offence is punishable by a custodial sentence so this was (theoretically) open to the court at the time of sentence or, by virtue of the ability to imprison under these circumstances.

An offender may breach the order not only by failing to fulfil a requirement but also by committing a further offence. In these circumstances the court who is dealing with the later offence can, along with passing a sentence for this latest crime, revoke the community order and sentence the offender in a way that it could do so at the time of the initial crime, i.e. if it is an imprisonable offence send the person to prison etc.

Suspended sentence of imprisonment

The suspended sentence of imprisonment has been in existence for only a relatively short period of time (Ashworth, 2000: 293), and in recent times was extremely controversial and was, indeed, *de facto* abolished for a time, being permitted only in exceptional circumstances (Ashworth, 2000: 293–6). Yet the CJA 2003 has reintroduced it (s.189, CJA 2003).

The essence of a suspended sentence of imprisonment is that it is a custodial sentence but one that does not require the offender to enter custody immediately but, rather, to stay at large on condition of being of good behaviour (Taylor et al., 2004: 243). Accordingly, a court should only pass a suspended sentence when it is satisfied that the offence is so serious that a custodial sentence should be imposed.

The 2003 Act permits a court to suspend a custodial sentence of not less than 28 weeks and no more than 51 weeks for a period of between six months and two years (s.189(1)(3) CJA 2003). Previously a suspended sentence merely acted as a 'sword of Damocles' above the head of the offender, but the revised suspended sentence differs in that it permits the court to make requirements on the offender. In essence, therefore, the suspended sentence of imprisonment allows some of the aspects of a community order to be imposed on an offender. This provides the court with a significant degree of flexibility since although the breach of a community order can lead to the offender being sentenced again, the suspended sentence of imprisonment sends a signal to the offender that they know exactly what the sentence to be imposed on them will be if they breach any of the requirements, i.e. a custodial sentence.

There is within the provisions of the CJA 2003 the ability of a court to review a suspended sentence (ss. 191–2, CJA 2003) i.e. to return the matter to the court to allow for the judge to monitor the progress of the sentence. Whilst, in theory, this may be a useful step and some judges have suggested a need for the court to be involved, it must be questioned how useful this provision will be given that the criminal justice system is already suffering delays due to the volume of work it has provided to it. There may be an argument to suggest that the judge will be interested to see how the orders they made are working, but it is more likely that the courts will simply make the order and rely on the parties to seek a variation where required or to revisit the argument if breach occurs.

Custodial sentences

A sentence requiring the offender to be committed to gaol is perhaps the most well-known sentence and, in the context of sex offenders, one of the more popular measures. However, popularity by itself is an insufficient reason to send someone to prison and a person should only be imprisoned where it is necessary to do so. It is clear from the sexual offences guidelines that sexual offenders can ordinarily expect a custodial sentence, especially in relation to the offences that have been discussed in this book.

Before the enactment of the CJA 2003 the length of time a person spent in prison depended heavily on the length of the sentence imposed. Custodial sentences were divided into four categories:

- Sentences under 12 months
- Sentences of more than 12 months but less than four years
- Sentences of four years or more
- Life imprisonment

Leaving aside life imprisonment which will be discussed below, the sentence was divided into three segments. The first segment was the time served in prison. The second segment was the time served on licence and the third segment was the 'dead time' where, in essence, the defendant was not subject to any restrictions (Ashworth, 2000: 258). A sentence of under 12 months' imprisonment had only two segments. A person was eligible for release after 50 per cent of their sentence and the remaining 50 per cent was 'dead time' (s.33(1)(a) CJA 1991). Where a sentence of under four years was passed then the prisoner was released after 50 per cent, a person remained on licence until the 75 per cent point and the remaining 25 per cent was 'dead time' (s.33(1)(b) CJA 1991). A sentence of more than four years was more complicated. A person was eligible for release at the 50 per cent point (with the parole

board having the discretion to release) (s.35(1) CJA 1991). If he was not released he had to be released at the two-thirds point (s.33(2) CJA 1991) and regardless of when release occurred, a person remained on licence until the 75 per cent point and the remaining 25 per cent was 'dead time'.

The CJA 2003 has removed these rather complicated provisions and replaced it with a more streamlined version. In essence, the CJA 2003 divides custodial sentences into two types of sentence; determinate sentences and indeterminate sentences.

Determinate sentences

The first, and more usual, sentence is a determinate sentence, i.e. where a judge sentences a person to a fixed term of imprisonment (be it a period of weeks or years). At the time of writing (Autumn 2007) the law does not draw a distinction in the duration of the sentence although this is scheduled to change at some point with different rules eventually applying to custodial sentences under 12 months (see below).

The basic rule with determinate custodial sentences is that there are now only two segments to a sentence; the period spent in actual custody and the period spent on licence. The CJA 2003 is clear that licences now last the full-length of the sentence (s.249(1) CJA 2003) and a person must be released after one-half of the determinate sentence (s.244(1) (3) CJA 2003). This means that all those who are sentenced to a determinate period in custody will now serve one-half of their sentence in custody and the remainder on licence. Where a person is sentenced to a term of imprisonment greater than twelve months then the court can recommend conditions on the licence (s.238, CJA 2003) although the Secretary of State is not bound by these recommendations (he must merely 'have regard' to them) and so the decision remains an executive one.

Early release

Although an offender must be released after serving half of their sentence it is possible that they could be released even earlier. The CJA 2003 includes provision for certain offenders to be released up to 135 days early (s.246) although a curfew condition must be made (s.246(5) CJA 2003). A curfew condition restricts an offender to designated premises (usually his house) for set periods of the day (usually the night). The conditions will ordinarily also include provision for the offender to be fitted with an electronic tag to monitor this curfew. The curfew and tag would remain active until the half-way point although it is legally permissible for these to be extended by making them a condition of the licence. It is, realistically, unlikely that this would happen however.

Extended licence

In the late 1990s considerable focus was placed on those who commit sex offences and, in particular, how they should be sentenced after conviction. One of the key changes introduced by the *Crime and Disorder Act 1998* (later consolidated in the *Powers of Criminal Courts (Sentencing) Act 2000*) was the provision of an extended sentence, meaning an extended licence (s.58, CDA 1998; s.85, PCC(S)A 2000).

As has been noted above, a custodial sentence consists of two elements, the period of incarceration and a period on which an offender serves on licence. The licence period is a percentage of the custodial element and thus is ordinarily a mathematical exercise. The extended licence provisions were designed to permit a judge the discretion (for sexual and violent offenders) to extend the licence beyond that which it would ordinarily reach. Given that licences can carry conditions this means that an offender can be subject to additional supervision and control with the hope that this assists in the rehabilitation of an offender (see, for example, *R v Gilbert [2007] EWCA Crim 1244*). The 'stick' that was attached to an extended licence was that an offender who breaches the licence conviction is subject to recall to gaol (and this is an administrative recall). Of course, an extended licence means that a person is liable to return to gaol beyond that which they would ordinarily be and accordingly the courts have been careful to ensure that any extended licence is commensurate and justified (see Ashworth, 2000: 188).

Extended licences proved to be quite successful and were used in conjunction with sex offender treatment programmes, especially where a programme would ordinarily not be available to an offender as a result of the short length of the custodial sentence. It was used reasonably frequently for those convicted of offences relating to abusive images of children (see, for example, *R*

v Sear [2003] EWCA Crim 2560 where an 'average' case involved the use of an extended sentence).

The 'dangerousness' provisions of the CJA 2003 (see above) brought about a fundamental change in the extended licence provisions. The CJA 2003 repealed s.85, PCC(S)A 2000 meaning that for offences after the commencement date (4 April 2005) an extended sentence can only be passed under the CJA 2003 regime. The CJA 2003 restricts extended sentences to specified offences and is, in effect, the counterpart to imprisonment for public protection. Accordingly, if an offence is a serious specified offence (instead of a specified offence) then the court no longer has any power to pass an extended licence and must, if the criteria is satisfied, pass a sentence of imprisonment for public protection. The extension period for sexual offences cannot exceed eight years (s.227(4)(b) CJA 2003) and nor can the total sentence, custodial element plus extension, exceed the statutory maximum for the offence (s.227(5) CJA 2003 c.f. the position for imprisonment for public protection, below). For example:

> D has been convicted of possessing indecent images of children contrary to s.160, Criminal Justice Act 1988. The judge sentences D to an extended sentence and specifies the custodial element as being eighteen months. The maximum extended licence will therefore now be 36 months (as the maximum sentence for s.160 is five years' imprisonment).

The change between the PCC(S)A 2000 and CJA 2003 regimes is significant. Under the 2000 regime not only were there more offences that the sentence could be imposed for, but the criteria was wider. Indeed in *R v Gilbert [2007] EWCA Crim 1244* it was noted that the courts did not, under the previous regime, have to consider that there was a risk of serious harm to the public (at [8]). Currently, although the sentence may be desirable, for example in order to permit an offender to undertake a sex offender treatment programme, a court can only impose the sentence where they are satisfied that the offender poses a risk of serious harm to the public. The second significant change is how an offender is released from an extended sentence.

Under the extended licence (PCC(S)A 2000) scheme an offender was released in the usual way for offences regulated by the CJA 1991 and the licence would then apply until the end of the extension period. However, under the CJA 2003 a person is only *eligible* for release at the half-way point for the custodial element but may only be released at that point if the parole board order his release (s.247, CJA 2003). The parole board may only order the prisoner's release if they consider that it is no longer 'necessary for the protection of the public that the prisoner should be confined' (s.247(3) CJA 2003). If the parole board continue to refuse release then the prisoner will stay in gaol until the end of the custodial element at which point he has to be released (s.247(4) CJA 2003). Regardless at which point the prisoner is released he will remain on licence (and subject to recall to gaol) until the end of the extension time. An example may clarify this:

> *D has been sentenced to an extended sentence consisting of two years' in custody and three years' extended licence. D is eligible for release after spending one-year in gaol and must be released by the end of the second year. Regardless of when D is released he will be subject to a licence until the end of the fifth year (two years custody plus three years extension).*

Custodial sentences of under 12 months

The CJA 2003 intended for custodial sentences of less than 12 months to be radically different from how they operated pre-CJA 2003 and indeed now. The emphasis on short custodial sentences would be a variable custodial element and a licence period, with the intention that this may assist offenders in their effort not to re-offend. The scheme has not yet come into force, not least because there have been concerns whether the *National Offender Management Service* (NOMS) could cope with the increased workload that this would bring.

The framework for the new sentences of under 12 months is set out in s.181 of the CJA 2003 and, like the other determinate sentences, consists of two elements; the custodial element and the licence period (s.181(2)). The custodial element is between two and 13 weeks (s.181(5)) and the supervision period must be at least 26 weeks in length (s.181(6)) although the total sentence must not exceed 51 weeks (s.181(2)). Where two or more consecutive custody plus sentences are passed then the custodial element may not exceed 26 weeks and the total sentence must not exceed 65 weeks (s.181(7)). This may appear to be similar to the existing position but it is important to note that unlike with determinate sentences currently, the custodial and licence periods do not have to be equal. Accordingly, when this section is in force a judge could, if he so wished, impose a custodial term of six weeks and a licence period of 30 weeks.

Unlike longer determinate sentences where NOMS will decide the conditions of the licence, for offences under 12 months the court will have the power to attach conditions to the licence (s.181(3)), these being defined in s.182(1) as:

(a) an unpaid work requirement
(b) an activity requirement
(c) a programme requirement
(d) a prohibited activity requirement
(e) a curfew requirement
(f) an exclusion requirement
(g) a supervision requirement
(h) in a case where the offender is aged under 25, an attendance centre requirement.

These requirements are taken from the list of requirements within the community order and are defined in the same way. Potentially, this could make a short custodial sentence a more suitable punishment. Prior to the CJA 2003 coming into force there was very little point in sending a sex offender to prison for less than twelve months (since they would not receive any treatment programme either in prison or in the community), and under the current system (i.e. prior to s.181 coming into force) it remains problematic since the licence period is dependent on the custodial period and thus a short prison sentence is coupled with a short licence period which may be of little rehabilitative benefit.

Indeterminate sentences

Along with passing determinate sentences it is possible that a court may decide that it needs to pass an indeterminate sentence, i.e. although the term of imprisonment will be satisfied, the offender will only be released from prison when he no longer poses a risk to society. There are, following the CJA 2003, two forms of indeterminate sentence, a life sentence and imprisonment for public protection.

Life sentence

Many offences are punishable by a maximum term of life imprisonment, including several sexual offences. Murder is the only offence that is punishable *only* by life imprisonment and this is known as a mandatory life sentence. For our purposes the discussion concerns discretionary life sentence, i.e. where the court has the power to impose any sentence ranging from an absolute discharge to life imprisonment.

Prior to the CJA 2003 there was no statutory criteria governing when a judge should impose a discretionary life sentence and it has been suggested that the effect of the CJA 2003 is to replace previous practice (Ashworth, 2005: 210). Under this previous custom, a life sentence was restricted to grave cases where an offender posed a high risk of harm (ibid.). This meant that it was a comparatively rare sentence to be handed down by the courts. The CJA 2003 links the discretionary life sentence with the concept of 'dangerousness'.

Where a person is being sentenced for a serious specified offence and the court *'considers that the seriousness of the offences . . . is such as to justify the imposition of a sentence of imprisonment for life'* then the court must impose such a sentence (s.225(2) CJA 2003). However, the statute does not indicate what would make a case so serious as to justify the imposition of a life sentence and, accordingly, the courts will probably simply revert to previous custom and reserve such sentences for only the most serious of cases where it is not possible to accurately predict how long a person will remain a risk to the general public at the time of sentence (see *R v Chapman [2000] 1 Cr App R 7*).

It is important to note what life imprisonment actually means. Apart from the rare situations when a person will be told that a life sentence will mean they spend the rest of their life in gaol (see s.82A(4) *Powers of Criminal Courts (Sentencing) Act 2000* (PCC(S)A)), a prisoner will eventually be released. Identifying the minimum period a person must serve is discussed below. After the minimum period has been served a person can apply to the parole board for release and if they decide to release him then the Secretary of State must release the prisoner on licence (s.28, *Crime (Sentences) Act 1997* (C(S)A 1997). The licence lasts for the rest of that person's life (s.31, C(S)A 1997) unless it is revoked and a person is returned to prison.

Imprisonment for public protection

Imprisonment for public protection (IPP) has been discussed above and is an indeterminate sentence in that an offender will not be automatically released when his term of imprisonment ends. Indeed, the Court of Appeal has suggested that there are no significant differences between a life sentence and IPP (*R v*

Lang et al [2005] EWCA Crim 2864). In reality there are only two differences. The first is that it is not open to a court to say that a person is so dangerous that they may never be released (see above), and the second is that when a person subject to IPP is released on licence he may apply to the parole board after a period of at least ten years for his licence to be terminated (s.31A, C(S)A 1997). The parole board must decide whether the offender continues to pose a danger (s.31A(4) C(S)A 1997), and if they reject the application then an offender can re-apply every twelve months (s.31A(3) C(S)A 1997). In other words, although the licence *may* last the offender's lifetime it need not.

Determining the minimum period of detention

It has been noted that for both life sentences and IPP an offender will usually be told that he is eligible for release on licence (although the final decision on whether the offender is actually released lies with the parole board). How is the minimum period calculated? It is a relatively complicated process and it should ordinarily be explained in open court (*Consolidated Practice Direction, I.7.2*). The statutory framework governing the setting of the minimum period is set out in s.82A(2) PCC(S)A 2000. It requires the judge to consider the sentence he would have imposed had he not imposed either a life sentence or IPP. In other words, he must consider what the determinate sentence would have been. Although s.82A(2) does not expressly say so, it is clear that along with considering the seriousness of the offence and any aggravating factors, the judge must consider the mitigation too. The judge must then take account of the fact that if it were a determinate sentence the offender would be released after serving half his sentence (see above) and accordingly this notional figure should be halved. From this figure the period the prisoner has already spent in prison on remand (if applicable) will also be deducted, with the resulting figure being the minimum custodial period to be served.

One of the difficulties with this approach is that it could mean that a relatively low figure is produced. This is especially the case with IPP where the notional starting figure cannot exceed the statutory maximum (*Lang et al [2005] EWCA Crim 2864* at [10]). The pronouncement of a low figure (e.g. four years or six years) can cause problems in terms of public perceptions where the media tend to forget the fact that it is an indeterminate sentence and that, theoretically, the offender may never be released from prison. Where the determinate sentence is pronounced, although the actual length of time a person will serve is announced, the 'headline' figure tends to be the sentence. In terms of public perception, '12 years imprisonment' sounds significantly longer than 'a minimum of six years imprisonment' even though, in reality, the two terms are identical.

Sentencing guidelines

This section of the chapter will discuss the likely sentences that could be passed for the sentences discussed in this book, but before doing this it is necessary to consider factors that may influence the decision. Some factors have been discussed already but there are some further general factors that can either aggravate or mitigate a sentence and it would be prudent to discuss these.

Aggravating factors

Prior to the CJA 2003 being implemented the concept of aggravation was realistically left to the courts to determine and it had been suggested that:

> It is not difficult to think of a handful of aggravating factors which are well established . . . offences by groups or gangs; offences against young, elderly or otherwise vulnerable victims; offences involving the abuse of trust or authority; racially motivated offences; and offences involving planning or organisation.
>
> (Ashworth, 2000: 134)

Whilst, as it will be seen, this remains true, the CJA 2003 has introduced a number of statutory aggravating factors (Ashworth, 2005, 151). Perhaps the most notable of these being a previous conviction, although additional factors include committing the offence whilst on bail, committing a crime for a racist or religious purpose or against disability or on the grounds of sexual orientation (Ashworth, 2005: 153–5). Most of these are not commonly important in sexual offences although previous convictions are.

Previous convictions

An interesting factor that is often cited is that of previous convictions. It will be seen immediately below that where a person is convicted for the first time, or convicted rarely, then this may be

considered a mitigating factor. However, previous convictions are not necessarily a neutral characteristic either because where there are a number of relevant offences, especially in connection with sexual offences, it is not uncommon for the courts to consider this to be an aggravating factor. The CJA 2003 reinforced this by providing statutory authority for this proposition:

> In considering the seriousness of an offence . . . committed by an offender who has one or more previous convictions, the court must treat each previous conviction as an aggravating factor if . . . the court considers that it can be so treated having regard to –
> (a) the nature of the offence to which the conviction relates and its relevance to the current offence, and
> (b) the time that has elapsed since conviction.
>
> (s.143(2) CJA 2003)

This is an interesting provision because it expressly states that the provisions are mandatory – the court *shall* treat it as an aggravating factor, albeit this requirement being tempered slightly by the relevancy exceptions. However, this clearly states Parliament's intention that relevant previous convictions should be considered an aggravating factor rather than the loss of a mitigating factor (see below for further argument on this).

Employment

An interesting factor that has to be considered is whether the employment of an offender should be treated as an aggravating factor even when this is not a *prima facie* abuse of trust in connection with the victim. In many situations the employment status of an offender could amount to a mitigating factor because it is considered that they have done something to benefit society (see, for example, *R v Parvin [2005] EWCA Crim 3502* where the appellant was a police officer). However, could it also be considered an aggravating factor? It could be argued that where a person is in a position of authority (e.g. judge, police officer, cleric, elected official) the crime could be considered to be especially serious as there is a breach of trust over the community. This appears to have been accepted by the courts:

It is critical that the public retain full confidence in our police force. A feature of the trust that must exist is that the public can expect that they will not be assaulted by officers even if they are being a nuisance. Any erosion of that basic but reasonable expectation will do profound harm to the good relationship that must exist between the police service.

(*R v Dunn [2003] 2 Cr App R (S) 535*
cited in Ashworth, 2005: 158)

This reasoning is perfectly understood where, as in the case above, the crime was committed by a police officer purporting to exercise their lawful authority. However, could this be extended further? Is the basis of the trust explained by the Court of Appeal that society will grant to certain people special powers of authority but on that basis they expect them not to act in a criminal manner? It has been suggested that this could be justified on the basis of deterrence, although Ashworth argues that given there are other consequences of conviction (most notably likely dismissal and public humiliation), it would appear difficult to accept the realism of deterrence (Ashworth, 2005: 158). Whilst this may be true will it arise as a matter of retribution, i.e. that society considers the actions of those in authority as serious.

The issue does not yet appear to be settled. The *Sentencing Advisory Panel* (SAP) produced guidance to the Court of Appeal on the sentencing of offences relating to child pornography, and in their consultation paper they stated:

. . . there are some circumstances in which the commission of such an offence by a defendant of good standing within the community may be regarded as aggravating rather than mitigating the seriousness of the offence.

(SAP, 2002a para 46)

By the time the actual advice was provided to the Court of Appeal this paragraph had been omitted (see, in particular, SAP, 2002b paras 40 and 45) and when the Court of Appeal itself issued the guideline (*R v Oliver et al [2002] EWCA Crim 2766* and see below), they did not see any need to reintroduce it. This has been followed by the definitive guideline where they have likewise failed to make any reference to the issue of good standing.

The issue of public standing is an interesting one and certainly from a political perspective it is possible to see any number of instances where people have lost their job over something that no ordinary member of the public would (e.g. sexual scandal etc.). It is often said that this happens because society expects certain standards and requires action to be taken when its officials fail to meet this standard. Could they, by analogy, demand a severe sentence notwithstanding the fact that the conviction itself will have significant consequences? (loss of job, reputation etc.) It could be argued that it does, but within the sexual context, apart from situations where the offence has been committed whilst in the position of authority (e.g. a police officer raping a woman on duty) and where this is undoubtedly a breach of trust, it does not appear that this is treated as an aggravating factor.

Abuse of trust

The term 'abuse of trust' is a variable concept. The SOA 2003 introduced a number of specific offences relating to situations where there is an abuse of a position of trust (ss. 16–24, SOA 2003). These offences relate to situations where an adult is in a position of responsibility over a child through, for example, being a teacher, foster-carer, guardian, doctor, etc. (see s.21, SOA 2003). However, within sentencing, the concept of 'abuse of trust' or abuse of authority is a much wider context and includes situations which would not be covered by the substantive abuse of trust offences but which nevertheless involves an abuse of trust with the child. Common examples of this could include childminders (*Attorney-General's Reference (No 125 of 2002) [2003] EWCA Crim 1166*), child group leaders (*R v MD(J) [2005] EWCA Crim 964*), or members of the clergy (*R v Coghlan [2006] EWCA Crim 1542*). It also includes familial relatives (*Attorney-General's Reference (No 112 of 2005) [2006] EWCA Crim 285*), as there is quite clearly a power imbalance in these situations.

The courts consider the abuse of a position of trust or authority (in this wider context) to be a significant aggravating feature. This considered position is not restricted to sex offences but also includes physical and, by implication, psychiatric harm (see, for example, SAP, 2007: 4). The approach adopted in these circumstances is that the culpability of the offender is greater (SGC, 2004: 5), and, accordingly, a sentence above the 'ordinary' guideline can be expected. This exists across all aspects of the law and can be of particular significance where the Internet is involved, for example, where teachers have been convicted of sexual offences facilitated by ICT (see, for example, *R v Wooton [2005] EWCA Crim 2137* and *R v Lister [2006] 1 Cr App R (S) 69*). It is clear that the courts are now alert to this and consider it, rightly, to be an aggravating factor.

Mitigating factors

Perhaps the more frequently cited changes to a sentence are in respect of the mitigating factors that are to be found in cases. Mitigation is a mixture of generic and personal mitigation and the latter, by its very nature, depends on the specific individual, but it is possible to identify some common mitigating factors:

- Previous good character
- A plea of guilty
- Worthy social contributions
- Personal characteristics such as age, health and frailty.

It is necessary to examine some of these characteristics, in particular to consider what role they should play in respect of a sex offence.

Good character

Whereas it has been seen that previous convictions can now be considered an aggravating factor, the absence of previous convictions has long been considered to be a mitigating factor (Ashworth, 2000: 141). The argument has its grounds in the proportionality principle and recognises that a lapse of judgement of an individual should not automatically be considered as serious as when a person has committed several offences before and thus demonstrates a pattern of behaviour. Indeed, this principle was traditionally carried forward so that an offender who had been previously convicted of an offence did not automatically lose full mitigation but instead there was a 'progressive loss of mitigation', i.e. the weight of mitigation given to previous character was reduced by each conviction until it (eventually) counted for nothing (Ashworth, 2005: 187–91).

Can this approach continue to be adopted? It has been argued that the CJA 2003 expressly states that its provisions are not to prevent relevant mitigation being recognised by the courts (s.166, CJA 2003 and see Taylor et al., 2004: 191–2). One reading, therefore, would be that since previous good character has previously

been recognised by the courts it could continue to be recognised. However, it is difficult to reconcile this with s.143(2) which requires previous convictions to be considered as an aggravating factor. That said, it should be noted that s.143 is not necessarily as strict as it may at first sight appear. The statute provides the court with a 'get-out' by stating that the provision only applies where the court is satisfied that a previous conviction can be 'reasonably' treated as aggravating the seriousness of an offence. Accordingly, where the court believes it is not reasonable then they are not bound to consider it an aggravating factor and may even consider it a mitigating factor. It has been suggested that this is particularly likely where the offences are of a disparate nature or where there has been a significant gap between the offending (Ashworth, 2005: 196–7).

It may seem common sense that a person who has not been convicted before should be dealt with more leniently than someone who has previous convictions, but should this apply in all circumstances? It is known that sexual offences are underreported and indeed some research suggests that people who have been convicted of a sexual offence have probably offended before but have never been caught (see, for example, Howitt, 1995: 28 *et seq.*). Given that there is this underreporting, is it right to give credit to an offender? Indeed, are there circumstances when an offence is so serious that previous good character should be considered irrelevant? It has been suggested that there may be (Ashworth, 2000: 141), and some sexual offences must undoubtedly come within this.

Plea of guilty

Perhaps the most potent form of mitigation is that of the plea of guilty. It has, in recent years, also been one of the most controversial forms of mitigation too. It is clear that mitigating a sentence for a guilty plea has a long tradition within English law (Ashworth, 2005: 163), but since 1994 it has received statutory recognition, with the latest version appearing in s.144, CJA 2003.

The justification for giving a discount for plea is normally said to encompass three reasons. First, it has been suggested that it demonstrates a degree of remorse on the offender and, therefore, this should be recognised as a factor in reducing the sentence from someone who has denied guilt throughout (Ashworth, 2000: 141). The second is that it saves time and money. Trials are very expensive and usually very time consuming. Accordingly, a person saving the courts the expense of money and time should be 'rewarded'. The third, and perhaps most relevant in connection with sex offences, is that a guilty plea means that witnesses, and in particular the victim, do not have to give evidence, something which could be extremely unpleasant (see, in general, Temkin, 2002: Ch. 4 and 5). Reducing the guilty plea in these circumstances ensures that someone who is guilty does not feel that they have nothing to lose by subjecting the victim to an arduous cross-examination and is thus an important public policy matter (see, in particular, *R v Millbery [2002] EWCA Crim 2891 at [27]–[28]*).

How does a judge quantify the discount to be awarded? If a principal reason for providing a 'reward' is to save money then should it alter depending on the stage a plea is given? The SGC thought it should and they produce a 'sliding scale' of discount (SGC, 2004: 5). The maximum discount would be one-third and this would be given when the plea comes at the 'first reasonable opportunity'. At the opposite end of the scale is when the plea is given 'at the door of the court' or even after the trial has commenced. Here, the suggestion is that a *maximum* of 10 per cent should be given (SGC, 2004: 5). However, the Council argues that even when it is a late plea some discount should be given. The proviso to this being:

> If the not guilty plea was entered and maintained for tactical reasons ... a late guilty plea should attract very little, if any, discount.
>
> (SGC, 2004: 5)

Tactical reasons could include remand privileges or to see whether the victim or witness will indeed turn up to give evidence. The latter is perhaps particularly appropriate to sexual cases and it is important that the courts do not acquiesce to such behaviour by rewarding such tactics.

'Red-handed' cases

Providing a discount for plea is not without criticism or controversy, however, and it has been questioned whether it should be used in all circumstances. The principal argument being whether the discount should be awarded for someone who has been caught 'red-handed', i.e.

the evidence is so strong at the time of arrest that an offender has, in effect, no option but to plead guilty. The SGC, when formulating the guideline, was adamant that this should not make any difference:

> Since the purpose of giving credit is to encourage those who are guilty to plead at the earliest opportunity, there is no reason why credit should be withheld or reduced on these grounds alone ...
>
> (SGC, 2004: 5)

On one level it can be understood why the SGC adopted this position. Just because someone is guilty does not mean they have to plead guilty. If no discount was to be awarded then it could be thought that an offender has nothing to lose by asking for a trial. Indeed, they arguably gain an advantage because if they expect to receive a custodial sentence then they will either prolong their liberty, if on bail, or have more favourable conditions if on remand, since remand prisoners are treated slightly better and their time on remand is deducted from their sentence. Rewarding a guilty plea may reduce the chances of this occurring. However, the difficulty with the SGC guideline is it concentrates on only one reason why the plea is tendered and not others. Some have suggested a principal difficulty with the guideline is that where an offender is caught 'red-handed' a plea of guilty may not mean there is any remorse and yet this is a principal reason for providing a discount (Ashworth, 2005: 165).

This issue exploded into public consciousness during the sentencing of Tanya French and Alan Webster in 2006. Alan Webster pleaded guilty to the indecent assault and rape of a twelve-week old baby. Tanya French pleaded guilty to indecent assault of the same baby with both also pleading guilty to taking indecent photographs of the baby. The photographs showed Webster raping the child and also both French and Webster of indecently assaulting the child. Accordingly, there was no doubt that they were guilty of the offences because the photographs served as evidence of the substantive offences. At trial Webster was given a life sentence for rape with the minimum period being set at six years. This was calculated by using a starting point of 18 years and deducting one-third as a discount for plea (leaving 12 years) which is then halved for the minimum term (see above).

The media reacted badly to this crime and the Home Secretary at the time, John Reid, considered the case to be unduly lenient and took the unusual action of writing to the Attorney-General to complain about the sentence. The Attorney-General appealed the sentences to the Court of Appeal as unduly lenient (a power that exists under s.36, *Criminal Justice Act 1988*). One of the grounds put forward was that granting a discount of one-third was too much where the offender was caught red-handed. Whilst the Court of Appeal sympathised with this submission they noted that the guideline had expressly stated that the full discount should be awarded under such circumstances and they doubted whether it would be possible to comply with s.172, CJA 2003 (which states that courts must have regard to guidelines) in such circumstances (*Attorney-General's References (Nos 14 and 15 of 2006) [2006] EWCA Crim 1335 at [52]*).

The controversy continued when Craig Sweeney was sentenced for the abduction and rape of a three-year-old girl. Again, Sweeney pleaded guilty in the face of overwhelming evidence and a full one-third discount was given which significantly reduced the minimum sentence that was imposed on him (reducing the notional term from 15 years to 10 years meaning he would serve a minimum of five years). Again the Home Secretary complained about the sentence, this time being joined by other members of the government and other senior politicians (see Gillespie, 2006c: 1154). The Lord Chancellor and the Attorney-General entered the row and noted that the judge had not acted improperly and that the sentences were in accordance with the law (ibid.). However, these cases did demonstrate a particular problem with the guideline and the SGC resolved to re-examine the issue.

At the time of writing the revised guideline has only been issued in draft form (SGC, 2007b), but if approved in its current form it will see a significant shift where an offender has been caught red-handed. There appears to be recognition that the common law did allow for a discount to be withheld when an offender was caught red-handed (*R v Landy (1995) 16 Cr App R (S) 908* and see Ashworth, 2000: 144), and the SGC has now decided that the full discount should not be automatically awarded. The clear presumption is that the discount should be given, but where the evidence is overwhelming then it has now been suggested that a maximum discount of 20 per cent should be given (SGC, 2007b: 7). This is a considerable reduction from

the one-third that would otherwise be given (SGC, 2007b: 6) but is still a significant discount.

Worthy social contributions

When discussing aggravating factors there was a discussion as to whether being in a position of standing should be an aggravating factor (see above), but Ashworth notes that making a social contribution through, for example, public service could act as a mitigating factor (Ashworth, 2005: 173). Such a discount is extremely controversial and Ashworth himself condemns this as 'social accounting'. This is undoubtedly correct and it becomes of less consequence in terms of sex offending where, as noted above, society may actually decide that such persons should show better restraint. That said, however, there are a number of cases where the courts have provided such a discount in respect of sex offences (see, for example, *R v S [2003] EWCA Crim 2055* and *R v PS [2003] EWCA Crim 1380*) but it is submitted that this should only happen in highly exceptional circumstances. An example of 'exceptional circumstances' that is often cited is *Reid (1982) 4 Cr App R (S) 280* where a burglar who had rescued three children from a blazing house whilst awaiting trial had his sentence reduced on this justification.

Specific offences

This final section of the chapter will briefly examine the likely sentences that could be expected in relation to the offences set out in the preceding chapters of this book.

Cyber-bullying and harassment

This is perhaps the most difficult of the crimes to discuss because it is, of course, the only non-sexual offence that has been discussed within the book. Accordingly, it does not feature in the SGC guidelines on sexual offences but some other limited guidance can be produced.

It will be remembered from Chapter 2 that there are a number of crimes that could be committed by this conduct and they should be considered separately.

Offences against the person

There is not, as yet, any guidance on the sentencing in relation to offences against the person. It will be remembered that this offence is based on the premise of causing psychiatric harm to a person (2.3.1.1 above). Where the offence is assault occasioning actual bodily harm (s.47, *Offences Against the Person Act 1861*) or inflicting grievous bodily harm (s.20, OAPA 1861) then the maximum sentence that can be imposed is five years' imprisonment. The courts would need medical evidence as to the degree of psychiatric harm caused to the victim but where this is significant then it is likely that a custodial sentence would be imposed where the offender is an adult.

Communication offences

It will be remembered that there are two communication offences of relevance. The first is contrary to s.127, *Communications Act 2003* and the second is s.1, *Malicious Communications Act 1988*. Both are summary-only offences and are punishable by a maximum of six months imprisonment. Again, no definitive guidance has been produced by the SGC and the offences are reported comparatively rarely.

As a summary-only offence it is less likely that an offender will receive a custodial sentence, but the courts do not rule out the possibility of a custodial sentence and such sentences have been passed before. Again, it is likely that issues such as distress and the nature of the communications would be the determining factor of any sentence.

Harassment

It will be remembered that the *Protection From Harassment Act 1997* was the most likely offence to be committed in these circumstances (see Chapter 2). Perhaps surprisingly, there has been little guidance given on offences relating to harassment. However, this may be explained by the fact that a wide-range of behaviour will be covered.

The 'simple' criminal offence of harassment (s.2, PFHA 1997) is a summary-only offence punishable by a maximum of six months' imprisonment (probably rising to 12 months' imprisonment eventually). A non-custodial disposition is much more likely in these circumstances, not least because if it were a more serious case of harassment it is likely the more serious criminal offence of s.4 would be satisfied. Section 4 is punishable by up to five years' imprisonment and a custodial sentence is more likely but is certainly in no way inevitable (see *R v Liddle; R v Hayes [2000] 1 Cr App R (S) 131* at

[134]). Particular questions that must be asked by the judge include the seriousness of the harassment and the harm (physical or psychological) that is caused to the victim (ibid.).

In Chapter 2 it was seen that one reason for using the PFHA 1997 was that upon conviction a restraining order could be imposed on the defendant (s.5, PFHA 1997). This is a significant deterrent and the courts have suggested that *'a short sharp [custodial] sentence may be appropriate'* where the order is breached (*R v Liddle; R v Hayes [2000] 1 Cr App R (S) 131* at *[134]*), with longer sentences being imposed for subsequent breaches.

Non-image based pornography

It was seen in Chapter 3 that the most likely offence for this type of material (until planned legislation comes into force) is the *Obscene Publications Act 1959*. It was also noted, however, that the use of this Act is comparatively rare and so there is limited guidance available.

The vast majority of sentencing decisions under the OPA 1959 relate to pornography relating to adults rather than to children (see *Current Sentencing Practice* §B10-1.3B) and it is thus likely to be of limited assistance. That said, it is notable that in many of these cases explicit reference is made to the fact that the material does not involve children and this is considered a significant mitigating factor (see, for example, *R v Xenofhontos and Mace (1992) 13 Cr. App. R (S) 580*). In most 'adult' cases a custodial sentence was imposed (*Current Sentencing Practice, op.cit*) and so the fact that the absence of children is a mitigating factor perhaps reinforces the fact that material involving children will invariably lead to a custodial sentence. This is perhaps confirmed by the case of *R v Travell [1997] 1 Cr App R (S) 52* where the material included line drawings of children in sexual contexts. The material was created by him but there was no evidence of any distribution and a sentence of three months' imprisonment was passed. It should be noted that the courts appreciation of such material has undoubtedly changed in the last decade and it is quite possible that a higher sentence would now be passed.

Indecent images

Indecent images of children was the subject of an advice to the Court of Appeal by the SAP under the pre-CJA 2003 regime. The advice paper issued

(SAP, 2002), was put together following a consultation exercise and the Court of Appeal broadly accepted the advice in *R v Oliver et al [2002] EWCA Crim 2766*. In a book of this length it is not intended to critique the original position (for a discussion on this see Gillespie, 2003) but rather to focus on the key issues set out in the definitive sentencing guideline (SGC, 2007) which altered, in part, the *Oliver* guideline.

As was noted in Chapter 4 the Court of Appeal, following the SAP's advice, adapted the COPINE typology to create five levels of indecent images. The SGC in 2007 has in turn adapted this typology again to take into account the fact that the SOA 2003 treats penetrative activity (including penetration of the mouth) as a serious matter. The new five-point scale is therefore:

1. Images depicting erotic posing with no sexual activity.
2. Non-penetrative sexual activity between children, or solo masturbation by a child.
3. Non-penetrative sexual activity between adults and children.
4. Penetrative sexual activity involving a child or children, or both children and adults.
5. Sadism or penetration of, or by, an animal.

(SGC, 2007: 109)

Pseudo-images should ordinarily be considered to be less serious than actual photographs although this is a presumption and can be rebutted (SGC, 2007: 109). This is an area I have been previously critical of since it is not always easy to tell the difference between photographs and pseudo-photographs (Gillespie, 2003: 82–3). The latest guideline does not alter this position but, admittedly, there is no evidence that this has been a problem over the last four years.

The age of the child

In the original advice (accepted by the Court of Appeal) the age of the child was not considered to be a factor that would either aggravate or mitigate the offence *by itself* (SAP, 2002: 13). The SGC has adopted a different approach, undoubtedly reflected by the fact that the SOA 2003 raised the age of 'a child' and because the SOA 2003 itself draws a distinction between ages more generally.

The SGC guideline draws a distinction between 16–18 year-old children, those aged 13 or over but under 16 and those under 13 (SGC, 2007: 110).

The principle of treating images of children aged 16 to 18 as slightly less serious than those under 16 is perhaps understandable and relatively uncontroversial. The SGC does, however, draw a distinction between the under 13 and states:

> *Starting points for sentencing for possession of indecent photographs should be higher where the victim is a child under 13.*
>
> (SGC, 2007: 110)

This, as has been noted, is a major shift and it does raise issues of proof. The SGC confirms this themselves by stating that where the age is not known then the court must, following established common law principles, treat the offender in a way favourable to the defendant. In other words, if there is conflict between the prosecution and defence as to whether a child is aged 12, 13 or 14 then unless the prosecution can prove this, the defendant should be sentenced on the basis that the child is over 13.

This may seem controversial but realistically it is not. Aging a child is notoriously difficult (see Gillespie, 2005a: 36) and in reality the police tend to differentiate between pubescent and pre-pubescent children. It is highly likely that a pre-pubescent child will be under the age of 13 and accordingly applying this approximation is likely to be successful.

Character

It was noted above that the issue of character or social-standing can sometimes be considered to be a mitigating factor. In the original advice the SAP had advised that, '*no special weight should be attached to good character in relation to these offences*' (SAP, 2002: 13). The Court of Appeal did not, however, mention this during *Oliver et al.* (see Gillespie, 2003: 87) and since that time it is not clear what the position as to character is. Unfortunately, the SGC does not reiterate its comments as to character and accordingly it would seem that good character may (subject to the discussion noted above) amount to mitigation in these cases.

Starting points

The starting points for sentencing differs depending on the classification of material and indeed the offence. They are summarised in Table 8.1:

Table 8.1 Starting points for sentencing

Offender commissioned or encouraged the production of level 4 or 5 images. Offender involved in the production of level 4 or 5 images.	6 years custody.
Level 4 or 5 images shown or distributed	3 years custody.
Offender involved in the production of, or has traded in, materials at levels 1–3.	2 years custody.
Possession of a large quantity of level 4 or 5 material for personal use only. Large number of level 3 images shown or distributed.	12 months custody
Possession of a large quantity of level 3 material for personal use. Possession of a small number of images at level 4 or 5. Large number of level 2 images shown or distributed. Small number of level 3 images shown or distributed.	26 weeks custody.
Possession of a large amount of material at level 2 or a small amount at level 3. Shown or distributed material at level 1 or 2 on a limited scale. Exchanged images at level 1 or 2 with other collectors but with no element of financial gain.	12 weeks custody.
Possession of a large amount of level 1 material and/or no more than a small amount of level 2, and the material is for personal use and has not been distributed or shown to others.	Community Order.

Grooming

It was noted in Chapter 5 that grooming takes place in a number of ways. In this section I seek to address only those who have been convicted of the offence of meeting a child following grooming contrary to s.15, SOA 2003.

The SGC notes that this is primarily an inchoate offence and thus where the offender is caught before he undertakes a substantive act the seriousness of the offence must be based on his intentions (SGC, 2007: 82). Presumably, where the offender has gone on to commit a substantive offence the seriousness of the grooming will be based on that offence. This may appear to be punishing an offender twice but it is not: it is a recognition that the grooming was a separate preparatory act that led to the eventual contact. It also recognises the separate harm that grooming can occur.

The SGC consider issues such as the sophistication of the grooming and the amount of planning involved would be aggravating factors together with an assessment of how close an offender came to succeeding in the crime (SGC, 2007: 82). The use of coercion or drugs and alcohol are also aggravating features (SGC, 2007: 83), the latter being particularly important as it may be used not only as a befriending tool but to make the child more placid and co-operative. Importantly, the issue of psychological injury caused to the victim by the grooming is also an aggravating factor. Although the SGC argue that

the harm caused to the victim will be less than when the substantive offence takes place there is no evidence to necessarily prove this. A sophisticated grooming process could cause psychological harm to a child, especially when they discover the improper motives of the offender. It is clearly important that where real harm has taken place that this is recognised by the courts.

The principal distinction in starting points is between penetrative or non penetrative activity and also in connection with the age of the child. As with other offences within the SOA 2003 the SGC considers the age of 13 to be a relevant marker. The starting points suggested are in Table 8.2.

Procurement

Procurement as a distinct course of conduct is comparatively rare and therefore does not come to the direct attention of the courts particularly frequently. This is, in part, because of the fact that in many cases the offender will have committed a substantive sex crime and it will therefore be more appropriate to charge the individual with this. However, it was seen in Chapter 6 that a number of cases have occurred and this, together with a careful analysis of the definitive sexual offences guideline should allow some predictions to be made.

The cases that were dealt with before the SOA 2003 came into force were all dealt with by

Table 8.2   Starting points in connection with children 13/16

Where the intent is to commit an assault by penetration or rape.	4 years custody (victim under 13) 2 years custody (victim under 16)
Where the intent is to coerce the child into sexual activity.	2 years custody (victim under 13) 18 months custody (victim under 16)
History of paying for penetrative sex with children under 18	15 years custody (victim under 13) 7 years custody (victim under 16) 3 years custody (victim under 18)
Penetrative sexual activity	12 years custody (victim under 13) 5 years custody (victim under 16) 2 years custody (victim under 18)
Non-penetrative sexual activity	5 years custody (victim under 13) 4 years custody (victim under 16) 12 months custody (victim under 18)

custodial sentence but it was seen in Chapter 6 that at the trial of one procurer, Luke Sadowski, the trial judge complained that the law was inadequate at dealing with such behaviour and that his powers were significantly limited. Sadowski was sentenced on the basis that the maximum sentence was only two years' imprisonment. If the circumstances were repeated today then it is likely that the conduct would be contrary to s.14, SOA 2003, punishable by a maximum term of 14 years' imprisonment.

The SGC, when considering s.14, noted that the behaviour involved with arranging a sex offence could be extremely wide (SGC, 2007: 66), and therefore the starting points etc. could vary depending on the nature of the offence. Importantly, the SGC also make the point that the dangerousness provisions (see above) should always be considered (SGC, 2007: 66). The guideline treats s.14 in a relatively complicated way. It does not provide starting points *per se* but rather it relates it to the conduct found within Sections 9–13, the sexual offences that are arranged.

Where the procurement is a commercial enterprise then the starting points *'should be increased above those for the relevant substantive [offences]'* (SGC, 2007: 67), but it does not say by how much. It has been noted that commercialism is considered a serious aggravating factor and thus the starting point should be significant. Where it is a non-commercial transaction then the starting points should be *'commensurate with that of the relevant [substantive offence]'* (SGC, 2007: 67). This does leave a slight loophole as to what happens where the procurement takes place

within a 'ring' of sex offenders, i.e. a sex offender makes available a child that he is aware of (perhaps, and even most likely, his own) without any charge. Is that a commercial enterprise? If there is no financial nature to the transaction it may seem that it will not be, but there is precedent for treating organised trading as a commercial transaction irrespective of a financial incentive (see the SAP's advice on offences relating to child pornography: SAP, 2002: 7). It is to be hoped that similar logic will be applied here.

Prostitution

The final set of offences that were examined in this book were that of prostitution. For the purposes of this section we will discuss only those circumstances where the child is the victim of prostitution, i.e. the offences contrary to Sections 47 to 51, SOA 2003.

Paying for a sexual service

It will be remembered that the SOA 2003 introduced a new offence which criminalised someone paying for a sexual service provided by a child (s.47, SOA 2003 and see Chapter 7). The definitive sexual offences guideline discusses this offence and provides guidance as to the correct sentence.

The sentence, like the Act, draws a distinction between the age of the child and the type of activity that has been paid for. The starting points are higher than those that would be given if a substantive child sex offence (e.g. sexual activity with a child (s.9, SOA 2003)), the justification for this being the fact that not only is the child being the subject of illegal sexual activity but (s)he is also being commercially exploited (SGC, 2007: 116). This is to be welcomed as an important message and one that the courts must heed.

The starting points suggested are in Table 8.3 below.

It can be seen that these starting points are quite high but there is a significant difference between activity with a child under 16 and activity with a child under 18. Whilst it is accepted that this reflects the ordinary age of consent, the fact remains that this is an exploitative position and it could be questioned whether the gap should be so significant given that they remain under the age of majority.

Arranging or facilitating child prostitution

It will be remembered that the SOA 2003 creates three new offences relating to those who control a child for the purposes of prostitution or pornography (ss. 48–50, SOA 2003 and see Chapters 4 and 7). These offences were designed to tackle those who introduced a child to commercial sexual exploitation or assisted in the exploitation of the children. The SGC notes that not everyone involved in these offences will necessarily do so for financial gain, but that all the starting points should be high to reflect the exploitation that exists alongside the substantive abuse (SGC, 2007: 120). Whilst this is to be welcomed it does not, by itself, answer the question as to whether these offences are necessary (see Gillespie, 2004a), since exploitation could be considered a serious aggravating factor where a substantive sex offence takes place.

Other important issues that the SGC address are the fact that where a number of children are involved then consecutive sentences should be used even though this may mean that the cumulative offences are significantly higher than a single offence (SGC, 2007: 120), and that the greater the role in the operation the higher the sentence should be. The suggested starting points are outlined in Table 8.3 below.

These starting points are interesting because they are not that different from the person who pays to have sexual activity with a child (above), this being particularly true where the activity is non-penetrative. The SGC do not give precise reasons why this should be so but it must be questioned whether this is necessarily appropriate. Whilst it is undoubtedly correct to criminalise those who pay for the sexual services of a child, the person who is exercising control over the child and who arranges for the child to be sold to further customers is exploiting the child in a particularly grave way. It is perhaps the fault of Parliament in not properly differentiating the sentences between s.47 on the one hand and ss. 48–50 on the other. It is to be hoped that the courts continue to bear in mind the principle that the greater the control the higher the sentence should be since this may be the way of ensuring that exploitation is punished.

Someone convicted of an offence under ss. 48–50 is not subject to the notification requirements of the SOA 2003 (see Chapter 9), something that appears to have little or no logic behind it (Gillespie, 2004a: 367).

Table 8.3 Starting points for organised sexual activity

Organised commercial exploitation (penetrative activity)	10 years custody (under 13) 8 years custody (under 16) 4 years custody (under 18)
Offender's involvement is minimal and not for personal gain (penetrative activity).	8 years custody (victim under 13) 5 years custody (victim under 16) 2 years custody (victim under 18)
Organised commercial exploitation (non-penetrative activity)	8 years custody (victim under 13) 6 years custody (victim under 16) 3 years custody (victim under 18)
Offender's involvement is minimal and not for personal gain (non-penetrative activity)	6 years custody (victim under 13) 3 years custody (victim under 16) 2 months custody (victim under 18)

CHAPTER 9

Ancillary Sentencing Issues

The last chapter looked at how an offender is sentenced, along with some of the more likely sentences in respect of the offences discussed in this book. By the very nature of this book it is necessary to keep matters relatively brief because the law of sentencing constantly changes and no two cases are the same. In this final substantive chapter, the consequences of sentencing will be discussed. In recent years the actual disposal of the offender (i.e. custodial or non-custodial sentence) is only one of a number of matters the courts have had to deal with when sentencing an offender. Indeed, it has been suggested that there are now so many orders a judge has to consider that there is a real danger that some are forgotten (Thomas, 2002: 475).

In this chapter the principal ancillary issues relating to convicted sex offenders will be discussed.

Notification requirements

Perhaps the most significant change in the sentencing of sex offenders was introduced in 1997 and is known more formally as notification requirements and more colloquially as the 'sex offenders register'. Technically, this is not an ancillary order or indeed any sort of order. Although a court will ordinarily explain that an offender is subject to the requirements, the courts have noted that they do not have the power to either apply or disapply them (see, for example the comments of the House of Lords in *R v Longworth [2006] UKHL 1 at [17]*). Whilst this is undoubtedly true (the legislation makes it clear that it is a consequence of a caution, conviction or special verdict), it is necessary to deal with the issue in this chapter because it is one of the most important consequences of a conviction for a sex offence.

The notification requirements are now contained within Part 2 of the SOA 2003 (ss. 80–93) but it originated in the *Sexual Offenders Act 1997*. The scheme was set up following a campaign by numerous pressure groups, most of whom wanted the right to be told when a sex offender was living in their community (Cobley, 1997: 690). The request was for a scheme similar to 'Megan's Law' in the USA, although this is a difficult concept since 'Megan's Law' is actually implemented in different ways by the individual states. However, the essence of 'Megan's Law' is that state authorities are under a duty to disclose details of high-risk sex offenders to the community.

The proposal for 'Megan's Law' was rejected in 1997 and has remained a live debate since. At the time of writing (Autumn 2007) the government have announced the results of a review of the issue of sex offender disclosure with the suggestion that legislation will be introduced to allow for greater access to information (see *Hansard, HC Deb, vol 461, col 761, 13 June 2007*). It has been questioned whether legislation is strictly necessary (Gillespie, 2007b), but the government appears to wish for greater clarity in this matter. However, at the time of writing the detail of the proposals has not been established nor is it strictly relevant to this book since community disclosure is generally not a matter relating to ICT. Nevertheless, as will be seen, many offenders who commit an offence facilitated by ICT will be subject to the notification scheme and, potentially, therefore, eventually the subject of disclosure.

To return to the issue of notification, it was accepted that a scheme that would allow law-enforcement and offender management agencies greater information about the location of sex offenders would be beneficial. The proposal was raised in the dying days of the last Conservative government and so it was thought that there would be insufficient Parliamentary time. However, the opposition parties agreed to support the proposal and thus the legislation was passed in very quick time (see Cobley, 1997: 691).

There seems little point in addressing the original scheme since it has been consolidated and replaced by Part 2 of the SOA 2003 but those interested in the original scheme and its amendments should consult Cobley, 1997; 2000. The SOA 2003, whilst clearly based on the 1997 scheme, contained new features that were aimed at improving and widening the scope of the notification requirements.

Initial notification

The SOA 2003 applies to all findings in respect of a sex offence against a child, including a caution but with the exception of an absolute discharge. It will be remembered that the position of discharges were discussed in the previous chapter, and the SOA 2003 clarifies the fact that a conditional discharge does require notification but an absolute discharge does not. This position is extremely controversial because it appears somewhat unfair to impose notification requirements on someone who accepts an administrative sanction (a caution) where there is no opportunity to test the evidence, but not to impose the requirements on someone who has the opportunity to test the evidence in a court and yet who receives an absolute discharge.

The argument for requiring notification for cautions is that a significant number of people accept cautions and that by accepting a caution, the person is admitting guilt. A caution should only be administered when there is sufficient evidence to justify a prosecution but there is some evidence to suggest that this does not always occur (Sanders and Young, 2000: 350–2) suggesting that the ability to test the evidence may be somewhat important. The idea that accepting a caution is an indication of guilt also misses the fact that there are many reasons why someone may wish to accept a caution and in respect of sex offences a primary reason may be the risk of publicity that a court trial will inevitably attract. It must be questioned whether a caution can correctly be said to be a correct avenue of disposition for sexual offences. Given the gravity of these crimes it could be suggested that where there is sufficient evidence to demonstrate guilt, a prosecution should be brought. Indeed, stopping cautions may mean that where a victim is reluctant to testify or would make a poor witness then the offender would escape without any form of punishment for their actions. However, can a caution in such circumstances be ethically correct? If it is known that the prosecution case is unlikely to succeed or is flawed, it would seem inappropriate to provide a caution under these circumstances.

That said, it is highly unlikely that this position will be changed and indeed in 2006, following a media furore over teachers who were allowed to continue in their profession despite being cautioned for a sex offence, the position of cautions was brought into 'List 99', a list of disqualified sex offenders (see Gillespie, 2006d, 2007b for further discussion on this).

A person who becomes subject to the notification requirements has three days in which to make his initial notification (s.83(1), SOA 2003) and, unlike in the original scheme, it is clear that this notification must take place in person at a police station rather than by post or telephone (s.87(1) SOA 2003). It will be seen, in Table 9.1, that the duration of notification requirements depends on the type and length of sentence but a person is required to notify when he is convicted (s.82(6) SOA 2003) and accordingly, if sentencing is adjourned, unless the prisoner is in gaol on remand, then the notification period begins and he has 72 hours to make this notification.

The information that must be notified is:

(a) The relevant offender's date of birth.
(b) His national insurance number.
(c) His name on the relevant date and, where he used one or more other names on that date, each of those names.
(d) His home address on the relevant date.
(e) His name on the date on which notification is given and, where he uses one or more other names on that date, each of those names.
(f) His home address on the date on which notification is given.
(g) The address of any other premises in the United Kingdom at which, at the time the notification is given, he regularly resides or stays.

(s.83(5) SOA 1997)

Items (c) and (e) and (d) and (f) are not duplicitous but are, instead, designed to tackle situations where, for example, an offender is known by a particular name on the date that he was sentenced for the offence and yet changes his name between then and notification. The principal addition to the requirements by the 2003 Act is that of the person's national insurance number which the state authorities frequently use as an index field on numerous databases, theoretically allowing them to cross-reference information held on the offender. The police are empowered to take the offender's fingerprints and/or a photograph of any part of the offender when this notification occurs. The purpose of this power is to assist the authorities in verifying the identity of the offender (s.87(4), SOA 2003).

Table 9.1 Notification requirements

Description of offender	Duration
A person who is sentenced to imprisonment for more than 30 months	Indefinitely.
A person who has been admitted to a hospital subject to a restriction order	Indefinitely
A person who is sentenced to imprisonment for more than 6 months but less than 30 months	10 years
A person who is sentenced to imprisonment for less than 6 months	7 years
A person who is admitted to hospital without being subject to a restriction order	7 years
A person cautioned*	2 years
A person given a conditional discharge	The duration of the discharge
A person of any other description (e.g. Fine, Community Sentence etc.)	5 years

*The Act actually says 'a person within subsection 80(1)(d)'. A discussion as to the possible implications of this is to be found below.

Duration of notification requirement

Section 82(1) SOA 2003 creates a table which details the duration of the notification requirements (see Table 9.1).

Where the offender is under 18 at the time of sentence or release from custody, the period is one-half of that contained within the table (s.82(2) SOA 2003). Rather embarrassingly, the SOA 2003 did not take account of other legislation proceeding through parliament at the time. As was noted in the previous chapter the *Criminal Justice Act 2003* introduced a new sentence, imprisonment for public protection (Chapter 8). This is an indeterminate sentence but s.82(1) did not recognise the sentence. Was such a sentence a term of imprisonment greater than 30 months (thus requiring indefinite registration)? It was seen in the last chapter that a minimum term must be pronounced and, theoretically, an offender could be released after this period. If the minimum period was set at, for example, 26 months imprisonment, what is the duration of the notification requirements? It could be argued the sentence is actually less than 30 months' imprisonment. The counter argument, of course, is that if a person is not released at that point then it may equate to a sentence of greater than 30 months. Irrespective of the actual period of time spent in custody, it will be remembered that a sentence of imprisonment for public protection will only be imposed where the court considers the offender to be dangerous (Chapter 8). It may be logical to assume, therefore, that a different approach to notification requirements may then be necessary.

Eventually s.82(1), SOA 2003 was changed and s.57, *Violent Crime Reduction Act 2006* amends the section to state that where a sentence of imprisonment for public protection is passed then an offender is subject to the notification requirements for an indefinite period of time. There is no provision for the requirements to lapse and accordingly, indefinite actually means for the rest of the offenders' life.

Changes

Where a person changes his name, address or having stayed at a location for a qualifying period, they must notify this change within three days of the change (s.84(1), SOA 2003). This change must occur in the same way as with initial notification, i.e. in person at a designated police station.

A qualifying period is defined under s.84(6), SOA 2003 as:

(a) a period of 7 days, or
(b) two or more periods, in any period of 12 months, which taken together amount to 7 days.

At first sight this appears relatively straight-forward but the syntax of s.84(1)(c) makes clear that the offender must have *stayed* at the premises for a qualifying period rather than stayed *away* from registered premises. This can have implications, especially when it is remembered that it is a reactive duty (i.e. it happens within three days of the seventh day of the stay). A series of examples may assist in understanding the operation of this and some of the difficulties that arise.

> *A, a relevant sex offender, has registered his home address as 10, Strawberry Fields, Anytown. A then goes on holiday for 8 days to the 'Village Hotel', Anyvillage. A must notify the police of this change and should attend the police station at Anyvillage by the 8th day (his last day) to notify them.*
>
> *A, a relevant sex offender, has registered his home address as 10, Strawberry Fields, Anytown. A then goes on holiday for 14 days to the 'Village Hotel', Anyvillage. A must notify the police of this change and should attend the police station in Anyvillage by the 10th day (seven days qualifying period plus the three days permitted) to notify them.*
>
> *A, a relevant sex offender, has registered his home address as 10, Strawberry Fields, Anytown. A then goes on holiday for 4 days to the 'Village Hotel', Anyvillage in March. A need not notify the police of this holiday because he has not been away for a qualifying period of time. In September he returns to the 'Village Hotel' for 5 days. He has now been at an address for a combined total of more than 7 days. By the 9th day (his last) he must notify the Anyvillage police of his presence.*
>
> *A, a relevant sex offender, has registered his home address as 10, Strawberry Fields, Anytown. He goes to Blackpool on holiday for six weeks but changes his hotel every six days. A does not have to notify the police of his presence because he has never stayed in a set of premises for a qualifying period.*

The legislation permits a person to notify the police in advance of the change, including the address where they are to stay for a qualifying period (s.84(2) SOA 2003), but does not *require* it and thus, as was seen in the examples above, it is perfectly possible for a person to go on holiday for ten days and to notify their presence on the final day. If this person was a high-risk offender this means that, in essence, a person can have been present in an inappropriate environment (e.g. family holiday park etc.) for ten days without anyone knowing of his presence.

Whilst this may raise concerns in terms of high-risk offenders and one can foresee how a clever offender could bypass the provisions of the Act, it is, arguably, that the alternative of requiring notification for a much shorter period could increase the bureaucracy to the point whereby the system begins to break. One possible solution would be to use a *Sexual Offences Prevention Order* (SOPO) to regulate the length of time an offender can stay away from premises without notifying the police (for a discussion on SOPOs see below).

Foreign travel

Related to the issue of 'changes' is that of foreign travel. The SOA 2003 empowers the Home Secretary to make regulations regarding the steps that those who are subject to the notification requirements must take if they are travelling abroad. The Home Secretary has used this power and Parliament passed *The Sexual Offences Act 2003 (Travel Notifcation Requirements) Regulations 2004 (S.I. 2004/1220)*.

Where a person wishes to travel abroad for a period of three days or more then they must notify the police in advance of the trip (Reg. 5(1) SI 2004/1220). It is easy to contrast this with the position of domestic travel (above) where a person notifies after the qualifying period has elapsed, but this arguably confirms the argument that this is due to bureaucratic concerns. Where possible, an offender wishing to travel abroad must provide at least seven days notice of their intentions (Reg. 5(2)(a) SI 2004/1220), and in any event they must provide no less than 24 hours notice (reg 5(2)(b)). The reason for this timeframe is almost certainly to allow the authorities to apply for a banning order where they believe it is necessary to do so (below).

When the statutory instrument is read in conjunction with s.86(2) SOA 2003, the details to be notified to the police become apparent. These are:

- The date on which the offender will leave the country (s.86(2)(a)).
- The first country the offender will be travelling to and his point of arrival there (s.86(2)(b)).
- The arrival point in each subsequent country that the person will be travelling to (reg. 6(a)).
- The transport carriers he is using for each leg of the journey that involves travelling to different countries (reg. 6(b)).
- Details of his accommodation for the first night away (reg. 6(c)).
- The date at which he intends to return to the UK (reg. 6(d)).
- The point of arrival at which he will return to the UK (reg. 6(e)).

The detail required is significantly greater than that which was required under the 1997 scheme (see *Sex Offenders (Notice Requirements) (Foreign Travel) Regulations 2001. SI 2001/1846*) and this may be in part to combat sex tourism. The requirement to know all of the countries and points of arrival is almost certainly to permit the police, where they believe it necessary to do so, to contact their counterparts in other countries to provide details of their risk assessments etc. Potentially this could be useful as regards Internet offenders as it could be that someone is trying to meet someone they have met over the Internet and groomed or procured or, for example, someone who has been convicted of offences relating to child pornography and who wishes to go to a country where child sex tourism is prevalent and where they would have the opportunity to photograph children.

Banning travel

Whilst this is not strictly part of the notification requirements it is convenient to deal with this matter here. If the authorities, when notified by an offender that they wish to travel abroad, are concerned that the person poses a danger to children then they could apply to the Magistrates' Court for a foreign travel order (s.114, SOA 2003). An order can do one of three things:

- Prohibit the offender from travelling to any country outside the United Kingdom named in the order.
- Prohibit the offender from travelling to any country outside of the United Kingdom other than one named in the order.
- Prohibit the offender from travelling outside of the United Kingdom.

(s.117(2), SOA 2003)

Any order lasts a maximum of six months (s.117(1) SOA 2003) although there is nothing within the Act which would prevent the police from applying for subsequent orders. The three possible prohibitions noted above quite clearly become increasingly draconian and it is submitted therefore that the Magistrates will need to carefully consider the necessity and proportionality of the orders, i.e. if the police are concerned that the offender is trying to go to a particular country then the first form of the order may be more appropriate than the second.

This is clearly a flexible order that could help safeguard children outside the United Kingdom from serious sexual harm. The flexibility of the order is enhanced by the fact that it applies to any person who has been convicted of a relevant offence in the past, i.e. it is not restricted to those who are subject to the notification requirements.

With such a flexible order there is the potential for it to be abused but the courts are experienced at balancing the relevant factors and have shown through the use of comparable legislation (e.g. see the *Football (Disorder) Act 2000* in relation to football banning orders) that they take care as to their use.

Breach of the requirements

Where a person does not comply with the notification requirements imposed on them without any reasonable excuse (s.91(1)(a) SOA 2003) or provides information that (s)he knows is false (s.91(1)(b), SOA 2003), then they commit an offence that is triable either-way and punishable by a maximum of five years' imprisonment (s.91(2), SOA 2003). Breach is considered serious and statistics show that a custodial sentence is imposed in just over one-third of cases (SGC, 2007b).

Transitional arrangements

The 1997 and 2003 schemes are slightly different in terms of the duration of the notification requirements and the SOA 2003 does create transitional arrangements to take into account the difference between the regimes although in respect of police cautions the transitional arrangements may be controversial.

Section 81, SOA 2003 deals with the transitional arrangements and states that those who were convicted of an offence before the date this Act came into force (which was 1 May, see *Sexual Offences Act 2003 (Commencement) Order S.I. 2004/874*) are, upon commencement of this Act, subject to the (new) arrangements. Section 82, as has been noted already, governs the duration of the notification requirements and the unambiguous purpose of s.81 is, therefore, to ensure that offenders who were required to notify under the 1997 legislation are now subject to the 2003 regime for the duration set out in s.82.

A person who was given a police caution under the 1997 scheme was classified as a person 'of any other description' and accordingly needed to notify for a period of five years. However, a person who is cautioned under the SOA 2003 is only subject to the requirements for two years (s.82(1) SOA 2003). It would seem logical to assume that a person who was required to notify under the 1997 legislation would simply be governed under the 2003 Act but the Act itself complicates matters.

For reasons that are not clear, in connection with cautions the SOA 2003 makes reference to '*a person within section 80(1)(d)*' (s.82(1)). Section 80(1)(d) refers to those who are cautioned by the police after the commencement of the Act. Those who were subject to the 1997 arrangements are dealt with by s.81, SOA 2003. The entry in s.82(1) is the only time in the entire table where a reference is made to a statutory provision rather than to a type of sentence and a literal interpretation of the section must mean that it is only those who are within s.80(1)(d) who are required to notify for a period of two years, i.e. those cautioned after the commencement of the Act. The natural consequence of this is that a person who was cautioned before the commencement is a person 'of any other description' and is thus required to notify for a period of five years.

The implication of this is quite serious with a person who accepts a caution on 30 April 2004 having to notify their details for five years and the person who accepts a caution the next day on 1 May would be subject to the requirements for only two years. This position appears somewhat untenable, especially when it is remembered that this is an administrative sanction that does not allow the evidence held by the police to be tested. It is difficult to think of any justification for this disparity and it is to be hoped the courts interpret the legislation in such a way as to 'read in' the words 'or s.81(1)(d)' which would take into account those cautioned before the commencement of the Act. However, it will not be easy for the courts to do this because the wording of the legislation is quite clear, but it would seem the only just and reasonable solution (for further comment on this see Gillespie, 2005b).

Offences committed abroad

The notification requirements under Part 2 of the SOA 2003 automatically apply only to those who are convicted in a court in the United Kingdom, but the Act also makes provision for those who are convicted of an offence outside of the territory. Section 97, SOA 2003 permits the police to apply to the Magistrates' Court for a notification order. The provisions are quite complicated but, in essence, three conditions must be satisfied:

- A court outside the UK must have either convicted the offender regardless of whether he

was punished, or a finding must have been made which is the equivalent to a finding of guilt (s.97(2) SOA 2003). Section 99(1) SOA 2003 defines the circumstances when an offender has been convicted of a relevant offence but in essence it requires a person to be convicted of an offence that, if it had occurred in this country, would have come within Schedule 3.
- The condition above must be satisfied by an offence that took place after 1 September 1997 or the offender has been released from custody after that date (s.97(3) SOA 2003).
- If the table contained in s.82 were to have effect for the sentence passed, the offender notification period would still exist (s.97(4) SOA 2003).

Where these conditions are satisfied then the court *must* make a notification order (s.97(4) SOA 2003). The third condition can be explained by way of two examples:

> *D, was convicted by a foreign court and sentenced to imprisonment for a term of 36 months. This would attract the notification requirements indefinitely and thus when D enters the UK, the police could apply, and should be granted, a notification order.*
>
> *D, was convicted by a foreign court in 1998 and sentenced to a fine of £250. This would attract the notification requirements for a period of five years. If he entered the UK in 2004 the third condition would not be satisfied (as the notification period would have ended) and accordingly no order can be granted.*

If a notification order is made then the offender is subject to the notification requirements under the SOA 2003 as though he were convicted of an offence in this country (s.97(5) SOA 2003).

Sexual offences prevention orders

After notification requirements perhaps the next most important ancillary issue is that of the Sexual Offences Prevention Order (SOPO). A SOPO, unlike the notification requirements, is a discrete order that is within the discretion of the court and not an inevitable consequence of conviction.

The SOPO was introduced by the SOA 2003 (ss. 104–13) but it is actually the consolidation of two previous orders; the *Restraining Order* (s.5A, *Sexual Offenders Act 1997* (inserted by para 6(1), Schedule 5, *Criminal Justice and Court Services Act 2000*) and a *Sexual Offender Order* (s.2, *Crime and*

Disorder Act 1998). The original act was the sexual offender order (SOO) and this was established at the same time as the *Anti-Social Behaviour Order* (ASBO) (s.1, CDA 1998). The ASBO and SOO were the first of the quasi-criminal orders: they are technically civil orders and the civil evidential rules apply although it is now settled that the higher standard of proof (roughly equivalent to the criminal standard of proof) applies to these offences (see *R (on the application of McCann) v Manchester Crown Court [2002] UKHL 39*).

The SOO was introduced because there was concern that the notification requirements introduced by the SOA 1997 were not fully retrospective: they applied only to those who were convicted or cautioned after 1 September 1997 or those who were either released from gaol or still serving a community sentence after that date (s.1(3) SOA 1997). This meant that a significant number of offenders were not subject to the notification requirements. Administratively, it would have been difficult to have backdated the legislation to all offenders (although it would be theoretically possible since the courts have decided that it is not a punishment and thus the rule against retrospective law would not apply, see *Ibbotson v United Kingdom (1999) 27 EHRR CD 332*), and the concern was, in reality, concentrated on those that continued to pose a risk, something noted by the courts:

> There is no room for doubt about the mischief against which this legislation is directed, which is the risk of re-offending by sex offenders who have offended in the past and have shown a continuing propensity to offend ...
> (*B v Chief Constable of Avon & Somerset [2001] 1 All ER 562 at 571 per Lord Bingham CJ*)

As part of this rationale, an important feature of the scheme was that it applied to a person convicted of a sexual offence regardless of when they had been convicted, and if that person was not already subject to the notification requirements they became subject to them for the duration of the order (s.2(5), CDA 1998). This, as will be seen, continues to be the case with a SOPO.

Criteria for a SOPO

As has been noted already the SOPO is actually the combination of two previous orders and this is reflected in the criteria for a SOPO. There are two times when an order may be made. The first is at the time of sentence (s.104(2) SOA 2003) (this

being the equivalent of seeking a restraining order under s.5A, SOA 1997) and the second is upon application to the Magistrates' Court by the police (s.104(5) SOA 2003).

Where a SOPO is considered at the time of sentence, the court must be satisfied:

> ... it is necessary to make ... an order, for the purposes of protecting the public or any particular members of the public from serious sexual harm from the defendant.
> (s.104(1)(b) SOA 2003)

Where the police have applied for a SOPO then the court must be satisfied:

> ... that the defendant's behaviour since the appropriate date makes it necessary to make such an order, for the purposes of protecting the public or any particular members of the public from serious sexual harm from the defendant.
> (s.104(1)(a) SOA 2003)

It is clear, therefore, that the substantive criteria – 'protecting the public ... from serious sexual harm' – is the same for both forms of the order, but where it is by application then there is an additional criterion. Both forms of the order also share an additional criterion, which is the subject has been convicted of a qualifying offence.

Qualifying offences

The SOA 2003 has widened the list of offences that a person must have been convicted of before the police can apply for an order (s.104(b) SOA 2003) or before the court can impose a SOPO at the time of sentence (s.104(2) SOA 2003). Under the 1997 regime a SOO could only be imposed on someone who was convicted of a relevant sexual offence. These offences were listed within Schedule 1 of the SOA 1997 and included the principal sex offences against children. However, a criticism of the notification requirements and, by analogy, the SOO regime was that it did not necessarily cover all sexual predators.

Perhaps the most notable case of relevance here in recent years was the killing by Roy Whiting of Sarah Payne, an 8-year-old schoolgirl. Whiting was not convicted of a sex offence but of murder and thus even though it was known he was, historically, a sex offender, he is not subject to the notification requirements (in the unlikely event he is ever released from gaol). There was concern that where a sex offender kills a child it would often be unlikely for a sex charge to be brought since the sentence for murder is a mandatory life sentence and thus bringing an additional sex offence (rather than demonstrating the motivation for the killing was sexual) could not increase the sentence since life imprisonment is the most serious punishment that can be handed down. When the judge sets the 'tariff' for murder (see Chapter 8 for a discussion on a comparable procedure) he can take into account the sexual motivation and construe this as a serious aggravating factor. On that basis the CPS may decide not to 'risk' also charging a sex offence alongside murder since there is the risk that an acquittal could undermine the case as a whole. The SOA 2003 introduced a new offence of committing an offence with intent to commit a sex offence (s.62, SOA 2003) but it is questionable how often this will be used in conjunction with murder for the reasons set out above.

However, as has been noted already it is comparatively rare for a life sentence to mean an offender will spend the rest of his life in gaol but when a murderer is released they will not be subject to the notification requirements because murder is not a sex offence. Concern was raised as to what could happen if a murderer began to act in an inappropriate way. It was decided prudent to widen the application of SOPO to include certain non-sexual offences and these are contained in Schedule 5 of the SOA 2003 and this includes murder, manslaughter and kidnapping, together with many non-fatal offences. Nevertheless, it is important to note that even though non-sexual offenders have been brought within the remit the criterion has not changed. The offender must still pose a risk of 'serious sexual harm' and accordingly the risk that he will commit a non-sexual offence within Schedule 5 (e.g. a crime of violence) would not be sufficient for an order to be made.

It is not known whether extending SOPOs to non-sexual offenders will make any practical difference since it is likely the vast majority of subjects will have been convicted of a sexual rather than non-sexual offence. Also, where a person has been convicted of murder they will be subject to a 'life-licence' meaning that they could be 'controlled' through the use of conditions on the licence. That said, it may prove useful for some other offences, most notably manslaughter where previously there have been examples of people who have been convicted of sexually-motivated manslaughter where a life-licence was not imposed and, accordingly, the SOPO may prove useful.

The final point to note in respect of the offences is that Schedule 5 usefully includes offences contrary to ss. 48–50, SOA 2003. It will be remembered that these are the offences that relate to the involvement of a child in pornography or prostitution (Chapters 4 and 7). For reasons known only to the government these offences were not contained within Schedule 3 meaning that an offender convicted of an offence is not subject to the notification requirements but their inclusion within Schedule 5 means that they are subject to a SOPO either at the time of conviction or at a later date if their behaviour gives grounds for concern.

Appropriate date

Where an application for a SOPO is made then the offender must have acted 'since the appropriate date' in a way that makes the court believe it is necessary to make a SOPO but what does this mean? The Act provides its own definition:

> 'Appropriate date' . . . means the date or (as the case may be) the first date on which he was convicted, found or cautioned [of an offence].
>
> (s.106(8) SOA 2003)

The only real effect that this has is it means that the police cannot rely on the conduct of the defendant in the commission of the original offence, i.e. the offender must have acted in a way that leads the police to reasonably believe an order is required (see s.104(5)(b) SOA 2003) *after* the date he was convicted. The words 'or (as the case may be) the first date on which he was convicted' were additions to the SOA 2003 and were designed to overrule a previous decision of the courts. In *Hopson v Chief Constable of North Wales [2002] EWHC 2430* the Divisional Court held that the term 'relevant date' within s.2, CDA 1998 meant the date of the last criminal conviction. This was because these words were not present. This led to an SOO being quashed because the behaviour that gave concern was then followed by criminal behaviour for which he was convicted. The Divisional Court held that the meaning of 'relevant date' (the term used in the CDA 1998 rather than 'appropriate date') could change depending on the offender's history.

If *Hopson* was to occur again it would be dealt with differently because, of course, it is now possible for a SOPO to be imposed at the time of conviction (s.104(2) SOA 2003). Accordingly, the police, instead of making an application where the behaviour was contemporaneous, would simply ask for an order at the time of conviction (at the time of *Hopson*, restraining orders (s.5A, SOA 1997) were not yet in force). Given that this is possible it would appear somewhat unusual for the wording to have changed, but it is perhaps to take account of the fact that counsel at trial may fail to make an application for a SOPO at the time of sentence. However, it does potentially mean that a SOPO can be granted on the basis of future offending rather than behaviour but it is questionable whether there will be any practical disadvantage to a defendant as a result of this.

Risk of serious sexual harm

Perhaps the most notable criterion is that it must be 'necessary for the purpose of protecting the public ... from serious sexual harm from the defendant' (s.104(1) SOA 2003). What does this mean? It has been held that 'necessary' means something more than simply 'desirable' (*R v D* [2005] EWCA Crim 2951) i.e. the court must not consider these orders to be automatic and they must assess that each offender meets the criteria for an order. The words that are perhaps more problematic are the risk of 'serious sexual harm' which are further clarified by the Act as meaning:

> ... protecting the public in the United Kingdom or any particular members of that public from serious physical or psychological harm, caused by the defendant committing one or more offences listed in Schedule 3.
>
> (s.106(3) SOA 2003)

This involves predictions as to two issues. The first is that an offender will commit one or more future sexual offences listed in Schedule 3 (which are the sex offences to which notification requirements attach). The second prediction which must be made is that members of the public must be caused serious physical or psychological harm by this future offending. The two need not necessarily be equated. Whilst some offences will almost certainly involve serious physical or psychological injuries being suffered by the very nature of the offence, some will not and it may depend, for example, on the way the crime may be committed or a victim. This does complicate the criteria although it is something that a judge may be advised on in a pre-sentence report.

A question that has been raised in the field of ICT-based crimes is whether serious harm will be caused by the commission of other 'virtual' crimes. Where the conduct amounts to 'grooming' it is quite likely that the psychological harm for this can be proven because the abuse of relationship/trust that is implicit within this conduct can be psychologically distressing. Will future downloading of indecent images of children lead to a risk of serious harm? In *R v Beaney* [2004] EWCA Crim 449 the Court of Appeal held that it would:

> *It is plain that the particular members of the public who might be at risk of serious harm are the children who are forced to pose, or, worse, to participate in sexual conduct for the purposes of enabling these images to be produced and disseminated. They would undoubtedly be subject to a real risk ... to serious psychological injury ... Would they have been subjected to that risk from people ... who simply downloaded the images and viewed them ...? We think they would. The serious psychological injury which they would be at risk of being subjected to arises not merely from what they are being forced to do, but also from their knowledge that what they are being forced to do would be viewed by others. It is not difficult to imagine the humiliation and lack of self-worth which they are likely to feel.*
>
> (at [8]–[9])

This demonstrates that the courts are prepared to look beyond contact offending and recognise the significant damage that Internet offending could cause. It was confirmed in *R v Collard* [2004] EWCA Crim 1664 that the implication of *Beaney* was that any case involving an offence contrary to s.160, *Criminal Justice Act 1988* or s.1, *Protection of Children Act 1978* was capable of leading to a SOPO although this would, of course, be subject to the question as to whether the offender was likely to re-offend.

An astute reader will realise that there is a striking similarity between the criteria for a SOPO and the criteria for being considered dangerous under the *Criminal Justice Act 2003* (see Chapter 8). This certainly did not escape academic commentators and counsel, and one eminent commentator suggested that the criteria were, in effect, identical and that if a judge ruled that an offender was not dangerous within the meaning of the CJA 2003 he could not then impose a SOPO (Thomas, 2006a: 360). The basis of this argument is that the provisions are certainly very similar. For example, a court can impose a sentence of imprisonment for public protection where:

. . . the court is of the opinion that there is a significant risk to members of the public of serious harm occasioned by the commission by him of further specified offences.
(s.225(1)(b) CJA 2003)

If, Thomas argued, 'serious sexual harm' includes physical and psychological injury then this must inevitably mean that serious sexual harm is within 'serious harm' for the purposes of the CJA 2003. On the face of it, therefore, this would appear to be a compelling argument since the terms are so close. However, it misses one crucial point which is the risk of harm. A SOPO can be made where there is 'a risk' whereas imprisonment for public protection can only be imposed where there is a 'significant risk'. This may seem semantics but in *R v Lang et al [2005] EWCA Crim 2864* it was held that for the purposes of the CJA 2003 this means *'the risk identified must be significant . . . [meaning] "noteworthy, of considerable amount or importance"'* (at [17(i)]) whereas a SOPO can be made where it is more than *'simply desirable'* (*R v D [2005] EWCA Crim 2951 at [10]*).

Inevitably the courts were called upon to rule on this matter. In *R v Rampley [2006] EWCA Crim 2203* it was accepted that whilst the *'terminology employed in the two Acts is very similar'* (at [21]) but that not only was the degree of risk different (as discussed above) but also that the type of future offending was different. This was followed by the case of *R v Richards [2006] EWCA Crim 2519* where the arguments were more fully argued, including specific reference to the article by Thomas. The Court of Appeal emphasised that there were differences between the two Acts (at [25]) and they concluded that the *'statutes were not intended to be and are not linked so as to enable the provisions of one of them to override the other'* (at [26]).

This, it is submitted, has to be correct since otherwise it would, in effect, neuter the provisions for a SOPO, especially at the time of sentence. Indeed, it would probably make little sense to impose a SOPO at the same time as imposing a sentence of imprisonment for public protection since an offender subject to IPP will not be released until the parole board considers he no longer poses a danger to society (see Chapter 8). Accordingly, it would be unlikely that he would require a SOPO whilst in gaol and upon his release the prohibitions of a SOPO could undoubtedly be imposed as a condition of his licence. Breach of a licence should lead to

automatic executive recall to prison, with a recalled prisoner not being released until the parole board consider that he is safe to be released again, and the licence only being discharged when the Parole Board believes it is safe to do so (s.31(A), *Crime (Sentences) Act 1997*).

Effect of an order

The nature of a SOPO was neatly summarised by the then Lord Chief Justice, Lord Bingham, when referring to a SOO:

The rationale of section 2 [of the CDA 1998] was, by means of an injunctive order, to seek to avoid the contingency of any further suffering by any further victim. It would of course be to the advantage of a defendant if he were to be saved from further re-offending.
(*B v Chief Constable of Avon & Somerset [2001] 1 All ER 562*)

The basis of a SOPO is the notion of 'an injunctive order', i.e. a person is being told what they cannot do and not what they *should* do. It must be questioned whether this prohibition is necessarily that problematic. For example, let us take an example of an offender where there is a belief that the sex offender notification requirements are insufficient to manage his behaviour. The police are concerned that the offender can stay away for a 'qualifying period' (see above) without them being notified. They wish to ensure that he notifies the police when he wishes to stay overnight. Assuming that the rest of the criteria for a SOPO is satisfied (e.g. because he is high-risk and when he has been staying away there have been concerns about his behaviour) this would appear an example of something that falls outside of a SOPO since requiring him to notify is a positive rather than negative requirement. However it is just as easy to reword the requirement. So instead of it being 'you shall notify the police when staying away from your home premises' it is transformed to, 'you shall not stay overnight in any premises other than your notified residential premises without notifying the police in advance'. This becomes a negative obligation and so theoretically within the scope of a SOPO.

All requirements must be necessary to prevent members of the public from suffering serious sexual harm (s.107(2) SOA 2003). In other words, it must be shown that the requirements requested do have the potential to save a person from serious sexual harm rather than them being, for example, merely of assistance in managing the sex offender. Although not expressly stated in the statute it is also clear that any requirements must also be proportionate to the risk that is posed. Both the police and the court imposing a SOPO are public authorities within the meaning of the *Human Rights Act 1998*. A requirement within a SOPO will inevitably interfere with the right of a defendant's respect for private life (Article 8(1), *European Convention on Human Rights*) since Article 8 is concerned with the right to go about one's life without interference from those in authority (see *Glaser v United Kingdom (2001) 33 EHRR 1*). An infringement of Article 8(1) need not be problematic given that Article 8(2) allows for such interferences to be justified. There will be little problem in the requirements meeting the criteria that they are in accordance with the law and for a legitimate aim and s.107(2) is designed to address the necessity point. However, a disproportionate requirement could render the Article 8(2) justification invalid.

That said, it is important to note that the courts do have considerable latitude but the concept of proportionality has led the courts to be careful as to how they design SOPOs. Issues of particular relevance to us are the requirements that may be imposed on those who use ICT to facilitate their abuse. It may be thought that at the time of sentence an offender who has abused ICT and whom it is thought may abuse ICT in the future, may require a SOPO to prevent future harmful conduct. However, can a prohibition not to use the Internet be justified?

It was noted in Chapter 1 that although the Internet undoubtedly has a 'darker side' to it, within modern society it has now become entrenched. The 'online generation' has become established and with the growth of broadband and wi-fi technology people now move seamlessly between the online and offline world. Many jobs will require access to technology that uses an Internet connection including virtually any call-centre. A prohibition against the Internet *per se* may be difficult to justify since it could mean an offender would commit a criminal offence simply by undertaking his work. The courts have recognised this and normally stated that such prohibitions should include a rider saying that it is permissible for legitimate business use (see *R v Collard [2005] 1 Cr App R (S) 34*). However, it is important to note that the courts have never said that this is an absolute rule and certainly where there is a particularly

dangerous offender it may be that an absolute prohibition can be justified; the key to proportionality is ensuring that care is taken to look at the individual offender and not simply common practice used elsewhere.

Duration of the order

A SOPO is either passed for an indeterminate period (i.e. until a further order is made or the order is discharged) or for a determinate period, in which case it must be for no less than five years (s.107(1) SOA 2003). Whilst the applicant must normally indicate how long they wish the order to last, it is ultimately a decision for the court and it has the power to make an order for an indeterminate period of time even where the application is for a determinate period (*Jones v Greater Manchester Police Authority [2001] EWHC Admin 189 at [22]*).

The SOA 2003 expressly provides for the variation, renewal or discharge of a SOPO (s.108). It is only the police and the subject who have the right to petition the court in this way although it is worth noting that the definition of 'the police' is extended to include the chief constable of an area where they believe the offender will come to (s.108(2)(c) SOA 2003). The court may vary the order as it seeks fit but new prohibitions may only be added where they are necessary to protect the public from serious sexual harm (s.108(5), SOA 2003). An order can only be discharged within five years of the order being made if the subject *and* the police agree (s.108(6) SOA 2003). It is highly unlikely that this situation will ever arise but Parliament is, it is argued, correct to provide for the theoretical possibility that the police may agree to discharge an order early and given the Damocles-type situation the subject of an offender finds him or herself under, it is only right that the courts have the opportunity to discharge this burden where consent is reached.

Breach of a SOPO

Although a SOPO has been described as an injunctive order (*B v Chief Constable of Avon & Somerset [2001] 1 All ER 562*), breach of the order does not, like with an injunction, amount to contempt of court but instead constitutes a discrete criminal offence (s.113, SOA 2003). The offence is triable either-way and is punishable by a maximum term of five years imprisonment (s.113(2) SOA 2003). It is important to note at the outset that breach itself is not punishable by up to five years imprisonment, but that it constitutes an offence that is so punished. This may appear semantics, but it is not, because it means the police will investigate any potential breach and the CPS may prosecute for the breach, after considering the relevant prosecutorial tests. This does mean that it is quite possible that an offender may breach an order but be not prosecuted and thus escape any punishment.

The offence is not one of strict-liability. A defence exists where a person can prove that they had a reasonable excuse for doing the act (s.113(1) SOA 2003). No guidance has been produced on what 'reasonable excuse' means and it will inevitably depend on the facts of each case. It is important to note that 'reasonable excuse' means that an offender will be judged against an objective rather than subjective test.

Whilst it has been recognised that prohibitions need not amount to a criminal offence, it is quite possible that the act of breach will in itself be criminal. For example, if a prohibition says that a person must not access pornographic images and the subject accesses and downloads an indecent image of a child, he will be liable for an offence under s.113, SOA 2003 *and* an offence contrary to s.1, *Protection of Children Act 1978*. This is not duplicitous because it does amount to two separate convictions. It is indeed possible for consecutive sentences to be imposed under these circumstances although the totality principle often means that this will not occur.

Breach of a SOPO is not a sexual offence in its own right and does not attract notification requirements. That said, it is likely that any breach would lead to the SOPO being extended which automatically means the notification requirements will continue. It is also notable that it is not a 'specified offence' for the purposes of the CJA 2003 and accordingly it is not possible to pass an extended sentence for breach (see Chapter 8 and *R v Lewis [2006] EWCA Crim 2225*). That does not prohibit a court from imposing an extended sentence or sentence of imprisonment for public protection (whichever is applicable) for a substantive offence at the same time as breach. This may mean that prosecuting authorities have to consider quite carefully which offence to charge where an act that constitutes a substantive sex offence amounts to the breach of a SOPO. The breach of a SOPO (and therefore the offence under s.113, SOA 2003) may be easier to prove,

but where it is thought that the offender is dangerous it may be more appropriate to also charge the substantive offence.

Disqualification from working with children

The third ancillary issue that needs to be addressed is disqualifying an offender from working with children. This is an important area and one that has been the subject of some controversy and change in recent years.

Disqualification by a court

The first issue to examine is how an offender may be disqualified by a court at the time of sentence. The power of a court to do so exists under the *Criminal Justice and Court Services Act 2000* (CJCSA), this being an initial recommendation of an inter-departmental government review on offending against children (see Cobley, 2005: 487). There are two forms of this court power. The first is when the court *must* disqualify the offender and the second is when the court *may* disqualify an offender. Common to both provisions are the courts that may disqualify an offender and the offences.

Courts

The power to disqualify an offender is given only to the 'senior courts' and this is defined as, '*the Crown Court, the Court of Appeal, a court-martial or the Courts-Martial Appeal Court*' (s.30(1) CJCSA 2000). Accordingly neither the Magistrates Court nor the High Court (sitting in its appellate or supervisory role) can impose a disqualification. It will be seen that this could become increasingly difficult to justify because of changes to automatic disqualification (see below) but there are currently no plans to alter this provision. It is not immediately clear why magistrates do not have the power to disqualify an offender although, admittedly, it will be relatively uncommon for magistrates to have jurisdiction in the cases where disqualification may become relevant.

Offences

A person must be convicted of an 'offence against a child' which is defined in s.26, CJCSA 2000 in three ways. The first is to commit an offence under paragraph 1 of Schedule 4, CJCSA 2000 (cruelty, infanticide, indecent images of children or abduction of a child by a parent and most sexual offences against a child). The second is to commit an offence contained in paragraph 2 against a child (murder, manslaughter, kidnapping, false imprisonment and certain non-fatal offences against the person). The third and final way is to commit an offence against a child contained in paragraph 3 (threats to kill, drugs offences, causing or allowing the death of a vulnerable child and certain preparatory offences).

In essence, this covers the vast majority of offences against children although it should be noted that the offences contained in Chapter 2 of this book (with the exception of the non-fatal offences) are not contained within this list and accordingly the conduct discussed in that chapter would not lead to court-ordered disqualification. This may increasingly become problematic and the government may in time have to reflect upon whether communication offences and harassment are, when committed against a child, brought within these provisions, at least on a discretionary basis.

Mandatory disqualification

The original scheme introduced by the CJCSA 2000 introduced mandatory disqualification for certain adult and juvenile offenders. For reasons of space it is not intended to examine the disqualification of juveniles (contained in s.29, CJCSA 2000). An adult will be disqualified by a court where he is convicted of a relevant offence (above) and a qualifying sentence is imposed (s.28(2) CJCSA 2000) or where a relevant order is made (this is principally in respect of those who are found not-guilty by reason of insanity etc. and so will not be discussed in this book). A 'qualifying sentence' is in essence a term of imprisonment of at least 12 months duration (s.30(1) CJCSA 2000).

Assuming that these requirements are met then a court must disqualify an offender unless:

> ... the court is satisfied, having regard to all the circumstances, that it is unlikely that the individual will commit any further offence against a child.
>
> (s.28(5) CJCSA 2000)

It is worth noting that the court must be satisfied the person will not commit any further offence against a child, not just one that is within Schedule 4. In *R v MG [2002] 2 Cr App R (S) 1* the Court of Appeal held that when considering whether the court was 'satisfied' that there would be no future offending, the balance of probabilities test would apply (at [18]). Accordingly, if a judge is satisfied that an offender will probably not offend against a child in the future then they need not disqualify an offender.

The mandatory nature of the requirements has been the subject of some criticism. In particular, it has been suggested that it is inappropriate because there is no requirement that an offender is either working with children or is ever likely to work with children before an order is made (see Thomas, 2003: 205). Of course, the counter-argument is that if a person is unsuitable to work with children then he should be told from the outset that he is not to work with children. The flaw in this riposte, however, is that it does not take account of the discretionary power a court possesses to disqualify an offender (see below). Indeed, it has been suggested that it would be more appropriate to repeal the mandatory requirements and rely solely on the discretionary provisions (Thomas, 2005: 803). This would, at least, ensure that the provisions would only apply to those who are thought to pose a danger to children. However, far from adopting such a stance, the government has made blanket disqualification more likely (see the discussion on automatic disqualification below).

Discretionary disqualification

The disqualification regime was relatively restricted in that it has been seen that only a senior court could make an order and only where a qualifying sentence was imposed. The courts expressed some regret at this (see *R v Bekus [2004] EWCA Crim 600* cited by Cobley, 2005: 488) and the government eventually decided to widen the disqualification regime.

The amendment was contained within the *Criminal Justice Act 2003* and it inserts a new provision within the CJCSA 2000 known as s.29A. This provision applies to both adults and juveniles when sentenced by a senior court (s.29A(1), CJCSA 2000). The discretion can be exercised when:

> ... the court is satisfied, having regard to all the circumstances, that it is likely that the individual will commit a further offence against a child ...
>
> (s.29A(2) CJCSA 2000))

It can be immediately seen that the test is, in effect, the opposite of the discretion contained within s.28 (see above). What standard of proof must the judge use when deciding whether it is satisfied? It will be remembered that for the purposes of s.28(4) (i.e. when it is using its discretion *not* to disqualify an offender) that it is the civil standard of proof (*R v MG [2002] 2 Cr App R (S) 1*) but should the same be true here?

The point has perhaps somewhat surprisingly not been considered by the courts directly. In *MG* the Court of Appeal, when deciding the civil standard applied, did so in part because they noted that this was the standard usually adopted when the prosecution had to prove something (at [18]). Where the court is considering its discretion not to disqualify someone it would be the defence who bear the burden of proving there is no danger of re-offending. However, when the court is considering exercising its discretion under s.29A, it is the prosecution that bear the burden of proving that the offender poses a risk of re-offending. Accordingly, it could be argued that the higher standard of proof should be required. This is perhaps reinforced by drawing a comparison to sexual offences prevention orders. SOPOs and disqualification orders both prevent an offender from doing something that would ordinarily be lawful. They both lead to the possibility of a criminal sanction for disobedience (see above and also below). It is clear that the standard of proof for a SOPO is the higher standard of proof (*R (on the application of McCann) v Manchester Crown Court [2002] UKHL 39*) and it is submitted the same is true of s.29A due to the implications of disqualification.

Automatic disqualification

The preceding section has noted that only the senior courts can disqualify an offender from working with children, albeit in recent years without the need for a qualifying sentence to be imposed. However there has, in recent years, been a tendency to increase the circumstances under which a person becomes automatically disqualified. This differs from mandatory disclosure since even mandatory disclosure requires an application to be made to the judge: the mandatory nature is simply in relation to the actions of the judge. This has caused some difficulties in the past. In Chapter 5 the conduct of Luke Sadowski was discussed. Sadowski was a trainee teacher at the time that he sought to

procure a girl and yet at his trial the prosecution forgot to ask for a disqualification order. At that time it was not possible to correct such an omission (although this has, at least, been remedied, see s.29B, CJCSA 2000).

Automatic disqualification, as its name suggests, occurs not because of any application to the court but simply as an administrative action resulting from relevant conduct. Some disqualifications occur because concerns are raised during civil proceedings (see *Protection of Children Act 1999*) but this book is concentrating on the criminal law and so reference will be made solely to those who are convicted or cautioned of a relevant criminal offence.

Central to the nature of automatic disclosure is the database known as 'List 99'. This is a document that has been in existence since 1926 but was recently placed onto a statutory basis (see s.142, *Education Act 2002*). The database is a list of people who are considered inappropriate to teach children. One of the ways that a person could be placed onto List 99 was being convicted of a relevant offence. In 2006 significant media controversy erupted because it was shown that those who had accepted police cautions for relevant sexual offences had not been disqualified from working with children (Gillespie, 2006: 19). A police caution is a formal finding of guilt and an adult may only be cautioned by the police where they admit their conduct and consent to having a caution administered (Gillespie, 2006: 23). It does not have the same status as a conviction since it is considered to be an administrative action that occurs instead of a prosecution (although this is only true of public prosecutions and a caution need not automatically prevent a private prosecution being brought, see *Jones v Whalley [2005] EWHC 93*), but it is an admission of guilt and can be cited as such in a criminal court.

From the media's perspective, absenting a person who is cautioned from List 99 meant that people who had admitted that they had offended against a child were still able to work with children. This logic would appear to have some strength behind it but it misses the fact that research has demonstrated that some people will accept a caution even in circumstances where there is insufficient evidence, in part because they fear the consequences of a public trial (Sanders and Young, 2000: 350–2; Soothill, 1997: 483). This undoubtedly meant that the decision to extend List 99 to include cautions became increasingly problematic but the government were determined to overhaul the system (Gillespie, 2006d).

After reviewing the position, the government introduced a twin-track approach to this area. The first was to modify, in the medium-term, List 99 and increasing the number of people who would become automatically disqualified (see Gillespie, 2007). The second track was to completely abolish the current system of disqualification and replace it with a single system. The legislation to do this has been passed (see *Safeguarding Vulnerable Groups Act 2006*) but no date has been given as to when the new system will be introduced. Its implications will be discussed below.

The current rules for automatic disqualification are set out under the authority of the *Education Act 2002* but are to be found in statutory instrument (see *Education (Prohibition from Teaching or Working with Children) Regulations 2003 SI 2003/1184* as amended by the *Education (Prohibition from Teaching or Working with Children) (Amendment) Regulations 2007 SI 2007/195*).

Regulation 8 discusses those who will be placed onto List 99 (more properly now referred to as the list operated under s.142 EA 2002). Inclusion on the list occurs in one of two ways. The first is automatic barring and the second is automatic inclusion.

Automatic barring

The first form of entry onto the list is through automatic barring. This is where a person comes within paragraphs 1–3 of Part 1, Schedule 2. In essence, this is where a person has been entered onto the list operated under the *Protection of Children Act 1999*, has been made the subject of a disqualification order by a court or has committed certain serious offences against children in the last 10 years. Those offences are:

- Rape
- Intercourse with a girl under 13 (now repealed)
- Assault by penetration
- Sexual assault of a child under 13
- Causing or inciting a child under 13 to engage in sexual activity by penetration.

The offence must have been committed against a child under 16. Where any of these criteria are met then the person is automatically on the list without the right to make any representations to the Secretary of State as to why he should not be so listed. A person will not be able to petition for removal from the list for at least a period of 10 years (reg 11, SI 2003/1184).

Automatic inclusion

The second method by which a person can be included on the list is through automatic inclusion and this is perhaps the more controversial. A person who is included on the list will be barred from working with children (see below) but will be able to make representations to the Secretary of State as to why they should not be included on the list (reg. 8A, SI 2003/1184). When making representations the person will be entitled to produce medical evidence (reg 8A(2)). The Secretary of State must then consider whether that person poses a risk to children and *'if it appears to the Secretary of State that [the person] is not unsuitable to work with children, the Secretary of State must revoke the direction'* (reg. 8A(3)).

No guidance is provided as to how the Secretary of State is to make this decision although we now know that it will no longer be the Secretary of State deciding this on their own, but instead they will be advised by an independent panel of experts (Gillespie, 2007: 10). No indication has been given as to who these experts are or indeed what their expertise is. Perhaps more importantly, however, is the fact that the statutory instrument does not make clear how this panel is to decide whether a person is 'unsuitable' or not. It would certainly appear to be a much wider test than that which is required under the disqualification regime (above).

The exact criteria under which a person is to be automatically included onto the List are quite complicated and it is not strictly necessary to consider them here in detail (for a more complete discussion on them see Gillespie, 2007b: 3–10). For our purposes it is sufficient to concentrate on one way that a person can be automatically included, that being where he is convicted or cautioned of a relevant offence. The relevant offences are set out principally in Part 4 of Schedule 2 to the Statutory Instrument. There are over 60 offences prescribed ranging from infanticide to nearly all of the sexual offences contained within the SOA 2003 and also including drug offences. Interestingly, however, non-fatal offences (including harassment) are not included and accordingly the conduct discussed in Chapter 2 (Cyber-bullying and Harassment) will continue to be outside of the scope of this provision.

Under the previous List 99 regime a person who was convicted of a relevant offence was only placed on the list if they worked with children (see Gillespie, 2006d: 24). This position has now been altered and anyone, regardless of whether they have ever worked with a child or not, is now automatically placed on the list (reg. 8, SI 2003/1184, cf. previous reg. 8(1)(a)(ii) and see Gillespie, 2007b: 9). This is undoubtedly controversial, in part for the reasons discussed by Thomas in relation to court-ordered disqualification (see above) and could also cause logistical difficulties. It has been noted already that everybody who comes within this provision is able to make representations to the Secretary of State. There is nothing to lose by not making representations since it does not affect the duration of the disqualification and arguably everything to gain since if the representations succeed then the disqualification is ended. Under the previous regime a person convicted of most of these crimes was not able to make representations and so it is logical to assume the number of representations will rise.

Assuming the representations are rejected by the Secretary of State (and it is likely that the vast majority will be), then the offender is also given the right to representation before the Care Standards Tribunal (reg.10, SI 2003/1184). The CST has to decide whether to revoke the direction and does so on the basis of a finding as to whether the person is unsuitable to work with children (reg.8(3) SI 2003/1184). Under the previous system the CST could vary a direction (by, for example, limiting the direction to prohibiting work with a certain age-group or sex) (Gillespie, 2006d: 25), but this power has been abolished. Again it must be questioned whether the practicalities of this have been considered. Everyone has the right to petition the CST although a hearing will occur where leave is granted (reg.10A(2) SI 2003/1184). Whilst the requirement of leave will limit the number of cases proceeding to a full tribunal hearing, there will still be a significant increase in the number of people who will appeal to the tribunal since before these new rules came into force in 2007 a person convicted of most of these offences could not appeal. Is the CST sufficiently staffed to meet this increase? In addition, we do not yet have clear guidance on the test that will be applied in deciding whether an appeal will succeed.

The number of people that may wish to make representations to the Secretary of State and appeal will be increased by the fact that a formal police caution for a relevant offence will also lead to automatic inclusion. This is extremely controversial (Gillespie, 2007: 6), not least because it will now be incumbent on the police to explain the consequences of accepting a caution. There has been some doubt as to whether police officers explained the consequences of a caution under normal circumstances (Sanders and Young, 2000: 351), and yet now, whenever an offender receives a caution for a specified offence, they must be notified of the fact that they are now automatically disqualified from working with children. Is this realistic? Will a police inspector who is faced with administering a caution remember to inform every offender of the consequences of a caution? The Department for Education and Skills thinks that it will occur (DfES, 2006: 3.09), but they did not say why they had such confidence. It is to be hoped that information is provided since the absence of providing information would inevitably lead to a defence against any criminal proceedings (see below) and indeed possibly to a judicial review of the legality of the caution itself (see the arguments raised in *R (on the application of R) v Durham Constabulary [2005] UKHL 21* where this issue was, it is submitted, never fully addressed). It should be noted that not being told of the listing will not lead to the disqualification itself being considered invalid (see, for example, *Hardy v Secretary of State for Education and Skills [2006] 0815.PC*).

Enforcing disqualification

Disqualifying a person from working with a child, either by the court or automatically, is only sensible if it can be enforced. An offender who is disqualified commits an offence if '*he knowingly applies for, offers to do, accepts or does any work in a regulated position*' (s.35(1) CJCSA 2000). It can be seen that the crime is not just that a person does work with children but merely applying for a post, or accepting a post that has been offered, will also suffice. The meaning of 'regulated position' is defined in s.36 and covers a wide range of positions that relate to having both supervised and unsupervised contact with children.

It is important to note that the offence is not one of strict liability. Not only does s.35(1) state that the offender must knowingly apply for work involving children (and thus where it is not immediately clear that the position is actually a regulated offence then liability may not arise), but there is also a limited defence. That said, the defence is limited to the circumstances of an offender not knowing, and could not be reasonably expected to know, that he is disqualified (s.35(3) CJCSA 2000). Realistically, it will be extremely rare for an offender not to know he is disqualified although it is perhaps more likely given the recent change in automatic disqualification.

For our purposes, a person is disqualified if they are disqualified from working with a child by a court order (s.35(4)(d), CJCSA 2000), or have been placed onto List 99 (s.35(4)(b) CJCSA 2000), and it becomes crucial, therefore, that an offender who is, for example, cautioned or convicted of an offence under, and is accordingly placed onto, List 99, is told of the consequences of the finding.

Disqualification: the future

The *Safeguarding Vulnerable Groups Act 2006* (SVGA) was established as a result of the *Bichard Inquiry* into the murder by Ian Huntley of the schoolgirls Holly Wells and Jessica Chapman (see Gillespie, 2007b: 1). The Act will completely alter the way that offenders are vetted and prevented from working with children. When the SVGA comes into force the disqualification regime noted above and List 99 will cease to apply (see s.63 and sch.10, SVGA 2006). In its place will be a new system of vetting and barring those who should not work with children.

The new vetting and barring arrangements will be operated by an independent agency known as the *Independent Barring Board* (IBB). This body, rather than the courts or the Secretary of State, will make the decisions as to who should be allowed to work with children, although in many circumstances the decision to bar someone will, initially at least, be automatic. Few details have been given as to how the IBB will be constituted or indeed work (Gillespie, 2007b: 11), although it is likely that these details will become clearer sometime in early 2008.

The principal change to the regime is that the system will become somewhat dynamic: the new procedure is based on the premise of constant vigilance and vetting. A person who wishes to work with children will be required to apply, as now, for a Criminal Records Check (Gillespie,

2007: 13). If there is no relevant information then they will be allowed to work with children and become 'subject to monitoring' (s.24, VCRA 2006). If there is information (e.g. intelligence, conviction, caution, etc.), then the matter is passed to the IBB who will decide whether a person will be allowed to work with children.

A person who is entitled to work with children is 'subject to monitoring' and what this means is that if information comes to light that a person is no longer suitable to work with children then the employer and employee will be automatically told of this decision (s.26, VCRA 2006). When this occurs a person becomes barred from working with children pending any appeals or submissions to the IBB. In this way it is hoped that it will eliminate the problems of the past whereby some employers were not notified of the actions of an employee and the information would only come to light as and when the employee chose to move jobs.

Given that one way a person becomes ineligible to work with children under the new scheme is through conviction or caution it is not yet clear whether this will be communicated to a person. Someone who is barred from working with a child commits a criminal offence if they seek to work with children (s.7(1), VCRA 2006: the offence is analogous to the existing liability discussed above), and so whether a person is told or not is crucial (for further argument on this see Gillespie, 2007b: 15).

Human rights

A disqualification order prevents an offender doing something that would otherwise be considered lawful, the right to work with children. This inevitably raised issues in terms of human rights legislation. The focus on challenges to the legislation has been twofold; the first is that a disqualification order is punitive and the second is that it is an interference with the rights of individual freedom.

Punishment

The first challenge that was brought concerned the possibility that a disqualification order is a punishment. In this context there are two principal arguments. The first is that it is something that a judge must consider when deciding the totality of the sentence (i.e. a sentence may be reduced because disqualification has been ordered), and the second is that if it is a punishment then it should only apply to offenders who commit an offence after the implementation of the relevant legislation. This is because there is a general common-law presumption against retrospective punishment and/or in any event it would be contrary to Article 7, *European Convention on Human Rights*. Given that the legislation has continually evolved (above) then this could have significant implications.

The first case to consider this in depth was *R v Field; R v Young [2002] EWCA Crim 2913*. The Court of Appeal was specifically asked to rule on the compatibility of a disqualification order with Article 7 and they concluded it was compatible. They argued that the order was preventative rather than punitive, and that this could be demonstrated by the fact that a conviction is not required for its imposition (at [22] *et seq.*). Whilst this is true, it can only be imposed in the absence of a conviction where a special verdict has been reached (most notably through insanity). In those circumstances a person is expressly not guilty of a crime (*Trial of Lunatics Act 1883* and see Ormerod, 2005: 268), but a finding of fact is made as to culpability, and a disqualification order can be made where the person is considered to have committed the relevant offence even though he has not been convicted of it.

Aside from this there were other, and it is submitted more convincing, reasons why the order may be preventative. One issue is that it is expressly considered by statute not to be a punishment but, instead, an *addition* to punishment ([2002] EWCA Crim 2913 at [25]). The Court of Appeal also considered analogous provisions (including sex offender orders, as they then were, and football banning orders) before concluding they were preventative. Certainly this logic seems convincing although it has been argued that if they were truly preventative they would relate only to those who are likely to work with children (Thomas, 2003: 205). It is submitted that this argument is flawed, however, since the preventative nature is that it ensures that a person *cannot* work with children. Whilst a person may not have any present intention of working with children this can, of course, change, and the disqualification order ensures that such persons will not be able to seek or obtain relevant employment.

When this case was heard the discretionary disqualification system was not yet in force (above) but in *R v G [2005] EWCA Crim 1300* the

logic of *Field; Young* was upheld by another constitution of the Court of Appeal. Accordingly, it can be said that a disqualification order and, by implication, List 99 does not amount to a punishment and is accordingly not a matter for Article 7 or relevant to totality arguments.

Individual freedom

Human rights arguments against disqualification were concentrated on the notion of punishment, but in *R v G [2005] EWCA Crim 1300* a more comprehensive argument was put forward, alleging breaches of Articles 3 and 8 along with reiterating the Article 7 argument. As noted immediately above, the Article 7 argument was dismissed as being unsound.

Article 3 prohibits torture, inhuman and degrading treatment. The appellant sought to base his argument on the latter but the Court of Appeal quickly dismissed this argument noting that any shame or inconvenience brought by a disqualification order is not sufficient to infringe Article 3 ([2005] EWCA Crim 1300 at [17]). This is undoubtedly correct. The European Court of Human Rights has been quite clear that there is a minimum degree of severity before something can amount to degrading treatment under Article 3 (see, for example, *Costello-Roberts v United Kingdom (1995) 18 EHRR 12*), and it is simply not possible to argue that this is met here.

Article 8, however, is a much broader right and provides the *'right to respect for ... private and family life, his home and his correspondence'* (Article 8(1) ECHR). It was contended by the appellant that a disqualification order interferes with his private life in that it denies him employment opportunities. Arguably, such an argument could be sustained since the essence of Article 8 is the right to pursue one's life without arbitrary interference from the state (see, for example, *Glaser v United Kingdom (2001) 33 EHRR 1*), and employment may be relevant to this (*Niemietz v Germany (1993) 16 EHRR 97*). However, Article 8 is not an absolute right but is a qualified right, meaning that the state may interfere with a person's right if it is, *inter alia*, in accordance with law and necessary for the prevention of crime or disorder or the protection of health and morals (Article 8(2)). Prescribed by law simply means a legal basis to act and s.28, CJCSA 2000 certainly meets this criteria.

The Court of Appeal questioned whether it would amount to a breach of Article 8(1) ([2005]

EWCA Crim 1300 at [31], but argued that even if it were, it was within the provisions of Article 8(2) since it is obviously for the prevention of crime or the protection of morals. It is submitted the ultimate conclusion is undoubtedly correct and that there is no difficulty in construing the disqualification regime as a justified interference. There is more difficulty in the belief that it does not even breach Article 8(1) since it would seem to be an interference in a private life. However, the powerful impact of Article 8(2) renders this point moot.

CHAPTER 10

The Future

This book has examined many of the key issues that have arisen in respect of tackling those who seek to exploit children through the use of information and communication technologies. In the preface I noted that this was a fast-moving area of law and this is undoubtedly true. This issue will sadly not go away. It is a sad fact of life that the abuse and exploitation of children has a long and shameful history and it shows no sign of receding. The law, and law enforcement agencies, must continue to adapt in order to ensure that children are safe from exploitation.

This will not be easy. The general public often misunderstand the characteristics of a sex offender, in part because of the way in which they are portrayed in the press. Many sex offenders are extremely clever and calculating. In the same way that lawyers and police try to find new ways of extending the law (or its application) to cover new threats, so their 'shadows' on the other side find new ways of exploiting gaps or loopholes in the law. It is frequently likened to a 'fight' or 'battle' against child exploitation and there is a degree of truth to this. It requires a lot of effort, thinking and resources.

In this final chapter I seek to discuss some of the challenges that are beginning to appear and to identify where the next battlegrounds will be.

Technological challenges

Perhaps the most obvious starting point is to examine what technological challenges will be brought about. To some extent this is the least predictable of all areas since the pace of technology is incredible. Technology is not going to stand still: firms will be forever trying to push the technical boundaries, this demand being fuelled by consumers who want the latest gadget.

3G mobile telephones

The most likely immediate impact will be the growth of 3G mobile technology. 3G has been progressing very slowly since the licences were bought several years ago but the costs of those licences mean that the mobile phone operators will need to make a success of this technology. The telephone handsets themselves were not sufficiently advanced to easily exploit the 3G technology: they were bulky and when using video-calling/conferencing or the high-speed Internet services their batteries were prone to be run down quickly.

However, mobile telephones are becoming increasingly advanced and they are also becoming cheaper. It is likely that over the coming years the proportion of the population who begin to use 3G technology will rise. It is known that children and young people are a target market for the mobile telephone industry and accordingly it is likely that they will account for a significant proportion of this market. The mobile industry is spending a lot of time and money, in advance of this growth, to consider their corporate responsibility in terms of accessibility of content, chat-rooms etc. Providing 'always-on' Internet coverage through a mobile telephone means there are whole new issues of privacy etc. The ability to record – and stream live – pictures and video from the 3G handsets also raises further issues about safety, particularly in the context of cyber-bullying and harassment.

Japan, perhaps unsurprisingly, is leading the way as regards mobile telephones. There, 3G technology has become almost commonplace and this has led to a wide number of sites being set up specifically for the teenage market. Dating has become more common both through the use of the Internet and mobile telephones, something that has begun to be recognised in the UK too (Smithers, 2006: 5). However, in Japan there is a sinister side to this. Teenagers have begun to use the technology to create so-called 'compensated dating' where teenagers will perform sexual favours in return for gifts or money (Schofield, 2005: 6). The teenagers involved in this are middle-class, educated young teenagers, but they see the mobile phone and the Internet as a way of discreetly making money. In Chapter 7 it was noted that some teenagers in the UK are also acting as 'camgirls' offering sexualised content for gifts. 3G telephones allow this to be taken one step forward with high-quality, live pictures being broadcast. A programme of education will be necessary to accompany the growth in 3G.

Payment

Another challenge that is likely to raise its head is the growth of anonymous payment services. Throughout this book there has been a discussion of how certain operations identifying those who exploit children have been traced as a result of their financial dealings. Indeed, many law enforcement agencies have now embedded financial analysts within child protection units in order to assist them in identifying those who seek to exploit children. *Operation Ore*, the UK operation arising from *Landslide Productions*, was a classic example of this. The offenders were traced through the credit card numbers that they provided in order to subscribe to this site.

Offenders are starting to realise that they can be tracked online via their financial dealings and are becoming wary about providing credit card or bank details. Unfortunately, the growth of general commercial fraud through ICT has also increased. The media is awash with stories of databases that have been 'hacked' into in order to obtain credit card details, or bogus websites attempting to identify credit card or bank details (a new term has even been coined to identify such behaviour, that of 'phishing'). The difficulty that this general fraud creates is that it encourages new forms of payment to be created. E-commerce is big business with eBay, a single albeit popular company, posting first-quarter revenue figures totalling $1.77 billion in 2007 and that was simply their receipts, i.e. commission and trading fees etc. The total trading value on eBay in the first-quarter globally amounted $14.3 billion in the same quarter.

With e-commerce being as lucrative (and it was noted earlier in this book that the sex industry itself finds the Internet and related communication technologies a commercially successful operation, see also Lane, 2000), the industry is attempting to find 'new' and 'safe' ways of trading money. However, the privacy suspicions that people have with e-trading means that many of these new forms of payment are becoming anonymous, potentially creating new opportunities for those who wish to trade in the exploitation of children.

Mobile telephones

A simple new method of gaining payment is through the use of credit on mobile telephones.

Within everyday society it is becoming clear that telephones are being used to gain money. Look at the popular 'reality-TV' programmes that have occupied so much of the media's attention over recent years. A principal way of voting for these shows is through a 'premium-rate' text message. This works on the basis that along with being charged by an operator for the usual fee of sending a text-message a further fee will be deducted which will go the operator. The industry-funded regulator estimates that in connection with broadcasting alone this was worth £270m in the financial year 2006/7 (ICSTIS, 2007: 8).

However, it is not only voting where this system can be used. Children can download ringtones, wallpaper and images through SMS payment. They can also subscribe to websites and gaming sites through using their mobile telephone as payment (Papworth, 2006: 7). The particular issue with mobile telephones, of course, is that there are two forms of payment options for telephones. The first, contract, requires the owner to provide their full details and financial status so that the bill can be automatically paid by direct debit. The second method is the 'pay-as-you-go' system whereby the owner uses vouchers to build up a credit balance on their telephone which is gradually reduced as it is being used. A user who has a 'pay-as-you-go' telephone does not need to provide any details and can remain anonymous. It is still possible to access these premium services and use a mobile as payment with a 'pay-as-you-go' system so long as sufficient balance is on the telephone.

A regulator does exist for premium telephone lines (ICSTS) and it is likely that they would prevent the use of such technology for overtly offering illegal content (e.g. abusive images of children), but it would be relatively easy to circumvent such an approach by offering passwords instead of the direct content etc.

Pre-paid credit cards

Many sites on the Internet require a credit card. It is sometimes suggested that this is part of an age-verification system in that only those aged 18 or over have access to a credit card although many are sceptical about its use as a verification system since there is nothing to stop a child from using their parent's card to provide verification. Many others will use the credit card to provide straightforward commercial transactions and, as noted above, the classic example of this was *Landslide Productions* which offered illegal abusive images of children.

A traditional credit card will be linked to a bank account so that the full details of the person's identity and use can be obtained. It was through this that a significant number of offenders were caught in *Operation Ore*. From an e-commerce point of view, if a traditional credit card is the subject of fraud it is possible to build-up vast amounts of credit. A recent solution to this is the introduction of pre-paid credit cards. To an extent the name is a misnomer since a person does not have credit *per se* (i.e. allowed to build up a debt owed to someone else), but rather they are a reverse credit card in that there is a positive credit balance which reduces as it is used. In essence they work on the same principle as gift vouchers and gift cards that have been used for many years. The advantage of these cards, however, is that they can be used wherever credit cards are accepted: they access the same principal networks.

Currently within the UK a pre-paid credit card still requires some elementary checks to be performed on the person but this is still a new form of transaction in this country. In the USA, where their use is significantly more widespread, it is now possible to buy these cards with minimal identification, in much the same way as one purchases a 'pay-as-you-go' mobile telephone. It is also possible to 'top-up' the cards anonymously using anonymous purchasing systems (see below) or by handing over cash to a bank and asking them to update the card's balance. Since these cards can be used in exactly the same way as a credit card it provides an anonymous way of purchasing (or accessing) material on the Internet, potentially causing difficulties to investigators.

Anonymous payment systems

The final aspect of anonymous payment is through the provision of an anonymous payment service. Many banks and financial organisations provide third-party payment systems in order to limit the potential for fraud. Perhaps the classic example of this is PayPal, now owned by eBay Inc. PayPal is a secure payment system that works as follows:

A wishes to buy a book from B. Instead of sending his credit or debit card details (which could be intercepted by a third-party or abused by B) he uses PayPal. A tells PayPal to debit his card for the cost of the book. PayPal then send that money to B and deposit it in his bank account. In this way B doesn't know any of A's payment details but has been credited for the full amount of money.

Third-party payment systems offer a high-degree of protection and are successful. It should be noted that PayPal is not an anonymous system, both parties to a transaction must have notified their details and accordingly it would be possible for law enforcement agencies to track the history of one or more persons to this. However, other third-party systems operate on a purely anonymous basis. One of the largest such systems is InternetCash who make anonymity a selling point of their system. Instead of providing a named bank account a person who signs up to their service is allocated an account without having to provide any details. Money can then be transferred in and out of that account (including by purchasing pre-paid cards) and this balance is then used to fund transactions in the same way as other third-party payment systems. This system would cause law enforcement agencies significant problems since, as InternetCash themselves point out, if they do not have the personal details of anyone they cannot be required to disclose these.

It is anticipated that pre-paid credit cards and anonymous payment systems will eventually link up, potentially providing a truly anonymous payment system that could be used wherever a credit card is accepted. The potential for the abuse of this by those who wish to trade in illegal material is significant and it is something that law enforcement agencies and the financial regulators will have to consider in the near future.

Computer-generated images

An issue that has begun to become increasingly notable is in respect of computer-generated images of abuse. It was noted in Chapter 4 that computer-generated images portraying sexual activity with a child cannot be classed as an indecent photograph or pseudo-photograph of a child and are accordingly outside the remit of the *Protection of Children Act 1978*.

Where the images are traded then it is possible that the *Obscene Publications Act 1959* (as amended) could be used, although the number of prosecutions under this statute has been dropping for many years (Edwards, 1998). Criminalising such images could be controversial with at least one author suggesting that the motive for criminalising images that do not depict real children would be questionable (Williams, 2004: 257). Certainly in other countries the criminalisation of such images has had limited success (see, most notably, the case of *R v Sharpe [2001] 1 SCR 45* (Canada) and *Ashcroft v Free Speech Coalition (2002) 122 S.Ct.1389* (USA)) although other countries have succeeded in establishing legislation (see, for example, s.2(1), *Child Trafficking and Pornography Act 1998* (Ireland)).

In 2007 the Home Office, together with its sister agencies in Scotland and Northern Ireland, issued a consultation paper questioning whether GCI-based images of child sexual abuse should be criminalised (Home Office, 2007). The proposal originated from the *Home Secretary's Task Force on Child Protection on the Internet* after the police began to increasingly discover these images. The images detected show a computer-generated child or children engaging in sexual activity. Many of the images would be at the higher-end of the COPINE scale (see Chapter 4), involving scenes of sadism, bestiality and the penetration of what appears to be young children. However, of course, CGI images are not real children (although it is possible to convert a photograph into a CGI so that it can be manipulated easier), and so questions are raised as to the legality of such images.

At present it is not illegal to possess the images and accordingly, even where they are found alongside indecent images of children, it is technically not possible to either seize or forfeit them. The government conceded that there is no evidence to suggest a direct link between possession of this material and the increased risk of sexual offending against children (Home Office, 2007: 6), although Quayle et al. have noted that several studies do appear to suggest that images, including those produced by any means, can be used as part of a solicitation process (Quayle et al., 2006: 45 citing three studies). Of course, the difficulty with criminalising the images on the basis that they could be used to groom or solicit children is that the criminal law already criminalises the use of such images (showing even CGI images of child abuse to a child is contrary to s.12, *Sexual Offences Act 2003*). Can the fact that some offenders may use images to solicit children justify criminalising its possession?

Another popular argument advanced is that the use of pseudo-images may satisfy the fantasy and sexual urges of some sex offenders (see Williams, 2004: 253 for a summary of this argument), and certainly it is recognised that some offenders have claimed that possession of pornography led to their sexual frustration being released before a contact offence (Quayle et al., 2006: 61). However, there has been no research conducted as to the reality of this situation and indeed research has suggested that many offenders find examining the same class of material eventually leads to them no longer being sexually aroused, causing them to seek out more explicit images (Quayle et al., 2006: 61). The research on the use of pornography and its relationship with contact offending is undoubtedly contradictory and so does this mean it cannot be used? Williams has suggested:

> . . . [it] would be impossible to justify the criminalising of pseudo-images (where no child is used) on this ground without proof of a causal relationship between child pornography and the sexual assault or abuse of children.
> (Williams, 2004: 257)

Yet psychologists have remarked:

> Given the importance of this issue and in the absence of definitive knowledge, for practical purposes prudence suggests we must err on the side of caution and assume the balance lies in terms of the dangers of fantasy becoming reality.
> (Taylor and Quayle, 2003: 195)

This perhaps goes to the heart of the problem. Neither Williams nor Taylor and Quayle are suggesting that the research is anything other than problematic and that being the case it causes difficulties for the legislature in deciding what should be done. Is problematic material to be criminalised on the chance that it *may* save children from being exploited and abused or should the law only act where there is some determinative link shown? It is this conundrum that the Home Office sought to tackle when it consulted on CGI images.

Of course, the protection of the public is not the only reason why material could be banned. Whilst it is easier to justify banning material on the basis of harm, it is also true to say that the law also interferes on the basis of morals. Criminalising on the basis of morals is always controversial but it must be accepted that it does happen; indeed the law of obscenity must be largely based on these principles. The upholding of moral standards is recognised in the *European*

Convention on Human Rights as being a legitimate aim (see Article 10(2) and *Handyside v United Kingdom (1979) 1 EHRR 737*). Whilst the consultation does not expressly say this, perhaps this is the other possible justification for criminalising these images.

At the time of writing (Autumn 2007) no decision has been made as to whether to bring forward legislation to criminalise CGI's. However, if, as the *Task Force* believes, these images are being increasingly detected then it would seem that a decision, one way or another, will have to be made relatively soon.

Rediscovering the child

The chapters in this book have identified threats to children and in many of these behaviours an exploited child is at the heart of the operation. However, this is not always true and, perhaps surprisingly, an exploited child is rarely at the heart of an investigation into abusive images of children. This point has perhaps been best summarised as follows:

> By its very nature, law enforcement agencies tend to address individuals or groups of offenders, rather than processes or victims.
>
> (Taylor and Quayle, 2003: 204)

It is difficult to argue against this statement. Whilst the police, and other law enforcement agencies, do play an important role in the protection of children and since the late 1980s have been accustomed to working in an inter-agency forum designed to help safeguard children, their primary role is the enforcement of the criminal law. The law relating to abusive images of children concentrate on the fact that the possession, making, taking, showing or distribution of photographs is illegal. The focus of the law is therefore the image itself and not the person featured in the image.

Whilst, of course, some analysis is made of photographs this again has traditionally been in respect of the identification of an adult suspect within it. Several suspects have been charged and convicted of contact sex offences on the basis that a photograph has shown them to be sexually assaulting a child. It is difficult to argue against such evidence in court and, quite rightly, this leads to their conviction and imprisonment. Where there is this close nexus then it is quite

possible that the victim will be identified through the perpetrator disclosing the child's name, but this is certainly not true of every case where sometimes the victim remains unknown.

It is a sad reality that unfortunately the vast majority of children portrayed in indecent images are never identified (Taylor and Quayle, 2003: 204). In part, this is because the involvement of children in pornography is a secretive activity since the consequences involved with detection are significant (Holland, 2005: 76). However, it is also symptomatic of how the criminal justice system has treated this issue over the years. In 2004 Interpol reported that less than 300 children had been identified from images on the Internet although this is not necessarily a conclusive figure since not every identification will necessarily have been reported (Holland, 2005: 77). Even taking into account the fact not every identification will necessarily have been reported it is submitted that the total number of identifications will still be extremely small. When it is remembered that every child in an image is a victim of exploitation or abuse (Taylor and Quayle, 2003: 21), this means that potentially the criminal justice system is failing children.

Of course, a difficulty with the Internet, and related communication technologies, is that it is now a global problem. Accordingly, it may be difficult for an agency to identify and recover a child but, although it is conceded that these can be real obstacles, it does not provide a justification for not attempting to identify children. A real difficulty in this area has been the resources that have been made available to law enforcement agencies. The agencies are measured according to how they meet key performance indicators (Jewkes and Andrews, 2005: 50), and child protection rarely features in any business plan let alone a key-performance indicator. Even where child protection features there is frequently a misunderstanding as to how 'online abuse' fits into this category (Jewkes and Andrews, 2005: 53), meaning that it is neglected by many agencies.

That is not to say that identification does not happen. Greater Manchester Police pioneered victim identification for many years and other forces began to co-operate with the victim identification project operated by the COPINE unit in Cork, Dublin. Eventually, technology began to be used in order to facilitate identification. The UK pioneered the use of *Childbase* which uses facial-recognition technology (Sinclair and Sugar, 2005: 49). The technology allows officers to scan an image and it will be compared to the images already loaded onto the database. The computer can, through analysing the characteristics of a face, identify a person regardless of age. Accordingly an officer will be made aware of whether the image of a five-year-old child is the same person as another image where the child is now eight years old. This can be valuable since officers can be told, for example, whether the child has already been identified (and saved), or if they are continuing to identify the child, they now know what age to look for.

Identifying the child can be a very slow process in part because it is perhaps the ultimate example of painstaking detective work. Whilst the image itself may contain metadata, such as embedded data that identifies the make of a camera, the date it was taken etc. (Holland, 2005: 81), it is more often tiny clues that can assist. Holland provides an example of an identification undertaken by Greater Manchester Police (GMP). They were aware that the abuse occurred in Britain because of the architectural details of the house. Calling in an expert on architecture meant that they could identify the broad type of house where the abuse occurred (Holland, 2005: 82). From everyday packaging shown in the photograph (e.g. boxes) it was possible to identify the approximate date the abuse occurred. Through other clues (which are not mentioned in the chapter by Holland and which will not be mentioned here for obvious reasons), it was possible to locate the offender and identify the victims. The victims were recovered and the offender sentenced for his crimes. However, this was resource-intensive work and persuasion was required for GMP's senior officers to support the investigation (Holland, 2005: 83).

Clearly, it would be difficult for individual forces to attempt to replicate the excellent work of GMP with every image. A particular difficulty in this area is that there are 43 police forces in England and Wales, each with a territorial jurisdiction. Some forces will adopt a policy of not investigating crimes (any crime) outside of their force boundary. At the early stages of image analysis it will be rarely possible to identify the location quickly and easily.

Interpol has created an International Victim Identification Group that consists of over 20 countries (Holland, 2005: 87). This means that the Childbase database will increase in sophistication and where it is identified that an abusive act portrayed in an image is likely to have occurred in a particular country Interpol can refer this to the appropriate national body. Whilst this is welcome it is important that resources are put in place to allow that body to investigate. Although some individual police forces (e.g. GMP, Metropolitan Police) continue to operate identification programmes, the newly-created *Child Exploitation and Online Protection Centre* (CEOP) has taken national responsibility for attempting to identify children. It has created a specialist unit whose sole purpose is to attempt to identify victims, allowing them to be recovered.

Whilst this is to be welcomed it is a small unit, in part because it is resource-intensive. The criminal justice system has to consider the role of the victims in this crime and put in place sufficient resources to do more than merely criminalise those who access and distribute indecent images. Identifying victims is important to save them from the abuse and exploitation that is being perpetrated against them. That, by itself, is a worthy goal and should be sufficient incentive. However, there is also the reality that if the victims can be identified then it will often follow that the perpetrators of the abuse and exploitation, including the makers of the abusive images, will also be indentified and prosecuted.

References

'Louise' (1997) Children Unheard: A Young Person's Experience. In Barrett, D. (Ed.) *Child Prostitution in Britain: Dilemmas and Practical Responses*. London: Children's Society.

Addison, N. and Lawson-Cruttenden, T. (1998) *Harassment Law and Practice*. London: Blackstone Press.

Akdeniz, Y. (1997) Governance of Pornography and Child Porngraphy on The Global Internet. In Edwards, L. and Waelde, C. *Law and The Internet*. Oxford: Hart Publishing.

Akdeniz, Y. (2001) *Governing Pornography and Child Pornography on The Internet: The UK Approach*. 32 UWLALR 247.

Ashworth, A. (2000) *Sentencing and Criminal Justice*. 3rd edn. London: Butterworths.

Ashworth, A. (2002) Re-Drawing The Boundaries of Entrapment. *Criminal Law Review*, 161.

Ashworth, A. (2004) Commentary on R v Johnstone. *Criminal Law Review*, 244.

Ashworth, A. (2005) *Sentencing and Criminal Justice*. 4th edn. Cambridge: Cambridge University Press.

Ashworth, A. and Redmayne, M. (2005) *The Criminal Process*. 3rd edn. Oxford: OUP.

Ayre, P. and Barrett, D. (2000) Young People and Prostitution: an End to The Beginning? *Children and Society*, 14:1, 48–59.

Bamford, A. (2004) *Cyber-bullying*. AHISA Pastoral Care National Conference: www.ahisa.com.au/documents/conferences/PCC2004/bamford.pdf.

Barrett, D. and Melrose, M. (2003) Courting Controversy: Children Sexually Abused Through Prostitution. *Child and Family Law Quarterly*, 371.

Bennetto, J. (1999) Games Developer Held on Child Sex Charges. *The Times*, 15 December.

Bocij, P. and McFarlane, L. (2002) Online Harassment: Towards a Definition of Cyberstalking. *Prison Service Journal*, 31.

Bocij, P., Griffiths, M. and McFarlane, L. (2002) Cyberstalking: A New Challenge for Criminal Law. *The Criminal Lawyer*, 3.

Brown, A. and Barrett, D. (2002) *Knowledge of Evil: Child Prostitution and Child Sexual Abuse in Twentieth Century England*. Cullompton: Willan Publishing.

Carr, J. (2001) *Theme Paper on Child Pornography*: A Conference Paper Presented at The 2nd World Congress on The Commercial Sexual Exploitation of Children. Available Via The Internet at: www.Ecpat.Net/Eng/Ecpat_Inter/Projects/Monitoring/Wc2/Yokohama_Theme_Child_Por nography.Pdf

Carr, J. (2003) *Child Abuse, Child Pornography and The Internet*. London: NCH.

Chatterton, C. and Neil, T. (2007) The Legal Issue of Electronic Commerce and Communications. *Electronic Business Law*, 12.

Childnet International (2002) *The Need for The New Section 15 Grooming Offence*. Available Via The Internet at: Www.Childnet-Int.Org.

Clark, D. (2004) *Bevan and Lidstone's The Investigation of Crime*. 3rd edn. London: Lexisnexis Butterworths.

Clough, S. (2003) Student Teacher Who Asked for Child Sex is Jailed But Trial Judge Says His Sentencing Powers Are Inadequate. *The Daily Telegraph*, 12 August.

Cobley, C. (1997) Keeping Track of Sex Offenders: Part 1 of The Sex Offenders Act 1997. *Modern Law Review*, 690.

Cobley, C. (2000) *Sex Offenders: Law, Policy and Practice*. Bristol: Jordans.

Cobley, C. (2005) *Sex Offenders: Law, Policy and Practice*. 2nd edn. Bristol: Jordans.

Collins, S. and Cattermole, R. (2004) *Anti-Social Behaviour: Powers and Remedies*. London: Sweet and Maxwell.

Corbin, J. (2001) The W0nderland Club. *Panorama*. At Http://News.Bbc.Co.Uk/1/Hi/Programmes/Panorama/Archive/1166945.Stm

Cormie, A. (2003) *Speech at Mobile Frontiers: Past, Present and Future Internet Safety Conference*. Preston: University of Central Lancashire.

Criminal Justice System (2004) *Guidance on Part 2 of The Sexual Offences Act 2003*. London: Home Office. At: Http://Www.Homeoffice.Gov.Uk/Justice/Sentencing/Sexualoffencesbill/Guidance.Html

Cusick, L. (2002) Youth Prostitution: A Literature Review. *Child Abuse Review*, 230.

Deakin, S., Johnston, A. and Markesinis, B. (2003) *Markesinis and Deakin's Tort Law*. 5th edn. Oxford: OUP.

Dennis, I. (2002) *The Law of Evidence* (2nd Ed). London: Sweet and Maxwell.

Department of Health (2000) *Safeguarding Children Involved in Prostitution.* London: HMSO.

Dworkin, A. (2004) Pornography, Prostitution and a Beautiful and Tragic Recent History. In Stark, C. and Whisnant, R. *Not for Sale: Feminists Resisting Prostitution and Pornography.* North Melbourne: Spinifex.

Easton, S.M. (1994) *The Problem of Pornography: Regulation and The Right to Free Speech.* London: Routledge.

Edwards, L. (2000) Pornography and The Internet. In Edwards, L. and Waelde, C. *Law and the Internet.* Oxford: Hart Publishing.

Edwards, S.S.M. (1998) The Contemporary Application of The Obscene Publications Act 1959. *Criminal Law Review,* 843.

Edwards, S.S.M. (2000) Prosecuting 'Child Pornography'. *Journal of Social Welfare and Family Law,* 1.

Emmett, S. (2001) The Camgirls: How are Teenagers Persuading Complete Strangers to Send Them Gifts and Money? *The Guardian,* August 28.

Eneman, M. (2005) The New Face of Child Pornography. In Klang, M. and Murray, R. *Human Rights in The Digital Age.* London: Cavendish.

Fenwick, H. (2002) *Civil Liberties and Human Rights.* 3rd edn. London: Cavendish.

Ferguson, P.W. (2004) Reverse Burdens of Proof. *Scottish Law Times,* 22, 133–39.

Finch, E. (2001) *The Criminalisation of Stalking.* London: Cavendish.

Finch, E. (2002) Stalking The Perfect Stalking Law: an Evaluation of The Efficacy of The Protection From Harassment Act. *Criminal Law Review,* 703.

Fitzpatrick, D. (2005) Are The Court of Appeal and The Queen's Bench Divisional Court Now Attempting to Restrict The Use of ASBOs? *Justice of The Peace,* 591.

Gardner, S. (1998) Stalking. *Law Quarterly Review,* 33.

Gillespie, A.A. (2001) Children, Chatrooms and The Law. *Criminal Law Review,* 435.

Gillespie, A.A. (2002a) Child Protection on The Internet: Challenges for Criminal Law. *Child and Family Law Quarterly,* 411.

Gillespie, A.A. (2002b) Discharging Sex Offenders. *Criminal Law Review,* 53.

Gillespie, A.A. (2003) Sentences for Offences Involving Child Pornography. *Criminal Law Review,* 81.

Gillespie, A.A. (2004a) Tinkering With Child Pornography. *Criminal Law Review,* 361.

Gillespie, A.A. (2004b) 'Grooming': Definitions and The Law. *New Law Journal,* 586.

Gillespie, A.A. (2004c) Discharging Sex Offenders: R v Longworth. *Journal of Criminal Law,* 466.

Gillespie, A.A. (2004d) Child Pornography: Restraining Order. R v Beaney. *Journal of Criminal Law,* 278.

Gillespie, A.A. (2005a) Balancing Substantive and Evidential Law to Safeguard Children Effectively From Abuse. *International Journal of Evidence and Proof,* 29.

Gillespie, A.A. (2005b) Changing Registers. *New Law Journal,* 84.

Gillespie, A.A. (2006a) Cyber-Bullying and The Harassment of Teenagers: The Legal Response. *Journal of Social Welfare and Family Law,* 123.

Gillespie, A.A. (2006b) Offensive Communications and The Law. *Entertainment Law Review,* 236.

Gillespie, A.A. (2006c) The Spider's Web. *New Law Journal,* 1153.

Gillespie, A.A. (2006d) Caution Ahead: Teachers, Vetting and The Law. *Education and The Law,* 19.

Gillespie, A.A. (2007a) Diverting Children Involved in Prostitution. *Web Journal of Current Legal Issues.*

Gillespie, A.A. (2007b) Smoke and Mirrors. *New Law Journal,* 565.

Gillespie, A.A. (2007c) Barring Teachers: The New Vetting Arrangements. *Education and The Law,* 1.

Goddard, C., De Bortoli, L., Saunders, B.J. and Tucci, J. (2005) The Rapist's Camouflage: 'Child Prostitution'. *Child Abuse Review,* 275.

Grubin, D. (1998) *Sex Offending against Children: Understanding the Risk. Police Research Paper 99.* London: RDS, Home Office.

Hernandez, A.E. (2000) Self-Reported Contact Sexual Offenses by Participants in the Federal Bureau of Prisons' Sex Offender Treatment Program: Implications for Internet Sex Offenders. Presented at the 19th Research and Treatment Conference of the Association for the Treatment of Sexual Abusers, San Diego, CA, November 2000.

Hirst, M. (2003) *Jurisdiction and The Ambit of The Criminal Law.* Oxford: OUP.

Holland, G. (2005) Identifying Victims of Child Abuse Images: an Analysis of Successful Identifications. In Quayle, E. and Taylor, M.

(2005) *Viewing Child Pornography on The Internet.* Lyme Regis: Russell House Publishing.

Home Office (2001) *Consultation Paper on The Review of Part 1 of The Sex Offenders Act 1997.* London: Home Office.

Home Office (2006) *Consultation on The Draft Code of Practice for The Investigation of Protected Electronic Information.* London: Home Office.

Home Office (2007) *Consultation on The Possession of Non-Photographic Visual Depictions of Child Sexual Abuse.* London: Home Office.

Howitt, D. (1995) *Paedophiles and Sexual Offences Against Children.* London: John Wiley and Sons. Http://Www.Sentencing-Guidelines.Gov.Uk/Consultations/Closed/Index.Html

ICSTS (2007) *Annual Report for 2006/7.* London: ICSTS.

Ingrams, R. (2003) Sting in The Take: Thanks to The Internet, We Can Catch Criminals Before They've Offended. *The Observer*, 17 August.

Itzin, C. (2001) *Legislating Against Pornography Without Censorship.* In Itzin, C. (Ed.) *Pornography: Women, Violence and Civil Liberties.* Oxford: OUP.

Jewkes, Y. and Andrews, C. (2005) Policing The Filth: The Problems of Investigating Online Child Pornography in England and Wales. *Policing and Society*, 42.

Khan, A. (2004) Sexual Offences Act 2003. *Journal of Criminal Law*, 68, 220–26.

Knock, K. (2002) *The Police Perspective on Sex Offender Orders: A Preliminary Review of Policy and Practice.* Police Research Series Paper 155. London: RDS, Home Office.

Koffman, L. (2006) The Rise and Fall of Proportionality: The Failure of The Criminal Justice Act 1991. *Criminal Law Review*, 281.

Krone, T. (2005) International Police Operations Against Online Child Pornography. *Trends and Issues in Criminal Justice*, 1.

Lane, F.S. (2001) *Obscene Profits: The Entrepreneurs of Pornography in The Cyber Age.* London: Routledge.

Lewis, P. (2004) *Sexual Offences Act 2003: A Guide to The New Law.* London: Law Society Press.

Livingstone, S. and Bober, M. (2005) *UK Children Go Online: Final Report.* London: ESRC.

Long, B. (2002) Telephone Rape. In Long, B. and McLachlan, B. *The Hunt for Britain's Paedophiles.* London: Hodder and Staughton.

Long, B. (2002) They're Nice Men or Why Would Children Like Them? In Long, B. and McLachlan, B. *The Hunt for Britain's Paedophiles.* London: Hodder and Staughton.

Lovell, E. (2005) Children and the Use of Anti-Social Behaviour Orders. *Childright*, 217, 14.

Melrose, M. (2004) Young People Abused Through Prostitution: Some Observations for Practice. *Practice*, 17.

Mieszkowski, K. (2001) 'Candy from Strangers' http://www.salon.com/tech/feature/2001/08/13/cam_girls/index.html

Mulkerrins, J. (2004) In Terror of The Text Bullies. *The Times*, 8 July.

Nabokov, V. (1996) *Lolita.* London: Penguin Books.

NCH (2005) *Putting U in the Picture.* London: NCH Publications.

O'Connell, R. (2002) *Young People's Use of Chatrooms: Implications for Policy Strategies and Programs of Education.* Preston: University of Central Lancashire.

O'Connell, R. (2003) *A Typology of Child Cybersexploitation and Online Grooming Practices.* At: www.Uclan.Ac.Uk/Cru/.

O'Connell, R., Price, J. and Barrow, C. (2004) *Cyber Stalking, Abusive Cyber Sex and Online Grooming: A Programme of Education for Teenagers.* Preston: University of Central Lancashire.

Ormerod, D.C. (2000a) Commentary on DPP v Lau. *Criminal Law Review*, 580.

Ormerod, D.C. (2000b) Commentary on R v Bowden. *Criminal Law Review*, 381.

Ormerod, D.C. (2001) Commentary on R v Smethurst. *Criminal Law Review*, 657.

Ormerod, D.C. (2002a) Commentary on R v Smith; R v Jayson. *Criminal Law Review*, 659.

Ormerod, D.C. (2002b) Commentary on R v Looseley. *Criminal Law Review*, 301.

Ormerod, D.C. (2003) Commentary on Kelly v DPP. *Criminal Law Review*, 45

Ormerod, D.C. (2005) *Smith and Hogan's Criminal Law.* 11th edn. Oxford: OUP.

Ost, S. (2002) Children at Risk: Legal and Societal Perceptions of The Potential Threat That The Possession of Child Pornography Poses to Society. *Journal of Law and Society*, 436.

Ost, S. (2004) Getting to Grips With Sexual Grooming? The New Offence Under The Sexual Offences Act 2003. *Journal of Social Welfare and Family Law*, 147.

Owen, T. et al. (2005) *Blackstone's Guide to The Serious Organised Crime and Police Act 2005.* Oxford: OUP.

Palmer, T. (2004) *Just One Click: Sexual Abuse of Children and Young Children Through The Internet and Mobile Telephone Technology*. London: Barnardo's.

Papworth, J. (2006) Mobiles: The Hidden Message for Parents. *The Money Guardian*, 7 October.

Paris, M. (2003) The Sting in The Tail of Police Entrapment. *The Times*, 16 August.

Paterson, M. (2003) Girl, 12 Flies Off With Internet Ex-Marine. *Daily Telegraph*, 15 July.

Pearce, J. (2006) Finding The 'I' in Sexual Exploitation: Hearing The Voices of Sexually Exploited Young People in Policy and Practice. In Campbell, R. and O'Neil, M. *Sex Work Now*. Cullompton: Willan Publishing.

Phoenix, J. (2002) In The Name of Protection: Youth Prostitution Reforms in England and Wales. *Critical Social Policy*, 353.

Phoenix, J. (2003) Rethinking Youth Prostitution: National Provision at The Margins of Child Protection and Youth Justice. *Youth Justice*, 152–68.

Quayle, E. (2005) *Young People Who Sexually Abuse: The Role of New Technologies*. In Erooga, M. and Masson, H. (Eds.) *Children and Young People Who Sexually Abuse Others*. London: Routledge.

Quayle, E. and Taylor, M. (2001) Child Seduction and Self-Representation on The Internet *Cyberpsychology and Behaviour*, 597.

Quayle, E. and Taylor, M. (2002) Paedophiles, Pornography and The Internet: Assessment Issues. *British Journal of Social Work*, 863.

Quayle, E. et al. (2006) *Only Pictures? Therapeutic Work With Internet Sex Offenders*. Lyme Regis: Russell House Publishing.

Reed, C. (2004) *Internet Law: Text and Materials*. 2nd edn. Cambridge: Cambridge University Press.

Robertson, G. (1979) *Obscenity: An Account of Censorship Laws and their Enforcement in England and Wales*. London: Weidenfield and Nicolson.

Rook, P. and Ward, R. (2004) *Rook and Ward on Sexual Offences: Law and Practice*. 3rd edn. London: Sweet and Maxwell.

Rowan, D. (2002) Menace on the Net. *The Observer*, July 7.

Sanders, A. and Young, R. (2000) *Criminal Justice*. 2nd edn. London: Butterworths.

Schofield, J. (2005) New Technologies are making it much easier for Young People to use the Net without Adult Knowledge. *The Guardian*, May 10.

Selfe, D. and Burke, V. (2001) *Perspectives on Sex, Crime and Society*. 2nd edn. London: Cavendish.

Sentencing Advisory Panel (2002) *Offences Involving Child Pornography*. London: SAP.

Sentencing Advisory Panel (2004) *Consultation Guideline: Sexual Offences Act 2003*. London: SAP.

Sentencing Advisory Panel (2007) *Consultation Guideline: Overarching Principles: Assaults on Children and Cruelty to Children*. London: SAP.

Sentencing Guidelines Council (2004b) *Reduction in Sentence for a Guilty Plea*. London: SGC.

Sentencing Guidelines Council (2007a) *Guideline on Sexual Offences*. London: SGC.

Sentencing Guidelines Council (2007b) *Sentencing Statistics* (CD-ROM). London: SGC.

Sher, J. (2007) *One Child at A Time: Inside The Fight to Rescue Children From Online Predators*. London: Vision Paperbacks.

Silverman, J. and Wilson, D. (2002) *Innocence Betrayed: Paedophilia, The Media and Society*. Cambridge: Polity Press.

Simester, A.P. and Sullivan, G.R. (2004) *Criminal Law: Doctrine and Theory*. 2nd edn. Rev. Oxford: Hart.

Sinclair, R.L. and Sugar, D. (2005) *Internet Based Sexual Exploitation of Children and Youth*. Ottawa: NCECC.

Smith, J.C. (1986) Commentary on Gillick v West Norfolk and Wisbech Area Health Authority. *Criminal Law Review*, 113.

Smith, J.C. (1997) Commentary on Ireland; Burstow. *Criminal Law Review*, 810.

Smith, J.C. (1998) Commentary on R v Land. *Criminal Law Review*, 120.

Smith, J.H, (2002) *Internet Law and Regulation*. 3rd edn. London: Sweet and Maxwell.

Smithers, R. (2006) Youngsters Value Phones for Privacy From Parents. *The Guardian*, 19 September.

Soothill, K. (1997) A Cautionary Tale: The Sex Offenders Act 1997, The Police and Cautions. *Criminal Law Review*, 482.

Soothill, K. (2004) Parlour Games: The Value of an Internet Site Providing Punters' Views of Massage Parlours. *Police Journal*, 43.

Sparks, I. (2002) *Foreward*. Brown, A. and Barrett, D. *Knowledge of Evil: Child Prostitution and Child Sexual Abuse in Twentieth Century England*. Cullompton: Willan Publishing.

Squires, D. (2006) The Problem With Entrapment. *Oxford Journal of Legal Studies*, 351.

Tate, T. (1990) *Child Pornography: An Investigation*. London: Methuen.

Taylor, M. and Quayle, E. (2003) *Child Pornography: An Internet Crime*. London: Routledge.

Taylor, M., Holland, G. and Quayle, E. (2001) Typology of Paedophile Picture Collections. *Police Journal*, 97.

Taylor, R., Wasik, M. and Leng, R. (2004) *Blackstone's Guide to The Criminal Justice Act 2003*. Oxford: OUP.

Temkin, J. (2002) *Rape and The Legal Process*. 2nd edn. Oxford: OUP.

Temkin, J. and Ashworth, A. (2004) Rape, Sexual Assaults and the Problems of Consent. *Criminal Law Review* 328–46.

Terrett, A. and Monaghan, L. (2000) *The Internet: an Introduction for Lawyers*. In Edwards, L. and Waelde, C. (Eds.) *Law and The Internet: A Framework for Electronic Commerce*. Oxford: Hart.

Terry, K.J. and Tallon, J. (2004) *Child Sexual Abuse: A Review of The Literature*. Http://www. Nccbuscc.Org/Nrb/Johnjaystudy/ Litreview.Pdf

Thomas, D.A. (2002) The Sentencing Process. In McConville, M. and Wilson, G. *The Handbook of The Criminal Justice Process*. Oxford: OUP.

Thomas, D.A. (2003) Sentencing: Disqualification Order (Field; Young). *Criminal Law Review*, 204–5.

Thomas, D.A. (2005) Sentencing: Disqualification Order (R v G). *Criminal Law Review*, 800–4.

Thomas, D.A. (2006a) Comment on R v Lang. *Criminal Law Review*, 174.

Thomas, D.A. (2006b) Comment on Attorney-General's Reference (Nos 14 and 15 of 2006). *Criminal Law Review*, 943.

Thomas, D.A. (2007) Comment of R v Johnson. *Criminal Law Review*, 177.

Thompson, D. (Ed.) (1995) *The Concise Oxford Dictionary*. 9th edn. Oxford: OUP.

Thompson, R. (2003) Net 'Kids' Lure Paedophiles. *The Observer*, 17 August.

Travis, A. (2000) *Bound and Gagged: A Secret History of Obscenity in Britain*. London: Profile Books.

Verkaik, R. (2000) Judge Calls for Law to Stop Net Paedophile Attacks. *The Independent*, 23 May.

Von Hirsch, A. and Ashworth, A. (1998) *Principled Sentencing: Readings on Theory and Practice*. Oxford: Hart.

Wells, C. (1997) Stalking: The Criminal Law Response. *Criminal Law Review*, 463.

White, M. (2003) Too Close to See: Men, Women, and Webcams. *New Media and Society*, 7.

Williams, A. and Thompson, B. (2004a) Vigilance or Vigilantes: The Paulsgrove Riots and Policing Paedophiles in The Community. Part 1: The Long Slow Fuse. *Police Journal*, 99.

Williams, A. and Thompson, B. (2004b) Vigilance or Vigilantes: The Paulsgrove Riots and Policing Paedophiles in The Community. Part 2: The Lessons of Paulsgrove. *Police Journal*, 193.

Williams, G. (1988) The Logic of Exceptions. *Cambridge Law Journal*, 281.

Williams, K.S. (2004) Child Pornography Law: Does It Protect Children? *Journal of Social Welfare and Family Law*, 245.

Russell House Publishing Ltd

We publish a wide range of professional, reference and educational books including:

Only pictures? Therapeutic work with Internet sex offenders
Edited by Ethel Quayle, Marcus Erooga, et al.   ISBN 978-1-903855-68-3

Viewing child pornography on the Internet: Understanding the offence, managing the offender, helping the victims
Edited by Ethel Quayle and Max Taylor   ISBN 978-1-903855-69-0

Child sexual abuse and the Internet: Tackling the new frontier
Edited by Martin C. Calder   ISBN 978-1-903855-35-5

Contemporary treatment of adult male sex offenders
By Mark S. Carich and Martin C. Calder   ISBN 978-1-903855-19-5

Contemporary risk assessment in safeguarding children
Edited by Martin C. Calder   ISBN 978-1-905541-20-1

Safeguarding children and young people: A guide to integrated practice
By Steven Walker and Christina Thurston   ISBN 978-1-903855-90-4

For more details, please visit our website: *www.russellhouse.co.uk*

Or we can send you our catalogue if you contact us at:

Russell House Publishing Ltd,
4 St George's House, Uplyme Road Business Park,
Lyme Regis DT7 3LS, England,
Tel: 01297 443948
Fax: 01297 442722
Email: help@russellhouse.co.uk

For enquiries or renewal at
Quarles LRC
Tel: 01708 455011 – Extension 4009